THE MOTIVATION-COGNITION INTERFACE

This volume honors the work of Arie W. Kruglanski. It represents a collection of chapters written by Arie's former students, friends, and collaborators. The chapters are rather diverse and cover a variety of topics from politics, including international terrorism, to health related issues, such as addiction and self-control, to basic psychological principles, such as motivation and self-regulation, the formation of attitudes, social influence, and interpersonal relationships. What these chapters have in common is that they have all been inspired by Arie's revolutionary work on human motivation and represent the authors' attempt to apply the basic principles of motivation to the understanding of diverse phenomena.

Catalina E. Kopetz (PhD, University of Maryland, 2007) is Assistant Professor of Psychology at Wayne State University, USA. Her research focuses on the mechanisms that underlie multiple goal pursuit and management of goal conflict and their implications for risk taking (i.e. overeating, substance use, risky sexual behavior, drunk driving). She has published in prestigious journals spanning social and clinical psychology, prevention sciences, psychopharmacology, behavioral and brain sciences, as well as journals appealing to a broader audience such as *Perspectives in Psychological Science, Current Directions in Psychological Science* and *Psychological Review*. Her research has been funded by the National Institutes of Health (including NIDA and NIAAA).

Ayelet Fishbach (PhD, Tel Aviv University, 1999) is the Jeffrey Breakenridge Keller Professor of Behavioral Science and Marketing at the University of Chicago, USA. Ayelet studies social psychology, management and consumer behavior. She is an expert on motivation and decision making. She has presented her research all over the world. Fishbach has been published in many psychology and marketing journals, including the *Journal of Consumer Research*, the *Journal of Marketing Research, Psychological Science* and the *Journal of Personality and Social Psychology*. She is on the editorial board of several journals, including the *Journal of Personality and Social Psychology* and the *Journal of Consumer Research*. Her research is regularly featured in the media, including WSJ, CNN, Chicago Tribune, NPR and was selected to be featured in the *New York Times*' "Annual Years in Ideas." Fishbach is furthermore the recipient of several international awards, including the Society of Experimental Social Psychology's Best Dissertation Award and the Fulbright Educational Foundation Award.

THE MOTIVATION-COGNITION INTERFACE

From the Lab to the Real World: A Festschrift in Honor of Arie W. Kruglanski

Edited by Catalina E. Kopetz and Ayelet Fishbach

Routledge
Taylor & Francis Group

NEW YORK AND LONDON

First published 2018
by Routledge
711 Third Avenue, New York, NY 10017

and by Routledge
2 Park Square, Milton Park, Abingdon, Oxon OX14 4RN

Routledge is an imprint of the Taylor & Francis Group, an informa business

Names: Kruglanski, Arie W., honoree. | Kopetz, Catalina E., editor. | Fishbach, Ayelet, editor.
Title: The motivation-cognition interface : from the lab to the real world : a festschrift in honor of Arie W. Kruglanski / [edited by] Catalina E. Kopetz and Ayelet Fish.
Description: New York : Routledge, 2017. | Includes bibliographical references and index.
Identifiers: LCCN 2016057910 | ISBN 9781138651074 (hb : alk. paper) | ISBN 9781138651081 (pb : alk. paper) | ISBN 9781315171388 (ebook)
Subjects: LCSH: Motivation (Psychology) | Self-control. | Cognition.
Classification: LCC BF503 .M68616 2017 | DDC 153.8–dc23
LC record available at https://lccn.loc.gov/2016057910

ISBN: 978-1-138-65107-4 (hbk)
ISBN: 978-1-138-65108-1 (pbk)
ISBN: 978-1-315-17138-8 (ebk)

Typeset in Bembo
by Taylor & Francis Books

CONTENTS

ILLUSTRATIONS

Figures

FOREWORD

In June 2016, a group of scholars from all around the globe gathered together at the University of Maryland to celebrate Arie Kruglanski. The group included past and present students, colleagues, and research collaborators. Naturally, these categories largely overlap. We would like to think of this group as Arie's friends. This group includes people studying rather varied topics from politics, including international terrorism, to health-related issues, such as addiction and self-control, to basic psychological principles, such as the formation of attitudes and interpersonal relationships. This group has one thing in common – we have all been lucky enough to cross paths with Arie Kruglanski at one point or another in our respective careers. Arie is our most inspiring collaborator.

The group spent the day the way academics do. We presented our research to one other, discussed our discoveries, and exchanged constructive feedback. We also shared some insights from our collaborations with Arie; how ideas were sparked, the breakthroughs in theory development, and how stimulated we felt in our many meetings with him. This book summarizes what many of us presented to the group on that day. Hopefully, this book also captures the magic of a room full of academics, all of whom came together to celebrate Arie. It was a room full of "Arie's people," exchanging their exciting discoveries and sharing their love of their mentor.

As you read this volume, you will realize just how rich and diverse Arie's contribution to the field of psychology has been. First, he has a unique approach, which has been guided by a quest for the basic principles of human judgment and behavior. The research he inspired is accordingly diverse, yet shares a fundamental goal – the authors of the essays in this book all wish to identify basic psychological principles, which we apply to diverse phenomena.

Second, Arie revolutionized motivation theory. He showed us just how much the principles of human motivation can explain the actions of the individual and society. He studies motivational phenomena such as regulatory mode, people's need for epistemic closure, intrinsic motivation, and he applies the principle of motivation to understand traditional social psychological phenomena such as conformity, interpersonal relationships, and the political and health-related issues that the society currently struggles with. The work of his collaborators reflects Arie's deep insights into human motivation.

We organized this book as a collection of essays that reflect both on Arie's work and on the work he inspired us to do on our own. We start with an introduction, written by Arie, that tells the journey of his research in psychology of over 50 years. We then present a collection of essays by his collaborators, organized by the order in which the origin ideas for the research were generated in Arie's scientific journey.

This volume is not only a summary of research inspired by Arie. It is also our way to express our gratitude to a great mentor, who provided guidance, inspiration, and friendship.

On behalf of the authors of the essays in this book,

Catalina and Ayelet

INTRODUCTION

A Journey with Friends: Reflections on the Present Volume

Arie W. Kruglanski

One of the most enjoyable aspects of my career as a social psychologist has been the experience of working with other people, graduate students and colleagues whose excitement, ideas and support made the enterprise so rewarding. Whether during "hard times" so frequent in the life of a scientist (e.g., when the empirical results refused to "cooperate" with the hypothesis, and even when they did, yet the reviewers stubbornly refused to see the light!), or during "good times" when the opposite miraculously happened, it was the shared reality with others that made the difference. Indeed, articles in this volume are written by some of my most cherished collaborators, and they represent the different facets of my work over the years.

On first blush, the present chapters may appear to bear little relation to each other. Nonetheless at root they do have a common denominator reflecting my ongoing fascination with the interface of motivation cognition and action. The bodies of work addressed here evolved over the years reflecting the various intellectual influences and environments that shaped my interests. They tell the story of my intellectual journey in psychology in the company of dear friends.

Attributional Beginnings

I came of age as a researcher toward the end of the 1960s, under the tutelage of Harold Kelley who at the time was developing his unique approach to causal attribution processes. Accordingly, my doctoral dissertation on interpersonal trust in supervisor-worker relations (Kruglanski, 1970) inspired by an earlier thesis by Lloyd Strickland was "attributional" to the core based on the idea that trust reflects the (*internal*) attribution of the actor's good performance to the actor rather than its attribution to an *external* force, namely, the supervisor's surveillance. At my first academic job at Tel Aviv University, I continued exploring the attributional paradigm by hypothesizing and demonstrating that the self-perception of intrinsic motivation and consequent performance depends on attribution of task-engagement to the self, that is "internally" rather than to "external" rewards.

My further reflection on these issues led to the (somewhat contrarian) conclusion that the "internal" "external" distinction so central to attribution theory in those days, really represents a quite different conceptual partition, namely that between "endogenous"-"exogenous" attributions (Kruglanski, 1975). An *endogenous* attribution represents the case where an activity is seen as its own end (i.e. is intrinsically motivated), whereas an *exogenous* attribution represents the case where it is seen as serving an ulterior end separate from the activity itself (i.e., the activity is extrinsically motivated). Why is this distinction more precise than the original differentiation between internal and external attributions. Simply because all human motivation is at once "internal" and "external"; it is internal because it is grounded in personal needs and it is external because it refers to desirable states of the world, or goal objects. In the present volume, these matters are creatively developed in the chapter by Kaitleen Wooley and Ayelet Fishbach on immediate and delayed rewards. In fact, Ayelet and I have decided to collaborate on an integrative paper that explores the implications of this view of intrinsic motivation for a wide ranging variety of phenomena, so stay tuned!

From Attribution Theory to Lay Epistemics

Still under the impact of Kelley's attribution theory and Popper's notions of hypothesis testing (that I avidly explored during my first sabbatical year spent at the University of North Carolina), I re-examined Kelley's ANOVA model and his attributional criteria (of consistency, consensus and uniqueness). This resulted in a formulation of my lay epistemic theory (Kruglanski, 1980) and the proposal of unique, rule-based, "propositional," mechanism of lay inference exhibiting the Aristotelian "if then" structure whereby people derive conclusions from what they perceive as relevant evidence. The notion of a unique inferential mechanism whereby people derive all their knowledge clashed with the prevailing Zeitgeist that assumed a duality of inferential processes (for a recent source book see Sherman, Gawronski & Trope, 2014), and led to my work on the "unimodel" (e.g., Kruglanski & Thompson, 1999; Kruglanski & Gigerenzer, 2011). A close partner in this enterprise was Hans-Peter Erb (Jennes) (e.g., Erb, Pierro, Mannetti, Spiegel, & Kruglanski, 2007). Jennes' chapter for this volume represents a spinoff of that work, aimed at exploring the implication that the essential process whereby minorities and majorities exert their influence on individuals is essentially the same (consistent with the unimodel), the only systematic difference between the two residing in the consensus rule ("if consensus then correct|") that is affirmed for majorities but not for minorities. Contrary to traditional views of minorities and majorities, and consistent with the unimodel, the Erb chapter elucidates the specific conditions under which minorities versus majorities would have the greater persuasive influence, revealing important motivational moderators of the consensus effect.

The Need for Cognitive Closure

According to theory, a central motivational underpinning of lay epistemics is the need for cognitive closure. This particular motivation functions as a stopping mechanism of hypothesis generation/information processing and it encompasses the twin processes of "seizing and freezing" whereby an individual decides on what constitutes the Truth in a given instance of judgment. Over the years, significant need for closure work has been carried out at several laboratories in different world locations (most prominently at Rome by the Pierro and Mannetti group, in Krakow by Malgorzata Kossowska's team, at Ghent by the Roets and van Hiel group, at Singapore by Ying Yi Hong and her colleagues, and at Maryland by our own lab) (for a recent review see Roets et al., 2015). Arne Roets chapter for the present volume describes the extensive need for closure work carried out by the Ghent group that drilled down on this concept's various implications and filled in important gaps of knowledge that the original theory merely hinted at.

Issues of epistemology and closure served as an intellectual fodder for my interaction with John Jost with whom I share the passions for philosophy and politics. What followed was an exciting collaboration on a range of topics including social constructionism (Jost & Kruglanski, 2002), meta-cognition (Jost, Kruglanski & Nelson, 1998), and most of all on our collaborative paper titled "political conservatism as motivated social cognition" (Jost, Glaser, Kruglanski & Sulloway, 2003) that evoked impassioned reactions from a wide range of readers and engaged us in mediatized debates with leading conservatives at home and abroad. John, Joanna and Chadly's paper for the present volume describes an intriguing follow up to that work that systematically addresses and deftly puts to rest the several critiques and methodological concerns that some commentators leveled against the original work.

Regulatory Mode Theory

The need for closure work as well as our prior research on endogenous and exogenous attribution reflects my longstanding fascination with motivational phenomena as they specifically intersect with cognitive processes. A different manifestation of this interest expressed itself in a theoretical and empirical project on the regulatory modes of *locomotion* and *assessment* undertaken jointly with Tory Higgins of Columbia University, and further developed through extensive collaboration with Antonio Pierro and Lucia Mannetti of the University of Rome

(Kruglanski et al., 2000; Higgins, Kruglanski, & Pierro, 2003; Kruglanski, Pierro, Mannetti, & Higgins, 2013; Pierro, Giacomantonio, Pica, Kruglanski, & Higgins, 2011). Roughly, the distinction between locomotion and assessment is one between thinking and doing; it turns out that people systematically differ on these dimensions, and that the emphasis on one versus the other has wide ranging effects on a variety of personal and social behaviors.

The regulatory mode research program proceeded apace and following the initial introduction of these concepts (Kruglanski et al., 2000) we published numerous theoretical and empirical articles on regulatory modes, among others papers comparing different cultures on locomotion and assessment (Higgins, Pierro, & Kruglanski, 2008), exploring the relation between the modes and time orientation (Kruglanski et al., 2016), and the relation between the modes and brain structures related to Parkinson's disease (Foerde, Braun, Higgins, & Shohamy, 2015). Tory Higgins' chapter for this volume describes exciting cutting-edge research on regulatory modes carried out by the Columbia group.

Goal Systems Theory

Both need for closure and regulatory modes represent specific motivations, that is, particular instances (or "contents") of the broad motivation construct. But my great theoretical challenge has been always to get to the underlying gist of things, and to conceptualize relations between phenomena at as abstract a level as possible (Kruglanski, 2004) (though no more abstract (!), as Einstein reputedly quipped). It is this penchant, I believe, that ultimately, prompted me to conceptualize the general goal concept as a cognitive structure (Kruglanski, 1996) and to subsequently develop the theory of goal systems that explored different types of goals-means architectures. Two contributors to the present volume were particularly active members of our lab when the goal systemic concepts were formulated and explored. Indeed, in their subsequent work they took goal systemic theory in exciting new directions. Catalina Kopetz, whose dissertation explored the fundamental multifinality constraint effect (Kopetz et al., 2011), explores in her chapter the surprising rationality of risky health behaviors, and Ed Orehek reviews his and his colleagues work on the instrumentality of interpersonal relations. Although the notion of "people as means" may strike some as cynical and callous, Ed's work actually explores the highly touted notion of "people who need people" (as in Barbra Streisand's well known song) whereby interpersonal relations depend on mutual instrumentality whereby friends and lovers serve each other's needs.

Significance Quest Theory

Finally, but of considerable importance, Jocelyn Bélanger's chapter (present volume) on radicalization and deradicalization touches on the most recent phase of my work commenced in reaction to the 9/11/2001 attacks on the U.S., and my conviction that social psychology has a great deal to contribute to understanding terrorism and radicalization. Our work brought to bear on this topic our general theorizing about motivation; this prompted a development of our new Significance Quest Theory that we subsequently tested in a variety of field as well as laboratory studies. Jocelyn was a member of the Maryland lab when our work on these topics was starting, and he contributed significantly to its evolution. Of particular interest was Joce's translation of our theoretical ideas into specific applied procedures designed to counter radicalization in specific at risk populations. It is this work that figures centrally in his chapter for the present volume.

In closing, I feel extremely fortunate for having the opportunity to work alongside the contributors to this volume who I regard as lifelong colleagues and dear friends. Our joint intellectual voyage was what lent my life meaning and filled it with excitement. I am profoundly honored by the publication of their work in the present volume, and eternally grateful for having them as companions on this journey.

References

Erb, H. P., Pierro, A., Mannetti, L., Spiegel, S., & Kruglanski, A. W. (2007). Biased processing of persuasive information: on the functional equivalence of cues and message arguments. *European Journal of Social Psychology, 37*(5), 1057–1075.

Foerde, K., Braun, E. K., Higgins, E. T., & Shohamy, D. (2015). Motivational modes and learning in Parkinson's disease. *Social Cognitive and Affective Neuroscience,* 10(8), 1066–1073.

Higgins, E. T., Kruglanski, A. W., & Pierro, A. (2003). Regulatory mode: Locomotion and assessment as distinct orientations. *Advances in Experimental Social Psychology, 35,* 293–344.

Higgins, E. T., Pierro, A., & Kruglanski, A. W. (2008). Re-thinking Culture and Personality: How Self-Regulatory Universals Create Cross-Cultural Differences. In R. M. Sorrentino & S. Yamagushi (Eds.), *Handbook of Motivation and Cognition across Cultures* (pp. 161–190). Cambridge, MA: Academic Press.

Jost, J. T., Glaser, J., Kruglanski, A. W., & Sulloway, F. J. (2003). Political conservatism as motivated social cognition. *Psychological Bulletin, 129*(3), 339.

Jost, J. T., & Kruglanski, A. W. (2002). The estrangement of social constructionism and experimental social psychology: History of the rift and prospects for reconciliation. *Personality and Social Psychology Review, 6*(3), 168–187.

Jost, J. T., Kruglanski, A. W., & Nelson, T. O. (1998). Social metacognition: An expansionist review. *Personality and Social Psychology Review, 2*(2), 137–154.

Köpetz, C., Faber, T., Fishbach, A., & Kruglanski, A. W. (2011). The multifinality constraints effect: how goal multiplicity narrows the means set to a focal end. *Journal of Personality and Social Psychology, 100*(5), 810.

Kruglanski, A. W. (1970). Attributing trustworthiness in supervisor-worker relations. *Journal of Experimental Social Psychology, 6*(2), 214–232.

Kruglanski, A. W. (1975). The endogenous-exogenous partition in attribution theory. *Psychological Review, 82*(6), 387.

Kruglanski, A. W. (1980). Lay epistemo-logic—process and contents: Another look at attribution theory. *Psychological Review, 87*(1), 70.

Kruglanski, A. W. (1996). Goals as knowledge structures. In P. M. Gollwitzer & J. A. Bargh (Eds.), *The psychology of action: Linking cognition and motivation to behavior* (pp. 599–618). New York: Guilford Press.

Kruglanski, A. W. (2004). The quest for the gist: On challenges of going abstract in social and personality psychology. *Personality and Social Psychology Review, 8*(2), 156–163.

Kruglanski, A. W., & Gigerenzer, G. (2011). Intuitive and deliberate judgments are based on common principles. *Psychological Review, 118*(1), 97.

Kruglanski, A. W., Pierro, A., & Higgins, E. T. (2016). Experience of Time by People on the Go A Theory of the Locomotion–Temporality Interface. *Personality and Social Psychology Review, 20*(2), 100–117.

Kruglanski, A. W., Pierro, A., Mannetti, L., & Higgins, T. E. (2013). The distinct psychologies of "looking" and "leaping": Assessment and locomotion as the springs of action. *Social and Personality Psychology Compass, 7*(2), 79–92.

Kruglanski, A. W., & Thompson, E. P. (1999). Persuasion by a single route: A view from the unimodel. *Psychological Inquiry, 10*(2), 83–109.

Kruglanski, A. W., Thompson, E. P., Higgins, E. T., Atash, M., Pierro, A., Shah, J. Y., & Spiegel, S. (2000). To "do the right thing" or to "just do it": locomotion and assessment as distinct self-regulatory imperatives. *Journal of Personality and Social Psychology, 79*(5), 793–815.

Pierro, A., Giacomantonio, M., Pica, G., Kruglanski, A. W., & Higgins, E. T. (2011). On the psychology of time in action: regulatory mode orientations and procrastination. *Journal of Personality and Social Psychology, 101*(6), 1317–1331.

Roets, A., Kruglanski, A. W., Kossowska, M., Pierro, A., & Hong, Y. Y. (2015). The Motivated Gatekeeper of Our Minds: New Directions in Need for Closure Theory and Research. *Advances in Experimental Social Psychology, 52*, 221–283.

Sherman, J. W., Gawronski, B., & Trope, Y. (Eds.). (2014). *Dual-process theories of the social mind*. New York: Guilford Publications.

1

WHEN INTRINSIC MOTIVATION AND IMMEDIATE REWARDS OVERLAP

Kaitlin Woolley and Ayelet Fishbach

Synopsis

Kruglanski et al. (2002) proposed that an activity (i.e., a means) is intrinsically motivated when it coincides with its goal (i.e., the reward for pursuing it). Based on this observation, we provide a framework for understanding intrinsic motivation using insights from research on immediate and delayed rewards. We explore the parallels between intrinsic (vs. extrinsic) motivation and immediate (vs. delayed) rewards and present support for three propositions. First, intrinsic (but not extrinsic) rewards are valued more in the present than with a temporal delay. For example, people value learning new things more in their present job than in previous and future jobs. Second, immediate rewards render the experience of an activity as more intrinsic. For example, receiving an immediate (vs. delayed) bonus payment increases the motivation to engage in a task during a free choice phase. Third, by increasing intrinsic motivation, immediate rewards increase persistence. For example, focusing on the positive taste of healthy food increases consumption compared with focusing on the delayed health benefits.

Introduction

Imagine someone intrinsically motivated to exercise; this person runs because she finds running inherently pleasurable. In contrast, the extrinsically motivated runner looks very different. This person is motivated to run not out of enjoyment, but for some external outcome such as losing weight or pleasing a partner. This distinction between intrinsic and extrinsic motivation has been widely studied, and can influence the quality of the experience and performance of these two runners based on their distinct motivations (Heath, 1999; Higgins & Trope, 1990; Kruglanski, 1975;

Mischel, Shoda, & Rodriguez, 1989; Ryan & Deci, 2000; Sansone & Harackiewicz, 1996; Wrzesniewski et al., 2014).

As another example, consider someone who exercises to pursue a long-term health goal, and while she runs, listens to music to improve her experience. Although this person does not find running inherently enjoyable, and is therefore not intrinsically motivated to run (i.e., does not receive an internal benefit), at the same time she does receive an immediate reward – the positive experience of listening to music. Intrinsic incentives – in the case of the intrinsically motivated runner, clearly differ from immediate rewards – in the case of the runner who listens to music while exercising, but is it possible that there is overlap in the psychological experience of intrinsic and immediate rewards? We address this possibility in the current chapter.

We start by providing an overview of research on intrinsic motivation, which has identified two separate incentives people can receive from goal pursuit. That is, people can receive intrinsic incentives, which are part of the experience of pursuing an activity and differ from extrinsic incentives, which are the outcomes of pursuit. We then address research on reward timing, specifically work on self-control, which documented a preference for immediate rewards that materialize sooner in time over delayed rewards that materialize later. Whereas intrinsic motivation and immediate rewards comprise separate areas of research and have typically been studied in isolation from one another, we suggest some degree of overlap exists between the psychology of both phenomenon (intrinsic–immediate vs. extrinsic–delayed). We explore recent research addressing this idea, and document novel insights of this overlap for understanding (1) People's valuation of intrinsic incentives (which is greater in the present than with a delay), (2) People's experience of immediate rewards (which render activities more intrinsically motivating), and (3) Implications of immediate rewards for increasing persistence in long-term goals, by increasing intrinsic motivation.

Intrinsic Motivation

An action is intrinsically motivating to the extent that it is internally derived as opposed to externally derived (e.g., Fishbach & Choi, 2012; Heath, 1999; Lepper, Greene & Nisbett, 1973; Sansone & Harackiewicz, 1996). For example, intrinsic motives include "learning new things" or satisfaction when "feeling good about oneself" and extrinsic motives are external to the task such as receiving pay or having job security (Heath, 1999). Some research identified certain contents that tend to be intrinsically motivating. Thus, research on self-determination theory offered a content-based definition of intrinsic motivation, which posits that an intrinsically motivated action serves at least one of three end goals: autonomy, competence and relatedness. In contrast, extrinsic actions serve more extrinsic ends and are pursued for tangible rewards or to avoid punishment (Ryan & Deci, 2000). This fruitful perspective inspired a large proportion of the research on intrinsic motivation;

however, it is limited in the sense that certain contents cannot be considered intrinsically motivating.

In contrast, Shah and Kruglanski (2000) offered a structure–perspective on intrinsic motivation that does not assume specific goal contents, and thus, for example, both hobbies and paid work can be similarly intrinsically (or extrinsically) motivating. Specifically, under the means-end fusion perspective, intrinsic motivation occurs when the activity (means) engaged in and the outcome (goal) the activity provides are closely associated such that there is a sense of inseparability between the two (Kruglanski et al., 2013). Thus pursuit, rather than attainment, is what is rewarding. The greater the fusion between an activity and its outcome, the greater the intrinsic motivation to engage in that activity. This structural approach to intrinsic motivation suggests that increasing the association between an activity and an important end goal will have beneficial outcomes for intrinsic motivation, by allowing the activity to cognitively fuse with the goal such that the means become "an end in itself" (Shah & Kruglanski, 2000). For example, to enhance one's intrinsic motivation to jog to get in shape, a person can (1) lessen the association between other activities and getting in shape (e.g., playing tennis) and (2) lessen the association between jogging and other goals (e.g., pleasing a romantic partner). In this way, the association between jogging and getting in shape becomes stronger, increasing one's intrinsic motivation to jog.

In general, these two theories of intrinsic motivation – based on content (Ryan & Deci, 2000) versus structure (Kruglanski et al., 2013; Shah & Kruglanski, 2000) – both distinguish intrinsic incentives as engaged in for their own sake from extrinsic incentives, which are means to an end. Further, these two theories of motivation share in the assumption that extrinsic incentives can undermine intrinsic interest in activity pursuit, although they differ with regards to the underlying process.

Specifically, work on intrinsic motivation has identified the role extrinsic incentives have in undermining motivation. Extrinsic incentives can undermine intrinsic motivation by (1) diluting the association between the activity and its intrinsic value such that the means no longer feel as effective in obtaining a particular goal (Kruglanski et al., 2002), (2) leading to inferences about activity enjoyment based on the presence of extrinsic incentives (Kruglanski et al., 1972; Lepper & Greene, 1978; Lepper et al., 1973), or (3) exerting external control over people's behavior, undermining satisfaction from autonomy and exploration (Deci & Ryan, 1985; Ryan & Deci, 2000). In addition to reducing enjoyment, providing extrinsic incentives has been found to reduce the likelihood of future activity engagement (Deci, Koestner, & Ryan., 1999; Kruglanski et al., 1972; Kruglanski et al., 1975). For example, after being offered an extrinsic incentive for coloring, children who were given the chance to color again without this incentive were less interested in coloring (Lepper et al., 1973). This undermining effect happens even when the extrinsic incentive stays intact; for example, young children were less likely to eat foods that were presented as instrumental for extrinsic goals (e.g., making them healthier, or better at reading and math; Maimaran & Fishbach, 2014).

We note that although cases of purely extrinsically motivated activities (e.g., going to the dentist) and purely intrinsically motivated activities (e.g., eating a delicious cake) do exist, it is more often the case that activities offer both intrinsic and extrinsic incentives to some degree (Etkin, 2016; Fishbach & Choi, 2012). For example, when riding a bike one can receive intrinsic incentives (enjoyable experience) as well as extrinsic incentives (improved health), and reading can be entertaining (intrinsic), while also offering educational benefits (extrinsic).

Having outlined research on intrinsic motivation, differentiating between intrinsic and extrinsic incentives, we next address work on self-control and intertemporal choice that examines tradeoffs between receiving immediate versus delayed rewards.

Self-Control Conflicts: Trading off Immediate and Delayed Rewards

Research on self-control and intertemporal choice present people with decisions that involve trading off costs and benefits over time. These lines of research distinguish between long-term (delayed) outcomes and short-term (immediate) outcomes. Whereas immediate rewards materialize during pursuit of an activity and arrive sooner, delayed rewards materialize later in time and are an outcome of pursuit (Ainslie & Haslam, 1992; Hoch & Loewenstein, 1991; Kivetz & Simonson, 2002; Mischel et al., 1989; Thaler, 1981; Trope & Fishbach, 2000).

In particular, research on intertemporal choice assumes the value of an outcome is discounted or diminished over time, and documents people's willingness to forgo somewhat larger future rewards in order to receive smaller rewards in the present (e.g., Ainslie & Haslam, 1992; Mischel et al., 1989). This work further documented that people are temporally inconsistent (often referred to as hyperbolic discounting, declining impatience, or present bias) such that their discount rates decline as the length of time to the outcome increases (e.g., Thaler, 1981). Time inconsistent preferences can produce preference reversals as the time to both the more immediate and more delayed outcomes diminishes (Ainslie, 1975). For example, a person who prefers $10 today over $12 in a week may also prefer $12 in 53 weeks over $10 in 52 weeks (Thaler, 1981; Urminsky & Zauberman, 2016).

Thus, although delayed rewards may be preferred from a distance, the valuation of immediate rewards increases as the opportunity to receive these rewards becomes available (Ainslie, 2001; Rachlin, 2000). And although people are generally able to balance their present and futures benefits, at times they can become extremely impatient such that they overvalue present relative to future outcomes (Dai & Fishbach, 2013; Hoch & Loewenstein, 1991). Work on discounting typically finds that the more immediately available the reward is, the greater the desire for receiving it is. This distinction has been analyzed for a number of self-control conflicts, for example, while the option of studying can overall dominate activity choice, on the night of the party, for a short and critical period, the option to party is significantly more attractive, potentially even more so than the option to study (Fishbach & Converse, 2010).

Although self-control dilemmas pose a conflict between collecting immediate and delayed rewards, with priorities set in advance such that a person prefers to forgo the immediate short-term reward to receive the delayed, long-term reward (Fishbach & Converse, 2010; Mischel, Cantor, & Feldman, 1996), we note it is often the case that activities pursued for their long-term rewards also offer immediate rewards during pursuit, to some extent. For example, studying at the library provides delayed rewards, such as an improved exam grade, and can also provide immediate rewards to the extent that the material is interesting, and while people often work out for delayed health reasons, it is also true that exercising can provide immediate rewards (e.g., improved mood while exercising). This is similar to our earlier point that intrinsic and extrinsic incentives also often co-occur during activity pursuit. In the next section, we further discuss recent research on commonalities between immediate rewards and intrinsic incentives.

Association between Intrinsic Incentives and Immediate Rewards

In examining the commonalities between research on intrinsic motivation and reward timing, we focus on intrinsic incentives and immediate rewards, and contrast these with extrinsic incentives and delayed rewards. Our analysis suggests that insofar as intrinsic incentives are defined as part of the experience of activity pursuit, and extrinsic incentives are defined as external outcomes that are delivered after pursuit (i.e., the structural definition; Kruglanski et al., 2002), motivation and self-control concepts overlap: intrinsic incentives are immediate and extrinsic incentives are delayed (Woolley & Fishbach, 2015). Further, since intrinsic incentives are inherent in activity engagement and typically arrive more immediately, they may be associated with immediate delivery even in the case when they are not more immediate.

Before continuing, we note this overlap is not complete; for one, immediate rewards include both rewards that are internal to the activity and rewards that are external to the activity. For example, a person can dine to enjoy the taste of the food (internal benefit), or dine purely for the social benefit of celebrating with friends over a meal (external benefit, e.g., a vegetarian at a steak house, where the food is not an intrinsic benefit). Both rewards, the taste of good food and socializing with friends, occur immediately during the eating activity, yet the former is internal and the latter is external to it. In addition, delayed rewards include both rewards that are internal and external to the activity. For example, a person can eat spicy food to develop an acquired taste, in which the benefit is inherent in eating, but arrives later after repeated exposure, or a person can eat healthy food to procure future weight-loss benefits. Whereas both eating activities lead to delayed outcomes and are not immediately gratifying, their rewards are internal or external to the food consumption. We do not suggest that these concepts – intrinsic and immediate – should be combined, rather, we suggest that intrinsic incentives and immediate rewards are often closely associated and experienced similarly.

To provide evidence for the association between intrinsic incentives and immediate delivery, we asked participants in one study to indicate when they believed intrinsic and extrinsic benefits of exercising would be delivered, either immediately while exercising or at a delay after exercising. Specifically, participants rated when they believed intrinsic incentives (e.g., enjoying, having fun) and extrinsic incentives (e.g., keeping in shape, improving health as a result of working out) would be delivered. As predicted, participants expected intrinsic incentives for exercising to arrive more immediately than extrinsic incentives (Woolley & Fishbach, 2015). Similar results were found using work-related incentives. Here, participants rated common intrinsic workplace incentives (i.e., learning new things, developing skills and abilities, accomplishing something worthwhile, and doing something that makes you feel good about yourself) along with common extrinsic workplace incentives (i.e., receiving a paycheck, fringe benefits, having job security, and receiving praise from a supervisor; from Heath, 1999). Intrinsic-work incentives were rated as arriving more immediately than extrinsic-work incentives, further documenting the association between intrinsic incentives and immediacy.

Taking the perspective that intrinsic incentives are associated with immediate rewards leads to a number of implications in terms of what people value and how to motivate persistence that we address in the remainder of the chapter. First, we outline research on the valuation of intrinsic incentives, demonstrating that people care more about intrinsic incentives when they arrive more immediately. That is, because intrinsic incentives are associated with immediacy, people value these incentives more when they are available, inside pursuit, than from a distance outside pursuit. We next discuss how immediate rewards serve to increase intrinsic motivation, showing the earlier delivery of rewards renders the experience of an activity more intrinsic. Therefore, one way to increase intrinsic motivation in an activity is to provide rewards that have a more immediate arrival. Lastly, we address implications of focusing on or adding in immediate rewards to activity pursuit for increasing persistence in long-term goals. Specifically, we demonstrate that by focusing on immediate rewards, which are valuable to people during pursuit, people are able to persist longer in activities that they care about pursuing.

Proposition 1: Intrinsic Incentives are Valued More when they are Immediate

By taking a perspective that intrinsic motivation and immediate rewards share some commonalties, our research has been able to generate predictions for what people care about and how to motivate persistence. We predicted and found that people value intrinsic incentives more during pursuit, when these incentives are delivered, than either before or after pursuit, when these incentives are not immediately experienced (Woolley & Fishbach, 2015). Because intrinsic incentives come from pursuing, rather than completing, an activity, and are rewarding immediately during activity pursuit, these intrinsic incentives are more attractive inside pursuit.

This proposition is also consistent with research showing that only when people are in a "hot state" do they appreciate the strength and influence of that state ("empathy gap," Loewenstein, 2000; Van Boven, Loewenstein, Welch, & Dunning, 2012). For example, only adults actively experiencing social pain fully appreciate the pain of emotional bullying for middle school children. Intrinsic incentives tend to be experiential, and therefore, undervaluing the strength of the experience when in a cold state outside pursuit could lead to an undervaluation of intrinsic incentives at a distance (outside pursuit).

In one study demonstrating the shift in importance of intrinsic incentives, gym-goers indicated how important intrinsic and extrinsic incentives were to them in deciding how long to currently work out (present pursuit) or in deciding how long to work out in the future (outside pursuit; Woolley & Fishbach, 2015). The items mapping onto intrinsic incentives included, for example, "having an enjoyable workout" and "having a workout that feels fun," whereas the items mapping onto extrinsic incentives included, for example, "keeping in shape" and "improving health as a result of working out." Gym-goers indicated that intrinsic incentives mattered more to them for their present workout than for a future workout, whereas extrinsic incentives were similarly valuable for present and future workouts (see Figure 1.1). This suggests that having an enjoyable workout is important when deciding how much to exercise in the moment, but people do not value enjoyment nearly as much when deciding how long to persist working out in the future. Further, this shift in valuation seems to be unique to intrinsic incentives; extrinsic incentives were not valued differently for present and future pursuits.

Not only does the value placed on intrinsic incentives diminish over temporal distance (inside vs. outside pursuit), but it also diminishes over social distance (self vs.

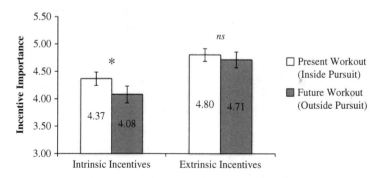

FIGURE 1.1 Intrinsic incentives are rated as more important inside pursuit of a present workout than outside pursuit of a future workout, whereas extrinsic incentives do not differ in importance for present and future pursuits

Note: lines in bars represent ± one *SE*

Source: Woolley & Fishbach, 2015

other). That is, people have the tendency to believe that they are more motivated by intrinsic incentives than are others (Heath, 1999). Whereas people are aware that intrinsic incentives matter for them, they underestimate the extent to which these incentives matter for others. For example, people feel that "learning new things" or "developing skills at work" are motivating factors for themselves, but they predict that this is less true for others. This finding may shed some light on why people believe others who pursue immediate desires (e.g., those who smoke or are overweight) lack willpower and self-control (Allon, 1982; Freeman, Shmueli, & Muraven, 2013; Puhl & Latner, 2007). That is, people may not realize the strength of intrinsic, immediate motives (in this case, temptation) for others, and just how hard it is to overcome them.

These effects on the valuation of intrinsic incentives have implications for how much people persist in activities in the moment versus anticipate persisting when they are reflecting on an upcoming activity. Specifically, intrinsic incentives may increase persistence in activities more than people realize at a distance when they are outside pursuit. Because people outside the activity are less aware that intrinsic incentives are important during pursuit, they fail to predict the influence of intrinsic incentives on their future task persistence. In one study demonstrating this, we examined the role of intrinsic incentives in pursuers' (inside pursuit) ability to follow through and persist in a task, compared with predictors' (outside pursuit) expectations for their own future persistence. Participants in this study were assigned to work on either a fun joke reading task or a boring computer manual reading task (high vs. low intrinsic incentives). The task further offered $0.10 or $0.05 bonus per trial (high vs. low extrinsic incentives). For pursuers inside pursuit, the presence of intrinsic incentives was the only factor driving their task persistence: they persisted longer when reading jokes than reading sections of a computer manual. However, predictors were blind to this and did not anticipate the role intrinsic incentives would play in shaping their persistence. Instead, predictors only expected extrinsic incentives to influence persistence: they expected to persist longer in the task that paid more (Woolley & Fishbach, 2015; Figure 1.2).

We next move to examine the role reward timing plays in influencing intrinsic motivation. We argue that the greater the temporal association is between an activity and its reward, the more the activity is perceived as intrinsically motivating. That is, immediate rewards can increase intrinsic motivation compared to delayed rewards.

Proposition 2: Reward Timing Increases Intrinsic Motivation

Not only do people value intrinsic rewards more when these are immediately available (e.g., inside perspective) than when they are at a distance (e.g., outside perspective), but they also perceive activities that offer immediate (vs. delayed) rewards as more intrinsically motivating.

According to Kruglanski's theory of means–end fusion outlined earlier, intrinsic motivation is derived from means that are closely associated with their end goals, and it

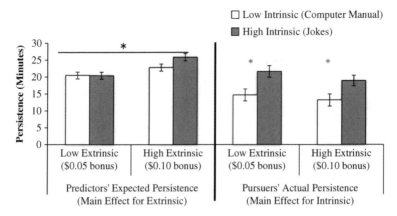

FIGURE 1.2 Predictors outside of a task reported their persistence (minutes completed) would only be influenced by extrinsic incentives (main effect for extrinsic), while pursuers' actual persistence was only influenced by intrinsic incentives (main effect for intrinsic)

Note: lines in bars represent $\pm$ one *SE*

Source: Woolley & Fishbach, 2015

is this sense of inseparability that makes the motivation intrinsic. This theory would predict that activities closely fused with goals are (1) perceived as more instrumental to goal attainment, (2) perceived as more intrinsically motivated, and (3) exhibit properties of the ends they serve. This content free theorization of intrinsic motivation creates a broader definition whereby activities need not be tied to specific goals (i.e., autonomy, competence, relatedness; Ryan & Deci, 2000). It thus suggests activities pursued for specific goals can be seen as intrinsic to the extent that there is a greater overlap between the specific activity and the goal it serves. For example, a person who bikes only to get in shape would be more intrinsically motivated (one means for one goal) than a person who bikes and runs in order to get in shape (two means for one goal).

In support of this, one study demonstrated that although typically seen as an extrinsic incentive, the presence of money can actually increase intrinsic motivation when the monetary reward is closely associated with the activity (Kruglanski et al., 1975). In this study, half of participants played a coin-toss game that is typically played for real money, and as such, receiving money is closely associated with the game. The other half of participants played a game with wooden blocks, an activity typically not associated with payment, where money was viewed as an extrinsic reward. The experimenters manipulated whether participants received money for the activity (coin-toss vs. block task) or not. In the coin-toss game, when money was intrinsic to the task, participants who received payment were more intrinsically motivated than those who did not receive payment. The opposite was true when money was extrinsic to the task; in this case, receiving money (vs. not) reduced intrinsic motivation. This study suggests that whenever money is closely associated with a task, its presence enhances intrinsic motivation as it provides a salient intrinsic cause for task performance.

On the basis of Kruglanski's theorizing that a close association between the activity and the end goal fosters intrinsic motivation, our research offers an approach for increasing intrinsic motivation. Specifically, we find that decreasing the temporal distance between a reward and an activity can lead the activity to be perceived as more intrinsically motivating. That is, because an earlier delivery of the reward strengthens the association between the activity and its reward, intrinsic motivation for the activity increases.

Our research finds that indeed a reward arriving more immediately increases intrinsic motivation to pursue an activity. In one study (Woolley & Fishbach, 2017), we had participants work on an experiment for a fixed payment. After starting the study, some participants learned of a bonus payment that was tied to reading an excerpt of a book. A third of participants learned this bonus would pay out immediately after they finished the reading task, while another third learned the bonus would be paid to them a month after completing the reading task. A final third of participants did not receive a bonus (no-reward control group). To assess intrinsic motivation, we had participants rate their experience as intrinsic (e.g., enjoyable, interesting), and also presented a free choice between continuing the reading task and switching to a new task. Other research suggested the hallmark of intrinsic motivation is choosing the task during free choice when no external incentives are offered (Deci, 1971; Deci et al., 1999). We find that participants who expected to receive their bonus immediately were more intrinsically motivated to work on their task, indicating that the reading task was more enjoyable and interesting than those receiving a delayed bonus or no bonus (Figure 1.3). Further, those who had previously received an immediate bonus for reading the book excerpt were more likely to choose to continue reading the excerpt during the free choice phase than those who previously received a delayed bonus (63.3% versus 44.4%) or no bonus (50.8%).

This study may seem inconsistent at first with research on the Over-justification Hypothesis (Lepper & Greene, 1978), which found that adding a reward to the pursuit of an intrinsic activity undermines (i.e., crowds out) intrinsic motivation to pursue that activity. However, a crowding out effect emerges whenever researchers introduce a reward for an activity that is otherwise not rewarded, and the key comparison is between the rewarded and non-rewarded treatments. In contrast, our research compares engagement in an activity that is typically rewarded and indeed, everyone is getting paid (although those in the control condition did not receive a bonus). Our key comparison is between those who received the bonus sooner versus later or versus no-bonus payment.

Notably, it is still possible that our results are inconsistent with the Over-justification Hypothesis, to the extent that this hypothesis predicts larger rewards

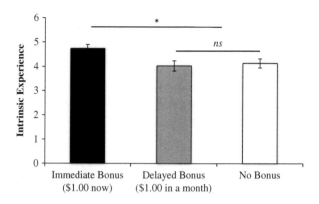

FIGURE 1.3 Expecting to receive an immediate bonus increased intrinsic interest in reading a book excerpt (e.g., how enjoyable, how interesting) compared with those expecting a delayed or no bonus

Note: lines in bars represent ± one *SE*

Source: Woolley & Fishbach, 2017

crowd out motivation more. Recall that research on intertemporal choice demonstrated a greater valuation of immediate (vs. delayed) rewards in the present. This could suggest that adding immediate and therefore, psychologically larger, rewards to activity pursuit will crowd out intrinsic motivation more. In contrast, we find that by decreasing the temporal distance between the reward and the activity, we increase intrinsic motivation, which suggests that the effect introduced by immediacy on activity-reward association strength is likely larger than the effect of immediacy on increased subjective reward magnitude.

In another study, participants received a reward (a chocolate truffle) either at the start of an experimental task (immediate condition) or only after they completed the task (delayed condition). Importantly, in both conditions participants were not allowed to eat the candy until after the study. As a measure of intrinsic motivation, participants then indicated how enjoyable the task was to work on. Those who received the reward immediately at the start of the task rated the experimental task as more enjoyable compared with those who received a delayed reward at the end of the experimental task.

These results are consistent with research on the Dilution Effect, which finds that as the association strength between an activity and its goal is decreased through the addition of multiple goals, intrinsic motivation is reduced (Orehek et al., 2012; Zhang, Fishbach, & Kruglanski, 2007). Rather than manipulate the activity-goal association through the number of goals received as an outcome of activity pursuit, we manipulate this association through the timing of reward delivery. In this way, we demonstrate that delivering a reward earlier in time increases intrinsic motivation for an activity; both the rated enjoyment and actual interest in pursuing a task in the future (i.e., free choice measure) increased when a reward was more immediate. In the next section, we move on to implications of this increase in intrinsic motivation for facilitating persistence in long-term goals.

Proposition 3: Harnessing Immediate Rewards and Intrinsic Motivation to Increase Persistence in Long-term Goals

Perceiving an activity that offers an immediate reward as more intrinsically motivating has implications for increasing engagement. Accordingly, we next explore whether immediate rewards increase engagement in an activity, even for activities primarily motivated by delayed rewards or extrinsic incentives.

Immediate Rewards Increase Long-term Goal Persistence

Can focusing attention on immediate rewards be beneficial in facilitating persistence in goals that serve long-term delayed rewards? On the one hand, people may perceive that short-term and long-term goals are in conflict, for example that healthy food is less tasty and tasty food is unhealthy (e.g., Raghunathan, Naylor, & Hoyer, 2006), and therefore emphasizing immediate rewards will make the activity appear less instrumental in the long-run. On the other hand, the pursuit of long-term goals does not always come at the expense of short-term interests (e.g., enjoying the taste of healthy food). Thus whenever people are intrinsically motivated to pursue activities that are associated with long-term goals, such as health or professional success, they come to receive both immediate and delayed rewards from the same action. Under such circumstances, people can increase their motivation by attending to immediate and intrinsic rewards of the action.

Some support for the notion that immediate rewards can facilitate long-term goal pursuit comes from previous research outlined above demonstrating the importance of the experience when inside activity pursuit (Woolley & Fishbach, 2015). During pursuit, the experience of the activity is salient and immediate, and immediate/intrinsic rewards are more valuable during pursuit than in advance. This suggests factoring in experience into option choice could facilitate persistence in an activity. More relevant for self-control behavior, to increase persistence in a long-term goal (e.g., exercising for health), a person could choose from a set of behaviors the one that is most enjoyable – immediately and intrinsically motivating – in order to increase engagement and persistence.

We first tested whether immediate and intrinsic rewards are more strongly associated with increased persistence in long-term goals compared with delayed and extrinsic rewards (Woolley & Fishbach, 2016a). We predicted that although activities such as studying and exercising first and foremost serve positive delayed outcomes, immediate rewards are more strongly associated with persistence in these long-term goals than are delayed rewards. We approached students studying in a library and measured how important their study materials were (delayed-extrinsic rewards), how enjoyable their study materials were (immediate-intrinsic rewards), and the total number of hours spent working on their materials that day. As predicted, immediate rewards more strongly predicted hours spent studying than delayed rewards. In another study, we approached gym-goers before they started using cardio machines at a gym. We recorded their valuation of delayed/extrinsic rewards (how important it was that their exercise was useful at keeping them in shape), their valuation of immediate/intrinsic rewards (how important it was that their exercise was enjoyable), and the number of minutes spent exercising. As predicted, the valuation of immediate rewards was a stronger predictor of minutes spent exercising than the valuation of delayed rewards. Having confirmed immediate rewards are associated with increased persistence in long-term goals (studying and exercising), we next moved to manipulating focus to immediate or delayed rewards inherent in long-term goals.

To test whether choosing based on immediate and intrinsic interests facilitates long-term goal pursuit, in one study we had participants choose between eating organic and non-organic carrots (Woolley & Fishbach, 2016b). We first confirmed that carrot consumption is mainly driven by health concerns for our population. We then manipulated participants' focus on immediate-intrinsic rewards ("Please choose the carrots you think are the tastiest and that you will enjoy eating the most. Since you'll be eating the carrots today, it's important you choose one that you like and find enjoyable to eat."), delayed-extrinsic rewards ("Please choose the carrots you think are the healthiest and that you will benefit the most from eating. Since you'll be eating the carrots today, it's important you choose one that is healthy and nutritious to eat."), or no rewards ("Please choose the carrots you think are more orange."). Participants made their selection and sampled the carrots, after which we recorded the amount of grams they consumed. In this choice set, the majority of people select the organic option – however they do so for different reasons: those in the immediate-rewards focus condition select organic carrots because they are tastier, whereas those in the delayed-rewards focus condition select organic carrots because they are healthier. We found that those choosing for immediate-rewards ate more of their selected carrots than those choosing for delayed-rewards, and more than the no rewards-focus control condition (Figure 1.4). This study suggests that focusing on immediate rewards increases consumption of a healthy food more than a neutral (control) and a delayed-rewards focus, even though participants report primarily eating carrots for delayed health rewards.

Other work supports the idea that focusing on immediate, experiential rewards boosts activity engagement during pursuit compared with focusing on delayed rewards (Fishbach & Choi, 2012). For activities offering both immediate and delayed rewards, focusing on the delayed reward may increase initiation, yet decrease persistence. In one study, pursuers who focused on the experience of folding origami (immediate reward) were more interested in continuing to engage in the activity than those focusing on their goals while creating origami (delayed reward). Focusing on the experience of pursuing the origami activity (immediate reward) increased

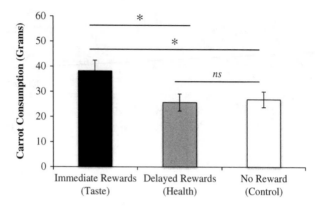

FIGURE 1.4 Choosing based on immediate rewards increases consumption of carrots more than choosing based on delayed rewards or no rewards

Note: lines in bars represent ± one *SE*

Source: Woolley & Fishbach, 2016b

pursuers' motivation to continue working on the activity compared with focusing on the activity's instrumentality (delayed reward).

These results showing a focus on immediate rewards can boost persistence in long-term goals, have implications for our understanding of self-control failures. When people fail to persist in certain long-term goals such as healthy eating or exercise behaviors, this may be because they do not perceive the activity as providing immediate benefits. For example, someone who stops an exercise program that is not enjoyable for her may be quitting because she believes the activity does not offer her the benefits that are important to her in the moment – immediate rewards. Future research can examine this possibility and also explore whether immediate rewards can help increase persistence in long-term goals by bypassing the need for self-control.

Adding Immediate Rewards that are Extrinsic to the Pursuit of Long-term Goals

The aforementioned research found that focusing on immediate-intrinsic rewards and thinking about the experience during activity pursuit helped facilitate continued activity engagement. Specifically, this work demonstrated that focusing on immediate rewards that are intrinsic to pursuing the activity helped to facilitate persistence. However, our theory also predicts that adding immediate rewards into activity pursuit increases goal persistence, even when these rewards are external to the activity. Although not inherent in activity pursuit, adding in external immediate rewards can increase persistence by boosting the positive experience of pursuit.

In line with this analysis, in one study high school students working on an in-class assignment were either allowed to add immediate rewards to the pursuit of their school work (immediate-rewards condition) or not (control condition). Students in the immediate rewards condition were given the opportunity to use fun colored pens, eat snacks, and listen to music while they worked. In a pilot test, we confirmed that students agreed adding these immediate rewards would make school work more fun. We find that students who received this combination of immediate rewards attempted to complete a greater percentage of their assignment than those in the control condition. Although these immediate rewards could be considered distracting, such that participants focus on the music and food rather than their work, this was not the case.

We were further interested in whether immediate rewards predict increased persistence in comparison with delayed rewards. We measured students' experience of immediate rewards while working on their assignment (e.g., "was working on this assignment fun?") as well as their experience of delayed rewards (e.g., "was working on this assignment important for understanding the materials?"). Presumably, students do their homework for long-term benefits (i.e., because it is important; not fun). However, we find students who reported experiencing more immediate-intrinsic rewards while working on their assignment attempted more math problems, with no effect of delayed-extrinsic rewards on persistence. Overall, our findings suggest adding immediate rewards can help high-school students work more on an assignment, without causing distraction.

In an effort to assist people facing self-control conflicts, other work has documented how adding rewards can influence motivation to engage in certain health behaviors. This research has found strong, positive short-term effects of financial incentives for inducing behavior change such as weight loss (John et al., 2011; Volpp et al., 2008), smoking cessation (Volpp et al., 2009), increased exercise (Acland & Levy, 2015; Charness & Gneezy, 2009), and adherence to medication (Volpp et al., 2008). One remaining question is what happens when these immediate rewards are removed? Research on intrinsic motivation could suggest the rewards, which are external to pursuit, crowd out intrinsic motivation such that removing the reward then removes interest in pursuing the incentivized activity (Deci & Ryan, 1985; Lepper & Greene, 1978). However, most studies do not find long-term negative effects of temporary incentives; in the absence of a reward, pursuit of the incentivized behavior can return to baseline (John et al., 2011; Volpp et al., 2006), with other research finding a positive impact of temporary incentives on behavior (Charness & Gneezy, 2009; Goswami & Urminsky, 2017; Volpp et al., 2009).

One possible strategy to increase the impact of financial incentives (and a possible area for developing interventions) is to connect the activity and reward more closely in time, rather than provide the reward with a delay after engaging in the activity. Through a closer temporal association, our research predicts that the reward could increase people's intrinsic motivation to engage in the behavior. A good example of this comes from evidence showing that bundling "should" behaviors that produce a delayed reward (e.g., exercising) with immediately gratifying "want" behaviors (e.g., listening to a popular novel) increases pursuit of the delayed behavior (Milkman, Minson, & Volpp, 2013). We note, however, that this intervention changes the actual experience of goal pursuit, not the perceived experience, and we would not expect continued persistence in the long-term goal absent the immediate reward.

Conclusions

We offer novel insights into work on both intrinsic motivation and research on immediate and delayed rewards. Whereas these theories have typically been studied in isolation from one another, we identify some commonalities between the two. Thus because intrinsic incentives are inherent in activity pursuit, they often arrive immediately and are associated with an immediate delivery.

In exploring the parallels between intrinsic incentives and immediate rewards (and between extrinsic incentives and delayed rewards), we came to three propositions. First, with regard to valuation of intrinsic incentives, we demonstrated that people care more about intrinsic incentives in the present than in the past or future. For example, people care more about learning new things for their present job than past and future jobs. Second, we demonstrated that immediate rewards increase intrinsic motivation because the reward (goal) becomes strongly associated with the activity (means). We specifically showed that an earlier delivery of a reward renders the experience of an activity more intrinsic. Receiving an earlier (vs. delayed) bonus, for example, increases intrinsic motivation to pursue a work task even after the bonus reward was removed. Third, we demonstrated that immediate rewards increase persistence in long-term (extrinsic) goals by increasing intrinsic motivation.

As a final note, we mention that we have no doubt that there are times when intrinsic incentives and immediate rewards are less likely to overlap, and recognize the distinct definitions and large bodies of literature on each of these motivational factors. However, we suggest an important, yet overlooked area of research on intrinsic motivation and reward timing – that the characteristics associated with each may have more in common than previously identified, and demonstrate the implications of this for fostering motivation.

References

Acland, D., & Levy, M. R. (2015). Naiveté, projection bias, and habit formation in gym attendance. *Management Science*, 61(1), 146–160.

Ainslie, G. (1975). Specious reward: a behavioral theory of impulsiveness and impulse control. *Psychological Bulletin*, 82(4), 463–496.

Ainslie, G. (2001). *Breakdown of will*. New York: Cambridge University Press.

Ainslie, G., & Haslam, N. (1992). *Hyperbolic discounting*. In G. Loewenstein & J. Elster (Eds.), *Choice over time* (pp. 57–92). New York: Russell Sage Foundation.

Allon, N. (1982). The stigma of overweight in everyday life. In B. B. Wolman (Ed.), *Psychological aspects of obesity: A handbook* (pp. 130–174). New York: Van Nostrand Reinhold.

Charness, G., & Gneezy, U. (2009). Incentives to exercise. *Econometrica*, 77(3), 909–931.

Dai, X., & Fishbach, A. (2013). When waiting to choose increases patience. *Organizational Behavior and Human Decision Processes*, 121, 256–266.

Deci, E. L. (1971). Effects of externally mediated rewards on intrinsic motivation. *Journal of Personality and Social Psychology*, *18*(1), 105–115.

Deci, E. L., Koestner, R., & Ryan, R. M. (1999). A meta-analytic review of experiments examining the effects of extrinsic rewards on intrinsic motivation. *Psychological Bulletin*, 125(6), 627–668.

Deci, E. L., & Ryan, R. M. (1985). *Intrinsic motivation and self-determination in human behavior*. New York: Plenum Press.

Etkin, J. (2016). The hidden cost of personal quantification. *Journal of Consumer Research*, 42 (6), 967–984.

Fishbach, A., & Choi, J. (2012). When thinking about goals undermines goal pursuit. *Organizational Behavior and Human Decision Processes*, 118(2), 99–107.

Fishbach, A., & Converse, B. A. (2010). Identifying and battling temptation. *Handbook of self-regulation: Research, theory and applications*, 2, 244–260.

Freeman, N., Shmueli, D., & Muraven, M. (2013). Lay theories of self-control influence judgments of individuals who have failed at self-control. *Journal of Applied Social Psychology*, 43(7), 1418–1427.

Goswami, I., & Urminsky, O. (2017). The dynamic effect of incentives on post-reward task engagement. *Journal of Experimental Psychology: General*, 146(1), 1–19.

Heath, C. (1999). On the social psychology of agency relationships: Lay theories of motivation overemphasize extrinsic incentives. *Organizational Behavior and Human Decision Processes*, 78(1), 25–62.

Higgins, E. T., & Trope, Y. (1990). Activity engagement theory: Implications of multiply identifiable input for intrinsic motivation. In R. M. Sorrentino & E. T. Higgins (Eds.), *Handbook of motivation and cognition: Foundations of social behavior* (pp. 229–264). New York: Guildford Press.

Hoch, S. J., & Loewenstein, G. F. (1991). Time-inconsistent preferences and consumer self-control. *Journal of Consumer Research*, 17, 492–507.

John, L. K., Loewenstein, G., Troxel, A. B., Norton, L., Fassbender, J. E., & Volpp, K. G. (2011). Financial incentives for extended weight loss: a randomized, controlled trial. *Journal of General Internal Medicine*, 26(6), 621–626.

Kivetz, R., & Simonson, I. (2002). Self-control for the righteous: Toward a theory of precommitment to indulgence. *Journal of Consumer Research*, 29(2), 199–217.

Kruglanski, A. W. (1975). The endogenous-exogenous partition in attribution theory. *Psychological Review*, 82(6), 387–406.

Kruglanski, A. W., Alon, S., & Lewis, T. (1972). Retrospective misattribution and task enjoyment. *Journal of Experimental Social Psychology*, 8(6), 493–501.

Kruglanski, A. W., Köpetz, C., Bélanger, J. J., Chun, W. Y., Orehek, E., & Fishbach, A. (2013). Features of multifinality. *Personality and Social Psychology Review*, 17(1), 22–39.

Kruglanski, A. W., Riter, A., Amitai, A., Margolin, B. S., Shabtai, L., & Zaksh, D. (1975). Can money enhance intrinsic motivation? A test of the content-consequence hypothesis. *Journal of Personality and Social Psychology*, 31(4), 744–750.

Kruglanski, A. W., Shah, J. Y., Fishbach, A., Friedman, R., Chun, W. Y., & Sleeth-Keppler, D. (2002). A theory of goal systems. *Advances in Experimental Social Psychology*, 34, 331–378.

Lepper, M. R., & Greene, D. (1978). *The hidden costs of rewards: New perspectives on the psychology of human motivation*. Oxford: Erlbaum.

Lepper, M. R., Greene, D., & Nisbett, R. E. (1973). Undermining children's intrinsic interest with extrinsic reward: A test of the "overjustification" hypothesis. *Journal of Personality and Social Psychology*, 28(1), 129–137.

Loewenstein, G. (2000). Emotions in economic theory and economic behavior. *The American Economic Review*, 90(2), 426–432.

Maimaran, M., & Fishbach, A. (2014). If it's useful and you know it, do you eat? Preschoolers refrain from instrumental food. *Journal of Consumer Research*, 41(3), 642–655.

Milkman, K. L., Minson, J. A., & Volpp, K. G. (2013). Holding the Hunger Games hostage at the gym: An evaluation of temptation bundling. *Management Science*, 60(2), 283–299.

Mischel, W., Cantor, N., & Feldman, S. (1996). Principles of self-regulation: The nature of willpower and self-control. In E. T. Higgins & A. W. Kruglanski (Eds.), *Social psychology: Handbook of basic principles* (pp. 329–360). New York: Guilford Press.

Mischel, W., Shoda, Y., & Rodriguez, M. I. (1989). Delay of gratification in children. *Science*, 244(4907), 933–938.

Orehek, E., Mauro, R., Kruglanski, A. W., & van der Bles, A. M. (2012). Prioritizing association strength versus value: The influence of self-regulatory modes on means evaluation in single goal and multigoal contexts. *Journal of Personality and Social Psychology*, 102(1), 22–31.

Puhl, R. M., & Latner, J. D. (2007). Stigma, obesity, and the health of the nation's children. *Psychological Bulletin*, 133(4), 557–580.

Rachlin, H. (2000). *The science of self-control*. Cambridge, MA: Harvard University Press.

Raghunathan, R., Naylor, R. W., & Hoyer, W. D. (2006). The unhealthy = tasty intuition and its effects on taste inferences, enjoyment, and choice of food products. *Journal of Marketing*, 70(4), 170–184.

Ryan, R. M., & Deci, E. L. (2000). Self-determination theory and the facilitation of intrinsic motivation, social development, and well-being. *American Psychologist*, 55(1), 68–78.

Sansone, C., & Harackiewicz, J. M. (1996). I don't feel like it: The function of interest in self-regulation. In L. L. Martin & A. Tesser (Eds.), *Striving and feeling: Interactions among goals, affect, and self-regulation* (pp. 203–228). Hillsdale, NJ: Erlbaum.

Shah, J. Y., & Kruglanski, A. W. (2000). Aspects of goal networks: Implications for self-regulation. In M. Boekaerts, P. R. Pintrich, & M. Zeidner (Eds.), *Handbook of self regulation* (pp. 85–110). San Diego, CA: Academic Press

Thaler, R. H. (1981). Some empirical evidence on dynamic inconsistency. *Economic Letters*, 8, 201–207.

Trope, Y., & Fishbach, A. (2000). Counteractive self-control in overcoming temptation. *Journal of Personality and Social Psychology*, 79(4), 493–506.

Urminsky, O., & Zauberman, G. (2016). The psychology of intertemporal preferences. In G. Keren & G. Wu (Eds.) *Blackwell Handbook of Judgment and Decision Making* (pp. 141–181). Oxford: Wiley-Blackwell.

Van Boven, L., Loewenstein, G., Welch, E., & Dunning, D. (2012). The illusion of courage in self-predictions: Mispredicting one's own behavior in embarrassing situations. *Journal of Behavioral Decision Making*, 25(1), 1–12.

Volpp, K. G., John, L. K., Troxel, A. B., Norton, L., Fassbender, J., & Loewenstein, G. (2008). Financial incentive–based approaches for weight loss: A randomized trial. *JAMA*, 300(22), 2631–2637.

Volpp, K. G., Levy, A. G., Asch, D. A., Berlin, J. A., Murphy, J. J., Gomez, A., Sox, H., Zhu, J., & Lerman, C. (2006). A randomized controlled trial of financial incentives for smoking cessation. *Cancer Epidemiology Biomarkers & Prevention*, 15(1), 12–18.

Volpp, K. G., Loewenstein, G., Troxel, A. B., Doshi, J., Price, M., Laskin, M., & Kimmel, S. E. (2008). A test of financial incentives to improve warfarin adherence. *BMC Health Services Research*, 8(1), 1–6.

Volpp, K. G., Troxel, A. B., Pauly, M. V., Glick, H. A., Puig, A., Asch, D. A., Galvin, R., Zhu, J., Wan, F., DeGuzman, J., Corbett, E., Weiner, J., & Audrain-McGovern, J. (2009). A randomized, controlled trial of financial incentives for smoking cessation. *New England Journal of Medicine*, 360(7), 699–709.

Woolley, K., & Fishbach, A. (2015). The experience matters more than you think: People value intrinsic incentives more inside than outside an activity. *Journal of Personality and Social Psychology*, 109(6), 968–982.

Woolley, K., & FishbachA. (2016a). Immediate rewards predict adherence to long-term goals. *Personality and Social Psychology Bulletin*, 43(2), 1–12, doi:10.1177/0146167216676480.

Woolley, K., & Fishbach, A. (2016b). For the fun of it: Harnessing immediate rewards to increase persistence in long-term goals. *Journal of Consumer Research*, 42(6), 952–966.

Woolley, K., & FishbachA. (2017). It's about time: Earlier rewards increase intrinsic motivation. (Working paper).

Wrzesniewski, A., Schwartz, B., Cong, X., Kane, M., Omar, A., & Kolditz, T. (2014). Multiple types of motives don't multiply the motivation of West Point cadets. *Proceedings of the National Academy of Sciences*, 111(30), 10990–10995.

Zhang, Y., Fishbach, A., & Kruglanski, A. W. (2007). The dilution model: how additional goals undermine the perceived instrumentality of a shared path. *Journal of Personality and Social Psychology*, 92(3), 389–401.

2

THE MOTIVATION-COGNITION INTERFACE IN CONFORMITY AND DEVIANCE

Hans-Peter Erb

Social influence phenomena lie at the very heart of the human nature and are thus a major theme in social psychology as a scientific discipline. Social psychologists have long been aware of the fact that influencing other individuals and being influenced by others are the necessary conditions of coordinated action. Social influence makes possible those achievements by groups, societies, and even mankind that require more than a single individual's motivation, will, decision, and execution. On the downside, individuals' sensitivity to what others feel, think, and do often results in effects seen as unwanted or even unwarranted. For example, the French sociologist Le Bon (1895/1960) presented a theory of "crowd behavior" according to which a mass of people can take command of an individual's self-control and personal responsibility. Interestingly, such negative effects of social influence were historically the first to attract researchers (see Pratkanis, 2007). At the latest, with the seminal studies and the by then astonishing results of Solomon Asch (1956), the social influence that a majority of others would exert on individual judgments entered social psychological research and was thereafter examined under the term *conformity*. It was not before Moscovici's (1980) formulation of his *conversion theory* (CT) that the influence of a minority of others also began to attract scientific attention. As going along with the minority contradicts what can be seen as the norm of "shared reality" (Echterhoff, Higgins, & Levine, 2009; Hardin & Higgins, 1996), it can be termed *deviance*. Conformity, as the mechanism that often secures social stability, and deviance, at times resulting in social change, build the major themes of the present chapter.

In 1990, Arie W. Kruglanski and Diane M. Mackie (Kruglanski & Mackie, 1990) published a paper in the *European Review of Social Psychology* in which they theoretically analyzed the most significant approaches to explain conformity and deviance at that time. As a young doctoral student who was interested specifically in conformity phenomena, I was very much fascinated by Kruglanski and Mackie's investigation into minority and majority influence, and their analyses have guided my own work on social influence ever since. In what follows, I will (briefly) re-develop Kruglanski and Mackie's (1990) basic notion that conformity and deviance can be traced back to the operation of consensus – that is, information on whether many versus few other people would agree over a certain issue or topic. Other than in alternative prominent conceptions (Deutsch & Gerard, 1955; Moscovici, 1980) that I will have to briefly discuss, the Kruglanski and Mackie analysis portrays the individual as rather flexible in that both low (minority) and high consensus (majority) positions can fulfill a variety of different motivations that the individual may have in a specific influence setting. This "consensus-based" approach leads to a number of predictions on which I will report empirical evidence. In particular, I will demonstrate that (a) consensus can have a crucial impact on human judgment, (b) consensus can interact with other variables to determine the extent to which individuals invest cognitive effort in a specific influence situation, and (c) some motivations, specifically the human pursuit for uniqueness and risk-seeking, can render the low consensus position attractive to the targets of social influence. I will conclude with a discussion of the theoretical and empirical assets of a consensus based approach as opposed to other theories of social influence.

In Disbelief of Popular Views

Kruglanski and Mackie (1990) started their discussion with "popular views" of majorities and minorities. First and foremost, they found that not only colloquial language, but also many scientific approaches accorded negative characteristics to minorities and positive characteristics to majorities by default. Often, minorities appear to be "small groups of oppressed and underprivileged" (Kruglanski & Mackie, 1990, p. 229) underdogs and are therefore considered less favorably, whereas majorities represent the social power of those with access to material, social, and psychological resources. And yet, Kruglanski and Mackie (1990) in their further analysis questioned that minorities are necessarily the oppressed, deprived, and basically the "bad" (Moscovici, 1980), and majorities necessarily those in demand of social power, in access to resources, and basically the "good." In fact, at times powerful minorities rule over the "silent majority" or represent "elites" like the members of a board of experts advising a nation's government. Thus, the "powerful might be few in number, and the underprivileged a horde or a handful" (Kruglanski & Mackie, 1990, p. 230). Accordingly, it would make no sense to associate conformity and deviance to characteristics that apparently can vary independently of minority and majority status.

Kruglanski and Mackie (1990) reached this conclusion on the basis of an extensive analysis of contemporary approaches, by then prominent theoretical models to explain minority and majority influence, and known empirical findings. I cannot engage into a detailed report of these fascinating considerations here, because this would go far beyond the present scope. Some examples may suffice. For instance, Kruglanski and Mackie (1990) found that neither minorities nor majorities would necessarily induce or satisfy needs or avoidance of non-specific closure (Kruglanski, 1989; Kruglanski & Webster, 1996). Instead, these authors argued that minorities and majorities can motivate targets of influence more or less to engage into processing of information related to the position they advocate. And perhaps most astonishing, at least at that time, Kruglanski and Mackie (1990) also found that a need for specific closure (Kruglanski, 1989) would not necessarily covary with minority versus majority source status. As they put it, "Whereas majorities are often seen as prestigious and desirable, and are therefore capable of arousing needs of specific closure, minorities can also be perceived in positive terms and thus be capable of arousing similar identification needs" (Kruglanski & Mackie, 1990, p. 243). The innovative and pioneering character of this corollary is hard to overestimate. It stood and still stands in stark contrast to two then and till this day prominent models aiming at the explanation of conformity and deviance, namely Mocovici's CT and Deutsch and Gerard's (1955) distinction between normative and informational influence. To fully understand Kruglanski and Mackie's (1990) analysis, I have to turn the reader's attention to these two models.

Conversion Theory and the Normative-informational Influence Distinction

Moscovici's (1976, 1980) CT was and still is one of the most influential models to explain social stability and social change and had an extremely energizing effect in particular on research into deviance and social change (see Wood et al., 1994, for a review of empirical findings). CT accorded qualitative differences to the processes that underlie minority and majority influence. As a starting point, this model holds that minorities are inevitably "... bad, because there are few who do it" (Moscovici, 1980, p. 210), whereas majorities generally represent positive valence.

Whenever an individual is in disagreement with a social majority, she or he would engage into a social comparison process without considering the details of the majority's matter of moment. Rather, the social conflict with the majority lies in the focus of the recipient's attention. To resolve the conflict with the majority, the target will show compliance, that is agreement with the majority in public in rather neglect of issue-relevant considerations. The driving force behind compliance is persuasion through threats of censure and ostracism to those who dare to deviate. Thus, the social power to reward conformity and to punish deviance, which CT unconditionally ascribes to majorities, reminds the individual of the stress and discomfort associated with dissent that she or he would immediately resolve. As such, majority influence is not substantiated, neither by extensive information processing of issue-relevant facts nor by a change of the target's inner conviction. It is short-lived and the change in attitudes vanishes as soon as the source of influence is no longer present. In short, conformity rests on the normative power of the majority by a rather neglect of the question whether the advocated position is correct or not.

Conversely, the social influence by minorities follows a qualitatively different psychological process. With reference to the minorities' lack of social power, CT holds that minorities can only be persuasive by presenting the content of their position. At first, a minority would have to evoke a climate of social unrest and change. This is accomplished by displaying a consistent behavioral style, in that the minority repeats their position unanimously and in a multitude of varying situations. The result is that the target will experience a cognitive conflict. Such conflict revolves around the question of whether the minority's position may be wrong or right. Subsequently, the target of the influence will engage into the extensive processing of information that relates to the content of the issue at hand – a process that is termed *validation* in CT. Validation leads to a slow, private, subtle, but constant change toward the minority position. The target will be reluctant to express her or his attitude change in public as long as the opposing majority still is in power and public punishment for deviance is imminent. Yet, the careful consideration of the minorities position will finally lead to long lasting attitude change, backed up by thorough information processing, and ultimately *conversion*.

CT's distinction between compliance and conversion perfectly maps onto the distinction between normative and informational influence that has guided much research on conformity and deviance ever since its formulation by Deutsch and Gerard (1955). According to this dual-process model, in normative influence the focal concern of the target is the social conflict with the influence source. As a result, conflict resolution rests on the surveillance of the target by the source which Deutsch and Gerard (1955) have ascribed as the critical impetus for mere conformity. Obviously, the basic idea of compliance with the majority position in terms of CT is tantamount to normative influence. More recent theorizing on normative influence is closely related to the concept of the individual's social identity concerns. According to those approaches (Crano, 2001, 2010; David & Turner, 2001; Tajfel & Turner, 1979; Turner, 1991), opinions held by an individual not only reflect subjective "knowledge" about a certain issue but fulfills identification needs. Agreement with the group's shared attitudes means adopting group membership as a feature defining the individual's self. As far as the minority is perceived as negative by default, identification needs can only be satisfied by majorities.

Conversely, informational influence is supposed to be based on the processing of issue-related information. As the social implications of opinion discrepancy are of less concern to the target, she or he is free to choose whether to follow or not.

If attitude revision occurs, however, such agreeing (Deutsch & Gerard, 1955) – or conversion in Moscovici's (1980) terms – is seen as "true" change that alters the target's mind independent of any social implications. The driving force behind conversion cannot be identification. Instead, the target is assumed to be motivated to hold "correct" attitudes and thus engage into in-depth and thorough processing of issue-related information – termed validation by Moscovici (1980) and systematic or central route processing by others at that time (Chaiken, Liberman, & Eagly, 1989; Petty & Cacioppo, 1986).

A Consensus Based View on Conformity and Deviance

It was and still is Kruglanski and Mackie's (1990) merit to have convincingly pointed out that both the distinction between compliance and conversion and the distinction between normative and informational influence likely assume rather specific circumstances that do not explain conformity and deviance in every context. As already mentioned above, minorities may not be always the "underdogs" and majorities not always those in power (see also Mucchi-Faina, Pacilli, & Pagliaro, 2011). Minorities at times are elites, and majorities can represent the notorious John Doe or the "sheep" that merely go along. Minorities and majorities may also represent a completely unspecified group, for example defined by nothing more than the number of those who endorse a certain position in an opinion poll drawn from a representative sample. Thus, the idea that majorities are those in social power and minorities necessarily have to compensate somehow for their lack in power seemed questionable to Kruglanski and Mackie (1990). Furthermore, the assumption that always conflict is in operation may be challenged as well. At the very least, sometimes targets may be confronted to issues that are novel or on which they have not formed an attitude yet. Another problem seems to be the distinction between superficial information processing in majority influence or normative influence, respectively, and in-depth processing in minority influence and informational influence. Indeed, some research has demonstrated that cognitive effort can vary independent of minority or majority status or in interaction of source status with other variables (see, for example, Baker & Petty, 1994; Mackie, 1987).

Following these considerations in their further analysis, Kruglanski and Mackie (1990) only found a single variable that necessarily varied with source status as a minority or a majority, namely social *consensus*. Minorities are fewer than majorities and thus consensus on minority positions is invariably lower than consensus on majority positions. If we agreed on this simple assumption, a number of new and innovative implications arise that have the potential to advance the understanding of social influence phenomena far beyond the restrictions that CT and the normative-informational distinction imply. For example, it should be possible that a variable as basic as *consensus per se* can build the basis of an attitude judgment even if conflict, identification needs, or variables that motivate low versus high effort in issue-related processing are not in operation. It also seems viable that processing motivation varies as a function of some variable in interaction with consensus. And furthermore, there should indeed exist motivational needs of specific closure that render the low consensus position attractive to the target, as the theoretical analysis of Kruglanski and Mackie (1990) suggested. These and related considerations guided my colleagues' and my own research into social influence phenomena.

Consensus Effects on Attitude Judgments

According to Kruglanski and Mackie's (1990) analysis, deviance and conformity have been connected to a multitude of variables assumed to produce, alter, mediate, and moderate the impact of minorities and majorities, and yet, the only variable that necessarily covaries with source status would be consensus. Much research suggests that consensus per se, or put otherwise, simply the information what few versus many others would think or do, is an omnipresent element of social life. Consensus makes people "know that they know" (Kelley, 1967) and has impact on attributional judgments. Consensus dictates what is ordinary, conventional, anticipated, and "in vogue." Consensus is the basis of democratic political systems, serves as a persuasive cue in advertising, and people care about opinion poll results that are often reported in the media. Thus, it seems that consensus is a variable to which the human mind is specifically tuned (Erb & Bohner, 2010; Prislin & Wood, 2005) and that consensus per se can affect information processing and subjective judgments.

The simplest test of this idea, sparked by my own understanding of the Kruglanski and Mackie (1990) work, involved experiments in which participants were exposed to a persuasive message attached to low versus high consensus, respectively (Erb, Bohner, Schmälzle, & Rank, 1998, see Hellmann & Erb, 2016, for related findings). In one study, for example, participants learned that the citizens of a city in a foreign country had discussed a (fictitious and therefore non-conflicting) tunnel building project in their city. The message that argued in favor of building the tunnel was ascribe to a socially irrelevant group of citizens in that foreign city, either a majority (high consensus) or a minority (low consensus). In a control condition no consensus information was provided. The operationalizations ensured that neither conflict in attitudes nor social threats of censure and ostracism were in operation.

Results (Table 2.1) showed that the cognitive responses of our participants were more favorable under high consensus and less favorable under low consensus when compared with the control condition. Perceived persuasiveness of the message and the valence of thoughts generated in response to the message (Greenwald, 1968; Petty & Cacioppo, 1986) was a linear function of consensus, although the message did not vary and was the same across conditions. Further analysis showed that this kind of "biased" message processing mediated the effect

TABLE 2.1 Thought Listing Measures and Attitude Index as a Function of Consensus Information (Study 1 in Erb, Bohner, Schmälzle, & Rank, 1998)

	Consensus Information		
	Low	High	None
(a) Perceived Persuasiveness	4.90	6.05	4.37
(b) Total Number of Thoughts	4.68	4.60	7.00
(c) Valence of Thoughts	-0.21	+0.08	-0.09
(d) Attitude Index	5.39	6.41	5.86

Note. Higher numbers indicate (a) higher perceived persuasiveness, range from 1: not at all convincing to 9: very convincing; (b) a higher amount of listed thoughts in a thought listing procedure in absolute numbers; (c) higher favorability of listed thoughts, range from −1: unfavorable to +1: favorable; higher favorability of attitudes, range from 1: unfavorable to 9: favorable.

of consensus on attitude judgments, resulting in favorable attitudes under high and unfavorable attitudes under low consensus (Figure 2.1). Measures that tapped into the cognitive effort in message processing showed that effort under both consensus conditions was lower than in the control condition where no consensus information had been provided. This result indicates that recipients can use mere consensus as a basis for information processing and subsequent attitude judgments. It also suggests that consensus calls to mind "heuristic" inferences that simplify information processing and attitude formation. It further indicates that conflicting findings that either minorities or majorities induce high processing effort are presumably due to other variables that interact with consensus in their effect on processing motivation. Most importantly, these effects occurred independently of social relevance and opinion discrepancy – those constructs that

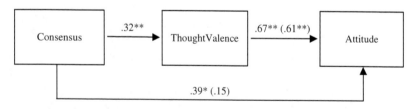

FIGURE 2.1 Direct effects and effects mediated by valenced cognitive responses of consensus (0 = low, 1 = high) on post-message attitude index (Study 1 in Erb, Bohner, Schmälzle, & Rank, 1998). Coefficients appearing above lines are beta weights for uncorrected paths. Coefficients in parentheses appearing below lines are beta weights for corrected paths.
Note: ★ p < .05, ★★ p < .01.

were ascribed major explanatory relevance in CT (Moscovici, 1980) and the normative-informational influence model (Deutsch & Gerard, 1955).

The Need for Non-specific Closure: Processing Effort in Minority and Majority Influence

In their analysis, Kruglanski and Mackie (1990, p. 245) did not find a single argument why consensus per se would lead to differential effort in message processing. They argued that minorities and majorities would neither be connected with the arousal nor with the opportunity to gratify needs for closure. Still, CT was definite in holding that minorities motivate in-depth processing of their messages, whereas the social conflict with the majority would hinder such processing (Moscovici, 1980). By contrast, Mackie (1987, p. 42) had argued that the high consensus position "is accepted as reflecting objective reality." Accordingly, targets of influence should be motivated to direct attention to the majority position, resulting in extensive message processing.

Interestingly, both of these contradictory assumptions found favorable empirical evidence. From a consensus perspective, the contradiction between Moscovici's (1980) and Mackie's (1987) findings points to the possibility that some factor interacted with consensus in its effect on processing effort in those studies. A closer inspection suggested that the attitude issues used in Mackie's (1987) studies were relatively unfamiliar to her participants and likely not related to strong convictions on side of the targets (e.g., the insurance of military balance in the Western hemisphere). On the other hand, in empirical tests of CT preexisting attitudes on side of the targets were strongly opposed to the position proposed by the influence source. Such discrepancies arose from conflicting assessments of colors in which a minority consistently insisted on calling a blue color green (e.g., Moscovici, Lage, & Naffrechoux, 1969; but see Martin, 1998) or from persuasive messages that contradicted important values such as European students' convictions regarding environmental conservation in the late 1970s and early 1980s (e.g., Moscovici, 1980).

A series of studies based on the consensus view (Erb, Bohner, Rank, & Einwiller, 2002; see Bohner, Dykema-Engblade, Tindale, & Meisenhelder, 2008, for related findings) addressed the hypothesis that a moderate level of opinion discrepancy would lead to the effect that the high consensus message will receive more attention (cf. Mackie, 1987), whereas under a high level of opinion discrepancy the low consensus message will receive more attention (cf. Moscovici, 1980), for the reasons outlined above. In a sample test of this prediction, preattitudes towards the fluoridation of drinking water in Germany were measured. The issue was chosen because pretesting had confirmed that attitudes toward this issue were either strongly opposed or moderate to begin with. Participants then received a persuasive message ostensibly forwarded by a minority or a majority. Also, argument quality was manipulated to assess the cognitive effort dedicated to message processing (cf. Petty & Cacioppo, 1986). Results showed that indeed low consensus sources attracted attention to their message when there was a strong conflict between preexisting attitudes on side of the targets and the position forwarded by the influence source. Under the condition of moderate preexisting attitudes, however, the high consensus message was processed more thoroughly. Thus, the components of Mackie's (1987) and Moscovici's (1980) theories obviously apply only to rather specific cases in which consensus interacts with some other variable, here the nature and strength of conflict with prior attitudes. In fact, the consensus view on minority and majority influence has proved useful, as it was able to reconcile the obviously contradictory findings by Moscovici (1980) and Mackie (1987). Furthermore, the data lend support to the notion that minorities and majorities per se do not covary with the need to (avoid) closure.

Minorities and Majorities and Motivational Needs for Specific Closure

As Kruglanski and Mackie (1990, pp. 243–244) have put it, "… minorities can also be perceived in positive terms…" and that therefore "… both minorities and majorities are capable of fulfilling needs for specific closure." They continued that

> the reason a majority (and thus its view) is particularly attractive to an individual may often be quite different from the reason a minority is attractive. For instance, majorities are likely to offer respectability and security, whereas minorities offer adventure and excitement. Thus, individuals who prefer respectability may be motivated to accept the majority position, whereas individuals who crave adventure may be motivated to accept the minority position.

At this point of the present discussion, it should have become clear that the idea of a motivational force to foster minority influence stood in stark contrast to concurrent models that aimed at explaining minority and majority influence at that time. The predominant belief was that minorities project a negative image to begin with and only factors able to compensate for their drawback to be few in numbers would explain why sometimes deviance and resulting social change could be observed. One such factor was the extensive processing of the minority's (convincing) arguments, as discussed above. Another example for such a factor is behavioral consistency that was ascribed significant explanatory relevance in CT (Moscovici, 1980), and, by the way, proved to play a major role in Asch's (1956) studies on majority influence as well. The trouble with these and a multitude of other compensating factors is that they likely promote the influence of a majority source, and they presumably foster the influence of other sources as well (like a colleague, your spouse, a politician, and so forth). It appears hardly astonishing to expect that any source of influence will be more successful in case it displays consistency and can muster convincing arguments in favor of its position. Technically speaking, such factors are likely to produce main effects and not interaction effects with consensus. As such, they are ineligible as potential explanatory constructs when it comes to deviance and conformity (which is not to say that they are uninteresting variables by their own).

Kruglanski and Mackie's (1990) analysis asks for something completely different. They expected that there exist motivational (and not compensatory) forces that promote not only majority influence (similar to what other models have proposed), but also minority influence (what other models have denied). Technically speaking, such forces would produce interaction effects with consensus, because a factor that promotes the influence of the many *because* they are many cannot at the same time promote the influence of the few, and vice versa. But what may such factors be?

(a) Minority Influence and the Need for Uniqueness

In fact, one of my colleagues and I (Imhoff & Erb, 2009) have already studied a motivational condition that alters the valence associated with "the minority" and makes the minority position attractive to fulfill a need for specific closure. In particular, at times individuals experience a feeling of being too similar to others and develop a *need for uniqueness* (NfU; e.g., Snyder & Fromkin, 1977, 1980; Schumpe & Erb, 2015; Schumpe, Herzberg, & Erb, 2016). In order to appear different from most others and demonstrate uniqueness, agreeing with a minority position would be more attractive than going along with the non-distinctive majority just like everyone else does. A low consensus position represents something "specific" that can distinguish the individual from the mere "sheep" and thus allows to (re-)gain a feeling of being unique.

In our first experiment, participants received bogus feedback in an alleged personality inventory. In one condition they learned that their personality was "specific" (the control condition), in another condition their personality was said to be "average", which we expected to trigger a high NfU (see Snyder & Fromkin, 1980, for a similar manipulation). In an ostensibly unrelated second study, participants read a persuasive message on a fictitious holiday resort area that was either ascribed to a minority or a majority of others. The control condition produced the well-established effect that the high consensus position received more favorable attitude judgments. Under high NfU, however, the minority was more influential than the majority, confirming the hypothesis that a high NfU makes the low consensus position more attractive to an individual than the high consensus position. The same result was found in a second study in which NfU was assessed as a personality trait (Snyder & Fromkin, 1977) rather than experimentally manipulated. In a third study, an additional condition involved a treatment that we expected to tap into the motivational nature of the observed effect (Kruglanski, 1996). In particular, in this condition participants received –

after the bogus feedback of being "average," but before the influence episode – the instruction to list a number of attributes that would describe them as a unique person when compared with others. We hypothesized that listing such attributes would allow our participants to regain a feeling of uniqueness and would consequently render the minority position less attractive. In confirmation of this hypothesis, attitude judgments, this time on a tunnel building project beneath a river in participants' own city, were no longer more favorable under minority influence. Once the NfU was met, the low consensus position did not appeal any more (Figure 2.2). This result speaks to the motivational nature of the observed effect and thus demonstrates that minorities are capable of fulfilling needs for specific closure.

(b) The Minority Decision – A Risky Choice

In their analysis, Kruglanski and Mackie (1990) have somehow intuitively associated majorities with "security" and minorities with "adventure," although at that time empirical research on the link between minorities and risk-seeking was rather scarce. In one study, Clark (1988) had tested the hypothesis that minorities would be more influential if they argued in favor of the "dominant value" within a group. His participants were exposed to the choice–dilemma scenarios developed by Kogan and Wallach (1964) to manipulate the dominant value. These

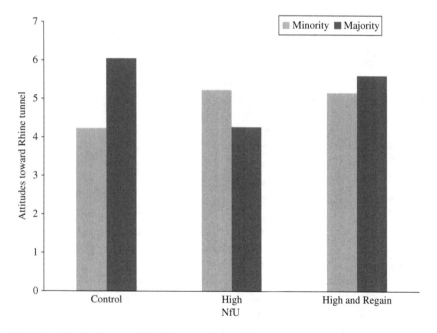

FIGURE 2.2 Attitudes toward Rhine tunnel (three items) as a function of NfU (Control/ High NfU/High NfU and Regain Uniqueness) and Consensus (Minority/ Majority) in Imhoff and Erb (2009), Study 3

scenarios are known to elicit the value of either risk taking or caution. The hypothesis was that a minority would be more influential when arguing in favor of risk in the risky scenarios and when arguing in favor of caution in the cautious scenarios. This prediction was only partially confirmed. The risky minority exerted influence in the risky scenarios, but the cautious minority had no influence in the cautious scenarios. Is it possible that minorities are somehow more related to risk than to caution?

Drawing on the consensus-based view on minorities that Kruglanski and Mackie (1990) have proposed, low consensus may have something to do with risk. If we equated low consensus with the low prevalence of the minority position, we can draw on research demonstrating that objects tend to be evaluated the more extreme the lower their prevalence. For example, attributional logic holds that failures are evaluated more negative and successes more positive when consensus among actors was low, whereas evaluations of failures and successes are moderately evaluated if consensus was high (e.g., Kelley, 1967). In their research on the scarcity principle, Ditto and Jemmott (1989) have demonstrated that the same (positive or negative) health condition was judged to have more extreme consequences when it was said to be rare among humans, as compared to when it was said to be common. Research on commodity theory (e.g., Brock & Brannon, 1992) and self-categorization (e.g., Simon & Hamilton, 1994) also attests to the idea that low prevalence elicits more extreme evaluations than high prevalence. We (Erb, Hilton, Bohner, & Roffey, 2015) have proposed that this asymmetry in valence renders the low consensus position a risk-oriented option. The reason is that an individual who shares an attitude or a decision with a minority of few others will be regarded as very unwise if wrong and extremely clever if correct. On the other hand, sharing a highly prevalent attitude or decision with a majority of many others does not hurt much if wrong, nor does it seem very rewarding if correct, because this holds true for nearly everybody else.

We (Erb et al., 2015) were able to confirm this hypothesis in a series of studies. The basic design involved an acting person that depending on conditions either opted for a minority position or a majority position, for example in a quiz show where the correct answer was unknown to the actor (and the participants) or in a public discussion meeting where a road building project of local interest was discussed. In one experiment, participants were exposed to the description of a TV game show where players competed in answering knowledge questions by either "yes" or "no." To answer a given question, the player would have to place her- or himself on one of two spaces on the stage, one representing yes and the other no. A certain "Mrs. G.," one of a total of 13 players simultaneously on stage, was said to have no idea what the correct answer was. After learning that depending on the condition "Mrs. G." had chosen the square where 2 (low consensus) versus 10 (high consensus) other people had placed themselves, participants were asked to evaluate her decision on risk-related adjectives of both negative and positive valence (e.g., risky, daring, cautious, over-anxious, etc.).

TABLE 2.2 Perception of Risk as a Function of Consensus (Low, High; Study 1 in Erb, Hilton, Bohner, & Roffey, 2015)

	Consensus	
	Low	High
Rash	4.04	2.74
Risk loving	7.07	2.78
Security-oriented	2.00	7.39
Risky	7.26	3.70
Adventurous	7.00	2.88
Over-anxious	1.70	5.39

Note. Higher numbers indicate a higher extent of agreement that the adjective describes the decision on scales ranging from: 1: absolutely not to 9: very much.

Results strongly confirmed that the minority decision was judged as more risk-inclined than the majority decision (Table 2.2).

Risk associated with the low consensus position appears to arise from amplified anticipated disapproval or approval either by oneself or by observers. Thus, the minority associated risk falls into the category of "social risk" (Weber et al., 2002). According to this conclusion, any uncommon attitude, decision, choice, or action may activate expectations that sorrow or satisfaction and related emotional responses to negative versus positive outcomes will be more distinct when consensus is low. From this view, one may expect that individuals will anticipate amplified emotional responses and accordingly choose common versus uncommon options as a function of anticipated negative versus positive outcomes. Accordingly, Mannetti, Pierro, and Kruglanski (2007) have argued that decisions to maintain the status quo (the cautious option) tended to be regretted less than decisions in favor of change (the more risky option), specifically when change was seen as less "normative" in the sense that it deviated from the "normal" (high consensus) position. It seems also straightforward to predict that contexts that promote risk will promote deviance (see the results by Clark, 1988). Interestingly, a study by Tindale, Sheffey, and Scott (1993) has already provided empirical evidence in favor of this hypothesis, although their experiment was designed to test a different hypothesis. Tindale and colleagues used the "Asian Disease Problem" (Kahneman & Tversky, 1979) in a group discussion setting. The problem can be framed in terms of either gains or losses. The loss version consistently fosters risky decisions, whereas the gain version yields risk-aversive decisions. In this study, minority influence was found in the loss, but not in the gain framing condition – a result that lends support to the above reasoning. It appears that in a context that promotes tendencies toward risk, the individual will be attracted to the minority position as low consensus is related to risk, whereas high consensus is related to caution. The nature and characteristics of these relations, however, need to be addressed in future research. At the very least, risk promoting situations seem to create conditions under which minorities may fulfill needs for specific closure (Kruglanski & Mackie, 1990, pp. 243–244).

Research on NfU and risk effects in minority and majority influence goes far beyond previous work because minority status can no longer be regarded as a negative feature in all situations. Whereas other models have discussed and examined variables that would compensate for the seemingly obstacle of being few in numbers, we have found the notion of "negative by default" suspect, chose a different approach, and found conditions that make the minority position attractive not despite but because the minority represents low consensus. Other than compensating conditions that likely promote the influence of the majority as well (the processing of strong arguments, behavioral consistency, etc.), NfU and presumably risk promote deviance while at the same time reduce conformity. This is exactly what Kruglanski and Mackie (1990) had in mind when speaking of minorities to be capable of fulfilling needs of specific closure.

Conclusion

In their concluding comments, Kruglanski and Mackie (1990) advised "… investigators of minority and majority influence … to focus their research efforts on defining the contexts in which differences between majorities and minorities will have significant implications for influence and those conditions under which they will not" (p. 255). They acknowledged that much of their analyses and conclusions have been speculative "… and as often as not, have rested on plausible conjectures rather than on 'hard' empirical facts" (p. 257). Since that time, some of the gaps between theory and data have been closed.

Guided by the elementary principle that consensus is the only variable that necessarily covariates with minority and majority status, the empirical research accumulated ever since Kruglanski and Mackie have published their analysis in 1990 yielded at least two conclusions.

(1) Consensus in itself – detached from variables like conflict or identification needs that other models portrayed as explanatory constructs – proved to have impact on information processing and judgment formation (Erb et al., 1998; Hellmann & Erb, 2016). It appears that consensus information can call to mind a heuristic inference, perhaps best described as "high consensus implies correctness" (Mackie, 1987; see also Bassili, 2003; Darke et al., 1998), that simplifies (biased) information processing and renders the majority position more positive than the minority position. (2) Some variables proved to interact with consensus in predictable ways. The extent and nature of conflict between the target's attitude prior to the influence attempt and the position proposed by the influence source produces different levels of non-specific closure and thus moderates the extent to which the target is willing to invest cognitive effort (Erb et al., 2002). In addition, variables like risk-seeking (Erb et al., 2015) and NfU (Imhoff & Erb, 2009) seem to call forth needs of specific closure that alter the advantage that majorities often have, render the minority status attractive,

and at the same time stall majority influence. This latter point provides empirical evidence in favor of Kruglanski and Mackie's (1990) opinion that minorities are not negative and majorities not positive in any case.

The research presented in this chapter is difficult to reconcile with the two alternative approaches that I have outlined above, namely Moscovici's (1980) CT and Deutsch and Gerard's (1955) normative-informational distinction, even though both can be found as widely accepted scientific knowledge in virtually every textbook of social psychology, have guided much research into conformity and deviance, and still remain vital elements of contemporary theorizing (see Martin & Hewstone, 2008). The reason is that these models closely connect the dichotomies of compliance versus conversion and normative versus informational influence to majority and minority sources, respectively. This rather mechanistic view may lead to the (erroneous) perception that individual responses are generally a function of the stimulus presented in the influence situation, or put otherwise, that minority and majority source information will produce *simple main effects* on attitudes, processing motivation, etc. Instead, the present analysis strongly suggests that researches should reason in terms of how and under what conditions consensus information – the stimulus of interest in the present context – will *interact* with the state of the target's mind in a given situation (see Erb, Kruglanski, Chun, Pierro, Mannetti, & Spiegel, 2003; Kruglanski, Erb, Pierro, Mannetti, & Chun, 2006).

In light of this perspective, an important question is what exactly the target finds relevant in a given situation. As an example, a person may encounter the information that a minority favors a certain attitudinal position. In case this person is not in strong conflict with the proposed position and experiences a high need for non-specific closure, she or he may follow the guiding rule that minority positions are often incorrect and will reject the influence attempt (e.g., Erb et al., 1998; Erb et al., 2002; Mackie, 1987). In a different situation, an individual may be in strong conflict and hence experience a high need to avoid closure and process the minority message extensively (Erb et al., 2002; Moscovici, 1980). In yet another situation, in which the individual experiences a high NfU, the minority stimulus may call to mind an inference like "a minority represents what only few others think." Then, the person will come up with a favorable judgment because subscribing to the minority view will promote the perception of being a unique person (Imhoff & Erb, 2009). This would represent a case of motivated reasoning (Kruglanski, 1999; Kunda, 1990) in that a motivational bias toward uniqueness triggers the use of low consensus information to form a favorable judgment.

Accordingly, the normative-informational distinction refers to two out of countless other motives with potential impact on conformity and deviance. Normative influence meets the need to belong and maintain a positive social identity (e.g., David & Turner, 1996; Turner, 1991) whereas informational influence refers to the need of holding accurate attitudes (e.g., Chaiken et al., 1989; Petty & Cacioppo, 1986) and related motives like the avoidance of closure (Kruglanski & Webster, 1996). The effect of NfU on minority influence, for example, seems to be difficult if not impossible to subsume under this dichotomy. It is difficult to be subsumed under CT's dichotomy of compliance versus conversion as well. The reasons are that neither was a cognitive conflict in operation, nor was the minority influence based on a validation process, nor was the influence indirect in the sense that it would have shown up in related but not the focal issue of concern (Imhoff & Erb, 2009).

The Kruglanski and Mackie (1990) approach, however, is not only critical with respect to the theorizing in other models. It offers an alternative view as well. The essential message of Kruglanski and Mackie's (1990) analysis is that consensus has to be seen as the only variable that necessarily covaries with the minority versus majority status of an influence source. Thus consensus can be assumed the key variable to explain conformity and deviance in attitudes. Intuitively, it makes perfect sense to ascribe such an outstanding status to this variable, when I consider the importance of consensus in many areas of public and social life, in democratic political systems, in science, and perhaps not the least when it comes to the question how to spend my leisure time with my friends. The extent of agreement creates not only psychological but also factual "reality."

In terms of theory, a focus on consensus liberates theorizing from the restrictions that CT and the normative-informative distinctions have established. These dual-process models have interrelated consensus with other factors like type of conflict, amount of effort in content-related information processing, fulfillment of specific identification needs on side of the target – just to name those which have been more extensively discussed in this chapter. As outlined above, a closer theoretical inspection and some empirical evidence suggest that these factors can vary independently of consensus. They gain explanatory relevance for conformity and deviance in case they produce interaction effects with consensus on information processing and attitude judgments, like, for example, the NfU. They cannot explain conformity and deviance when they produce mere main effects independent of consensus, like, for example, the consistency in behavior factor. Future research can easily profit from these considerations, for example in search of further conditions that render the low consensus position attractive to individuals. Insofar, even after so many years Kruglanski and Mackie's (1990) analysis has not suffered the loss of its strength as a theoretical guide for research on conformity and deviance phenomena.

References

Asch, S. E. (1956). Studies of independence and conformity: A minority of one against a unanimous majority. *Psychological Monographs*, 70, 1–70.

Baker, S. M., & Petty, R. E. (1994). Majority and minority influence: Source-position imbalance as a determinant of message scrutiny. *Journal of Personality and Social Psychology*, 67, 5–19.

Bassili, J. N. (2003). The minority slowness effect: Subtle inhibitions in the expression of views not shared by others. *Journal of Personality and Social Psychology*, 84, 261–276.

Bohner, G., Dykema-Engblade, A., Tindale, R. S., & Meisenhelder, H. (2008). Framing of majority and minority source information in persuasion: When and how "consensus implies correctness." *Social Psychology*, 39, 108–116.

Brock, T. C., & Brannon, L. A. (1992). Liberalization of commodity theory. *Basic and Applied Social Psychology, 13,* 135–144.

Chaiken, S., Liberman, A., & Eagly, A. H. (1989). Heuristic and systematic information processing within and beyond the persuasion context. In J. S. Uleman, & J. A. Bargh (Eds.), *Unintended thought* (pp. 212–252). New York: Guilford.

Clark III, R. D. (1988). On predicting minority influence. *European Journal of Social Psychology, 18,* 515–526.

Crano, W. D. (2001). Social influence, social identity, and ingroup leniency. In C. K. W. De Dreu, & N. K. De Vries (Eds.), *Group consensus and minority influence: Implications for innovation* (pp. 122–143). Oxford, UK: Blackwell.

Crano, W. D. (2010). Majority and minority influence in attitude formation and attitude change: Context/categorization – leniency contract theory. In R. Martin, & M. Hewstone (Eds.), *Minority influence and innovation: Antecedents, processes and consequences* (pp. 53–77). Hove, UK: Psychology.

Darke, P., Chaiken, S., Bohner, G., Einwiller, S., Erb, H.-P., & Hazlewood, D. (1998). Accuracy motivation, consensus information, and the law of large numbers: Effects on attitude judgment in the absence of argumentation. *Personality and Social Psychology Bulletin, 24,* 1205–1215.

David, B., & Turner, J. C. (1996). Studies in self-categorization and minority conversion: Is being a member of the outgroup an advantage? *British Journal of Social Psychology, 35,* 179–199.

David, B., & Turner, J. C. (2001). Majority and minority influence: A single process self-categorization analysis. In C. K. W. De Dreu, & N. K. De Vries (Eds.), *Group consensus and minority influence: Implications for innovation* (pp. 91–121). Oxford, UK: Blackwell.

Deutsch, M., & Gerard, H. B. (1955). A study of normative and informational influences upon individual judgement. *Journal of Abnormal and Social Psychology, 51,* 629–636.

Ditto, P. H., & Jemmott, J. B. (1989). From rarity to evaluative extremity: Effects of prevalence information on evaluations of positive and negative characteristics. *Journal of Personality and Social Psychology, 57,* 16–26.

Echterhoff, G., Higgins, E. T., & Levine, J. M. (2009). Shared reality: Experiencing commonality with others' inner states about the world. *Perspectives on Psychological Science, 4,* 496–521.

Erb, H.-P., & Bohner, G. (2010). Consensus as the key: Towards parsimony in explaining minority and majority influence. In R. Martin, & M. Hewstone (Eds.), *Minority influence and innovation: Antecedents, processes and consequences* (pp. 79–103). Hove, UK: Psychology.

Erb, H.-P., Bohner, G., Rank, S., & Einwiller, S. (2002). Processing minority and majority communications: The role of conflict with prior attitudes. *Personality and Social Psychology Bulletin, 28,* 1172–1182.

Erb, H.-P., Bohner, G., Schmälzle, K., & Rank, S. (1998). Beyond conflict and discrepancy: Cognitive bias in minority and majority influence. *Personality and Social Psychology Bulletin, 24,* 620–633.

Erb, H.-P., Hilton, D. J., Bohner, G., & Roffey, L. (2015). The minority decision – A risky choice. *Journal of Experimental Social Psychology, 57,* 43–50.

Erb, H.-P., Kruglanski, A. W., Chun, W. Y., Pierro, A., Mannetti, L., & Spiegel, S. (2003). Searching for commonalities in human judgment: The parametric unimodel and its dual-model alternatives. *European Review of Social Psychology, 14,* 1–47.

Greenwald, A. G. (1968). Cognitive learning, cognitive response to persuasion, and attitude change. In A. Greenwald, T. Brock, & T. Ostrom (Eds.), *Psychological foundations of attitudes* (pp. 148–170). New York: Academic Press.

Hardin, C. D., & Higgins, E. T. (1996). Shared reality: How social verification makes the subjective objective. In R. M. Sorrentino & E. T. Higgins (Eds.), *Handbook of motivation and cognition* (Vol. 3, pp. 28–84). New York: Guilford.

Hellmann, D. F., & Erb, H.-P. (2016). *Antecedents and consequences of processing survey results.* Manuscript submitted for publication.

Imhoff, R., & Erb, H.-P. (2009). What motivates nonconformity? Uniqueness seeking blocks majority influence. *Personality and Social Psychology Bulletin*, 35, 309–320.

Kahneman, D., & Tversky, A. (1979). Prospect theory: An analysis of decisions under risk. *Econometrica*, 47, 263–291.

Kelley, H. H. (1967). Attribution theory in social psychology. In D. Levine (Ed.), *Nebraska symposium on motivation* (Vol. 15, pp. 192–238). Lincoln, NE: University of Nebraska Press.

Kogan, N., & Wallach, M. (1964). *Risk taking: A study in cognition and personality.* New York: Holt, Rinehart, and Winston.

Kruglanski, A. W. (1989). *Lay epistemics and human knowledge: Cognitive and motivational bases.* New York: Plenum.

Kruglanski, A. W. (1996). Motivated social cognition: Principles of the interface. In E. T. Higgins & A. W. Kruglanski (Eds.), *Social psychology: Handbook of basic principles* (pp.493–529). New York: Guilford.

Kruglanski, A. W. (1999). Motivation, cognition, and reality: Three memos for the next generation of research. *Psychological Inquiry*, 10, 54–58.

Kruglanski, A. W., Erb, H.-P., Pierro, A., Mannetti, L., & Chun, W. Y. (2006). On parametric continuities in the world of binary either ors. *Psychological Inquiry*, 17, 153–165.

Kruglanski, A. W., & Klar, Y. (1987). A view from a bridge: Synthesizing the consistency and attribution paradigms from a lay epistemics perspective. *European Journal of Social Psychology*, 17, 211–241.

Kruglanski, A. W., & Mackie, D. M. (1990). Majority and minority influence: A judgmental process analysis. *European Review of Social Psychology*, 1, 229–261.

Kruglanski, A. W., & Webster, D. M. (1996). Motivated closing of the mind: "Seizing" and "freezing". *Psychological Review*, 103, 263–283.

Kunda, Z. (1990). The case of motivated reasoning. *Psychological Bulletin*, 108, 480–498.

Le Bon, G. (1895/1960). *The crowd* [Psychologie des foules]. New York: Viking Press.

Mackie, D. M. (1987). Systematic and nonsystematic processing of majority and minority persuasive communications. *Journal of Personality and Social Psychology*, 53, 41–52.

Mannetti, L., Pierro, A., & Kruglanski, A. W. (2007). Who regrets more after choosing a non-status quo option? Post decisional regret under need for cognitive closure. *Journal of Economic Psychology*, 28, 186–196.

Martin, R. (1998). Majority and minority influence using the afterimage paradigm: A series of attempted replications. *Journal of Experimental Social Psychology*, 34, 1–26.

Martin, R., & Hewstone, M. (2008). Majority versus minority influence, message processing and attitude change: The source-context-elaboration model. In M. P. Zanna (Ed.), *Advances in experimental social psychology* (Vol. 40, pp. 237–326). San Diego, CA: Academic Press.

Moscovici, S. (1976). *Social influence and social change.* London: Academic Press.

Moscovici, S. (1980). Toward a theory of conversion behavior. In L. Berkowitz (Ed.), *Advances in experimental social psychology* (Vol. 6, pp. 149–202). New York: Academic Press.

Moscovici, S., Lage, E., & Naffrechoux, M. (1969). Influence of a consistent minority on the responses of a majority in a color perception test. *Sociometry, 32*, 365–379.

Mucchi-Faina, A., Pacilli, M. G., & Pagliaro, S. (2011). Automatic reactions to the labels "minority" and "majority" are asymmetrical: Implications for minority and majority influence. *Social Influence, 6*, 181–196.

Petty, R. E., & Cacioppo, J. T. (1986). The elaboration likelihood model of persuasion. In L. Berkowitz (Ed.), *Advances in experimental social psychology* (Vol. 19, pp. 123–203). New York: Academic Press.

Pratkanis, A. R. (2007). An invitation to social influence research. In A. R. Pratkanis (Ed.), *The science of social influence* (pp. 1–15). New York: Psychology Press.

Prislin, R., & Wood, W. (2005). Social influence: The role of social consensus in attitudes and attitude change. In D. Albarracín, B. T. Johnson, & M. P. Zanna (Eds.), *The handbook of attitudes and attitude change* (pp. 671–706). Hillsdale, NJ: Erlbaum.

Schumpe, B. M., & Erb, H.-P. (2015). Humans and uniqueness. *Science Progress, 98*, 1–11.

Schumpe, B. M., Herzberg, P. Y., & Erb, H.-P. (2016). Assessing the need for uniqueness: Validation of the German NfU-G scale. *Personality and Individual Differences, 90*, 231–237.

Simon, B., & Hamilton, D. L. (1994). Self-stereotyping and social context: The effect relative in-group size and in-group status. *Journal of Personality and Social Psychology, 66*, 699–711.

Snyder, C. R., & Fromkin, H. L. (1977). Abnormality as a positive characteristic: The development and validation of a scale measuring need for uniqueness. *Journal of Abnormal Psychology, 86*, 518–527.

Snyder, C. R., & Fromkin, H. L. (1980). *Uniqueness, the human pursuit of difference.* New York: Pelnum.

Tajfel, H. (1981). *Human groups and social categories: Studies in social psychology.* Cambridge, UK: University Press.

Tajfel, H., & Turner, J. C. (1979). An integrative theory of intergroup conflict. In S. Worchel, & W. G. Austin (Eds.), *The social psychology of intergroup relations* (pp. 33–47). Monterey, CA: Brooks/Cole.

Tindale, R. S., Sheffey, S., & Scott, L. A. (1993). Framing and group decision making: Do cognitive changes parallel preference changes. *Organizational Behavior and Human Decision Processes, 55*, 470–485.

Turner, J. C. (1991). *Social influence.* Pacific Grove, CA: Brooks/Cole.

Turner, J. C., Hogg, M. A., Oakes, P. J., Reicher, S. D., & Wetherell, M. S. (1987). *Rediscovering the social group: A self-categorization theory.* Oxford, UK: Blackwell.

Weber, E. U., Blais, A.-R., & Betz, N. E. (2002). A domain-specific risk-attitude scale: Measuring risk perceptions and risk behaviors. *Journal of Behavioral Decision Making, 15*, 263–290.

Wood, W., Lundgren, S., Ouellette, J. A., Busceme, S., & Blackstone, T. (1994). Minority influence: A meta-analytic review of social influence processes. *Psychological Bulletin, 115*, 323–345.

3

THREE DECADES OF NEED FOR CLOSURE RESEARCH

About Epistemic Goals and (Not) Means

Arne Roets

Introduction

In 1980, Kruglanski presented the "theory of lay epistemology" in a *Psychological Review* paper outlining his ideas on the process of knowledge formation. Although originally introduced to provide a new perspective on attribution theory, Kruglanski's theory addressed a far broader aspect of the human psyche: how and why people construct knowledge the way they do. Given the broadness and fundamental nature of these questions, it should come as no surprise that over the next few decades the theory inspired a variety of productive research programs (for a brief overview, see Kruglanski, Dechesne, Orehek, & Pierro, 2009). Yet, of the many branches that sprouted from the Lay Epistemics Theory tree that Kruglanski had planted, one in particular proved to be especially fruitful: *Need For Closure (NFC)*. Not only did this branch produce some of the finest fruits thanks to the careful nurturing of Kruglanski himself, their seeds also spread and found fertile soil in various new terrains.

This chapter pays tribute to Arie Kruglanski's indispensable contribution to social psychology and beyond, addressing how his work on NFC has shed light on the underlying epistemic motivations that drive people in a broad diversity of everyday and not-so-everyday life. To this end, I sample from almost four decades of NFC research, elaborating on Arie Kruglanski's foundational work, how it has inspired other scholars in various fields, and how research on NFC has even allowed a more advanced insight in one of social psychology's classic works; Allport's seminal theory on the nature of prejudice. Importantly, throughout this chapter, I will argue that a focus on goals (i.e., attaining and/or maintaining closure) rather than means (e.g., specific information processing strategies) is crucial to a true understanding of NFC. Indeed, many different (and sometimes unexpected) ways can lead to the attainment of closure, and a goal perspective is key to fully appreciate the versatile effects of NFC on individual behavior as well as its intricate role in important social issues such as prejudice and extremism.

The Origin, Basics, and Applications of the NFC Theory

In developing his Lay Epistemics Theory, Kruglanski (1980) argued that knowledge formation (i.e., the epistemic process) basically consists of two major stages: the first is to gather information and generate hypotheses, the second is to reach an answer and hence form "knowledge." Need for closure then pertains to the human motivation that guides these two stages and the transition where "a belief crystallizes and turns from hesitant conjecture to a subjectively firm 'fact'" (Kruglanski & Webster, 1996, p. 266). In particular, NFC refers to the desire of completing the epistemic process, or as Kruglanski and Webster (1996) put it: "the individual's desire for a firm answer to a question and an aversion toward ambiguity" (p. 264).

Seizing and Freezing

Mapping onto the two stages of the epistemic process, NFC is argued to prompt two general proclivities, known as urgency and permanence (Kruglanski & Webster, 1996). The urgency tendency denotes an inclination to *seize* quickly on information that promises to bring about closure. Given the desirability of reaching closure and the undesirability of postponing it, individuals with a high need for closure may often leap to conclusions (i.e., "crystallized knowledge") based on partial or inconclusive information sampling and hypothesis generation. The subsequent permanence tendency, on the other hand, denotes the inclination to maintain closure by holding on to, or *freezing* the acquired knowledge. The freezing process strengthens the consolidation of knowledge, and immunizes it against contradictory information. Both the seizing and the freezing tendency serve to escape or avoid the aversive lack of closure, the first by terminating this state quickly, and the second by keeping it from recurring.

Early research on Need for Closure that arose from Lay Epistemics Theory mostly focused on situations that instigate high levels of NFC (e.g., Kruglanski & Freund, 1983). For example, time pressure by definition elicits the need to reach a conclusion quickly, making people more prone to seize early available answers. Time pressure generally also makes revisiting an answer more costly, hence motivating people to preserve or freeze their decision once it has been made. Yet, any situation wherein information processing is costly, difficult, laborious, or aversive can foster a heightened desire for closure, for example when the task at hand is dull (e.g., Webster, 1993a), laborious due to fatigue or intoxication (e.g., Webster, Richter & Kruglanski, 1996; Webster, 1993b), or if performance is impeded by external stressors such as environmental noise (e.g., Kruglanski, Webster, & Klem, 1993).[1]

Importantly, although NFC can be temporarily heightened by situational forces, people also substantially differ in their overall dispositional level of NFC. To measure dispositional or "trait" NFC, in the early nineties, Kruglanski and his team (Kruglanski, Webster, & Klem, 1993; Webster & Kruglanski, 1994) developed and validated the NFC scale. The scale, as well as its revised version (Roets & Van Hiel, 2007) taps into five central aspects of NFC: preference for order, preference for predictability, (need for) decisiveness, aversion for ambiguity, and closed-mindedness. In the two decades that followed, especially this individual differences aspect of NFC has attracted a great deal of interest from scholars in (social) psychology, and well beyond.

Basic NFC effects on Judgment and Decision Making

One of the most straightforward consequences of the inclination to seize and freeze pertains to the extent to which people sample information and generate hypotheses under high NFC. Indeed, the desire to reach closure quickly, and to subsequently maintain closure, should lead people to consider less information when making judgments. Several of the early studies on NFC confirmed this basic effect, while other studies further showed that the urgency-driven reliance on easily-accessible and early information, and the permanence-driven disregard of later information under high NFC, also affect a number of classic phenomena in (social) psychology. Some examples are listed in Box 3.1.

In addition, several studies examined NFC effects in intra- and inter-group contexts, and Kruglanski, Pierro, Mannetti & De Grada (2006) integrated these distinctly social NFC effects under the umbrella of *group centrism*. Specifically, the studies within this domain revealed that individuals under high NFC tend to protect the group and the epistemic security it provides in a number of ways (see Box 3.1 for examples).

NFC Effects in Other Fields

The accumulating body of research over a time span of nearly four decades has gained the NFC concept a prominent place within social and personality psychology (for a recent overview, see Roets, Kruglanski, Kossowska, Pierro, & Hong, 2015). But also beyond its "native fields," the seeds of NFC have taken root and inspired research within a variety of domains. Looking at only the past few years, this includes research in Finance, Public Health, Medical Decision Making, Psychiatry, Criminology, Education, Business and Administration, and a variety of Marketing and Consumer studies (see Box 3.1 for some examples).

Indeed, because the NFC theory is a framework for understanding the motivational aspects of human knowledge formation and decision making, it obviously also has broad applicability in other domains where judgment and decision making play a central role. Although the contribution of NFC research to other disciplines has far from reached its full potential yet, the growing number of studies that investigate NFC at the cross-roads of different disciplines is a promising indicator that Kruglanski's seminal ideas on the motivational forces in human knowledge formation are increasingly finding their way to other scientific disciplines.

BOX 3.1 A SAMPLE OF NFC EFFECTS: BASIC, GROUP-CENTERED, AND APPLIED

Less extensive information search (e.g., Mayseless & Kruglanski, 1987; Roets, Van Hiel, Cornelis, & Soetens, 2008)

Generation of fewer hypotheses (e.g., Mayseless & Kruglanski, 1987; Chirumbolo, Mannetti, Pierro, Areni, & Kruglanski, 2005)

Inflation of impressional primacy effects (e.g., Kruglanski & Freund, 1983; Freund, Kruglanski, & Shpitzajzen, 1985)

Strengthening of anchoring effects (e.g., Kruglanski & Freund, 1983; DeDreu, Koole, & Oldersma, 1999)

Increased attributional biases (e.g., Webster, 1993a; Webster & Kruglanski, 1994)

Increased effects of priming and use of accessible constructs (e.g., Ford & Kruglanski, 1995)

Preference for autocratic group decision structure (e.g., De Grada, Kruglanski, Mannetti, & Pierro, 1999; Pierro, Mannetti, De Grada, Livi, & Kruglanski, 2003)

Pressure toward opinion uniformity, rejection of opinion deviates, and dislike of membership diversity (e.g., Kruglanski & Webster, 1991)

In-group favoritism and out-group derogation (e.g., Pierro et al., 2003; Shah, Kruglanski, & Thompson, 1998)

Preference of smaller immediate promotions over a delayed, larger promotions [MARKETING] (Kim, 2013)

Dilution of tendency to update investment portfolios when the market changes [FINANCE] (Disatnik & Steinhart, 2015)

Reduced willingness to revise diagnoses in light of new evidence [MEDICAL DECISION MAKING] (Roets, Raman, Heytens, & Avonds, 2014)

Hence, with the broadening attention to NFC research in psychology as well as in other domains, a thorough understanding of the construct becomes ever so important. To this aim, the present chapter advocates to look beyond the typical NFC outcomes in order to appreciate the complexities and versatility of NFC as a motivational construct.

A Goal Versus Means Perspective to NFC

With hundreds of empirical articles, spanning several decades of research across a diversity of research domains, the basic behavioral outcomes of NFC are firmly established. That is, high levels of NFC *generally* lead people to reach conclusions quickly and often prematurely (cf. seizing) based on cognitive heuristics, and to display heightened resistance to alter these conclusions once made (cf. freezing), often by neglecting contradictory information.

Yet, ironically, exactly the robustness and consistency of these *"default"* NFC effects across a wide variety of studies, also makes the exact nature of the NFC construct prone to unwarranted simplification or misinterpretation. In particular, one may be inclined to explicitly or implicitly interpret or frame a high NFC as being akin to cognitive laziness, or a *lack* of cognitive motivation. Indeed, both novices and scholars well versed in NFC research have frequently (although maybe inadvertently) described high NFC as "lack of motivation to process information" in their work. Additionally, a too strong focus on the traditional outcomes and "default" NFC effects also brings the risk of defining NFC by the behavior it typically incites, which represents an interpretation of NFC from primarily a means perspective rather than the appropriate goals perspective. In the following, I will argue why, based on Kruglanski's original theorizing as well as empirical findings, such interpretations are unwarranted.

NFC as a Goal: The Presence versus Lack of Motivation

From the very conceptualization and throughout the subsequent stages of the development of the NFC construct and theorizing, Kruglanski (1989) proposed that NFC denotes the presence of a motivated tendency: a *goal* whose attainment gratifies the need in question (see also Kruglanski & Webster, 1996). Attesting to this idea, Roets and Van Hiel (2008) demonstrated that high (vs low) NFC individuals exhibited higher and cumulative levels of distress (indicated by galvanic skin conductance) when the need for closure was frustrated; i.e., when they engaged in a "trial-and-error task" where reaching closure is not immediately possible. These findings clearly attest to the assertion that NFC is the presence of motivation rather than the lack thereof. Indeed, if NFC were to represent a lack of motivation (e.g., a lack of need for cognition; Cacioppo, & Petty, 1982), high NFC individuals should not care about the task and, if anything, exhibit less distress. Moreover, a follow up study by Richter, Baeriswyl, and Roets (2012), showed that when closure was hard to achieve (in a hard vs an easier version of the task), participants with high NFC, but not those low in NFC, showed a corresponding increase in myocardial beta-adrenergic activity, a psychophysiological indicator of task investment. In other words, whereas low NFC participants tended to disengage when the task was more difficult, high NFC participants did not, and they actually *increased* their investment in the task to find the solution, and hence, closure.

These findings clearly indicate that people high in NFC are not just cognitive misers, for they are actually (more) willing to invest cognitive effort to achieve their goal of closure, if such effort is functional or necessary to the goal. Importantly, such willingness to adapt effort investment in function of closure attainment also signals that the means to reach closure are not fixed. Below, I elaborate on how this translates to behavioral measures of cognitive effort, in particular the extent of information sampling, as well as the degree to which people resist new information, and I argue that these are mere means to reach closure, rather than goals in themselves.

Different Ways to the Same Goal: Information Sampling Extent

Obviously, limiting information processing is often the quickest and most convenient way to attain and maintain closure. Yet, Kruglanski and Webster (1996) already explicitly stated that "need for closure may sometimes promote extensive information processing in instances in which closure is lacking" (p. 268), thereby clarifying that NFC is not defined by a particular means to achieve it. Indeed, several behavioral studies have demonstrated that the influence of NFC on information sampling actually depends on whether or not it really allows closure. For example, in a study by Kruglanski, Peri, and Zakai (1991), participants were asked to make a decision about the authorship of drawings based on a sample drawing. When participants had an initial hunch, those under high NFC indeed tended to search for *less* information compared to participants under low NFC (i.e., the "standard" NFC effect). However, when participants did not have an initial hunch in which they had some confidence, those under high (vs. low) NFC searched for *more* information in order to form a clear opinion and hence attain the desired closure. Similarly, in a consumer choice paradigm, Houghton and Grewal (2000) found that high NFC resulted in a less extensive information search, but only when participants supposedly already had well-formed and accessible opinions on the product. In a related study, Vermeir, Van Kenhove, and Hendrickx (2002) asked participants to choose between brands of unfamiliar products so that reliance on prior knowledge was eliminated. They found that in these situations, high NFC individuals initially sought significantly more information.

Hence, although numerous studies have shown that NFC is generally associated with limited information search, this is in fact only the case when there already is some initial, satisfactory basis for closure. If high NFC individuals, however, lack such a knowledge base on which they can relatively confidently rely, their efforts to sample information seem to equal or even exceed the efforts of low NFC individuals in their quest for a clear-cut answer.

Different Ways to the Same Goal: "Stick" or "Switch"

In addition to NFC effects on the extent of information sampling (which primarily refers to the seizing aspect), also the default effects on the tendency to maintain and protect acquired knowledge (cf. the freezing aspect) are subject to "reversal" under particular circumstances. This was already demonstrated by Kruglanski, Webster, and Klem (1993) who investigated the role of NFC in (resistance to) persuasion. In two experiments, they found that both situational and dispositional NFC can lead to either higher or lower susceptibility to persuasion, depending on whether earlier information allowed for a "definite opinion" before entering the discussion. In particular, if, based on sufficient initial information, participants had already formed a relatively clear opinion about a subject, high NFC participants increased freezing on this opinion and were consequentially less easily persuaded (*"Stick"*). However, if participants had not yet received enough information to form a definite opinion (and hence reach closure), the position and arguments of the persuader provided the most readily available means to reach a definite opinion and hence, the desired closure. As a result, in this condition, high levels of NFC facilitated adopting the persuader's opinion, and thus increased persuadability (*"Switch"*).

Similar evidence came from a particularly interesting study by Kosic, Kruglanski, Pierro, and Mannetti (2004) who examined the impact of NFC on the acculturation patterns of Polish and Croatian immigrants in Italy. They found that acculturation patterns were interactively determined by immigrants' NFC and their reference group upon arrival. Specifically, if the immigrants arrived in the host country together with other co-ethnics, higher levels of NFC were associated with a stronger tendency to adhere to the culture of origin (*"Stick"*) and thus decreased their tendency to assimilate to the host culture. In contrast, if on arrival they found themselves without other co-ethnics, higher levels of NFC augmented their tendency to embrace and assimilate to the host culture, and consequently reduced their adherence to the culture of origin (*"Switch"*). These findings indicate that in order to reduce the considerable uncertainty associated with arrival in a new country, high NFC immigrants turned to whichever cultural reference framework was most capable of providing closure; in the company of other co-ethnics, freezing on the culture of origin provides most immediate closure, whereas in the absence of the co-ethnic reference group, assimilation to the host country provides closure best. Hence, in the latter situation high NFC individuals, more so than their low NFC counterparts, relinquished their original framework and switched to (i.e. seized) a new framework, which had become more suitable to satisfy their closure needs.

In sum, the goal is always to have and/or maintain closure. Yet, whether this goal is best served through stubborn resistance or through eager adoption of a new perspective, depends on variables like the degree of original certainty and whether or not the new frame provides a better alternative to reach and maintain closure. This mechanism has important implications for understanding relevant social phenomena in the real world, such as the above acculturation strategies adopted by immigrants, but possibly also other domains, such as political and voter dynamics. In particular, although high NFC individuals should generally be conservative and supportive of the political (party) establishment (see e.g., Jost, Glaser, Kruglanski, & Sulloway, 2003), this commitment is unlikely to be absolute and should probably not be taken for granted. That is, a radical "switch" in allegiance by NFC individuals is possible under a combination of two conditions: 1) the traditional political powers or establishment are believed to no longer provide the desired epistemic security and certainty, *and* 2) an alternative (candidate, party, or movement) is available that provides (the promise of) clear answers and solutions, and hence epistemic security. Although at the present time, empirical evidence for this assertion is lacking, key electoral transition moments, such as the 2016 US presidential nomination elections (ongoing at the time this chapter was written) seem to provide a perfect opportunity to investigate such mechanisms.

Another interesting example along these lines is the adoption of (violent) extremism, an issue that has become increasingly relevant to societies worldwide (and, not surprisingly, has also captured Arie Kruglanski's research interest for the past few years). Most extremists do not start out as radicals from the beginning, but rather "convert" to extremist ideologies. Again, an unsophisticated interpretation of NFC theory would suggest that high NFC protects people from such conversion, because they are less persuadable by default. However, the opposite seems to be true. Especially in environments of uncertainty and loss of significance (which in themselves increase NFC), extremism is most appealing to people high in NFC, exactly because of its unambiguous nature, and the definite answers and epistemic security it seems to provide (see Kruglanski, Belanger, Gelfand, Gunaratna, Hettiarachchi, Reinares, Orehek, Sasota, & Sharvit, 2013; Kruglanski, Gelfand, Belanger, Schori-Eyal, Moyano, Trujillo, Gunaratna, and Hetiarachchi, 2014.

Allport's Classic Work on Prejudice through the Lens of a NFC Goals and Means Perspective

The substantial literature on NFC effects in various domains described above testifies that the Lay Epistemics framework and the construct of NFC have a much broader reach than merely being an alternative perspective on attribution theory; the context in which they were originally developed. Yet in my view, one of the most remarkable features of the NFC construct is that it may provide valuable insights, reinterpretations and even "corrections" of one of the most influential works in the history of social psychology: Allport's (1954) seminal work on "The nature of prejudice." In recent work (Roets & Van Hiel, 2011a; Roets et al., 2015), we pointed out that the need for closure shows a striking similarity with Allport's description of the "prejudice-prone personality." Allport argued that prejudice stems from a particular way of thinking (rather than a specific feeling towards a specific group) and that this way of thinking is shaped by motivated cognition. In particular, when delineating the motivated cognition that characterizes the "prejudiced personality," Allport description bears an uncanny, almost verbatim similarity to the core concepts from NFC theory. Indeed, his description focused on high preference for order, feelings of insecurity in the absence of clear answers, an inclination to latch on to what is familiar, abhorrence of hesitation, intolerance of ambiguity, failure to see different perspectives, a general urge for quick and definite answers, and a tendency to cling to past solutions (see Roets & Van Hiel, 2011a, for a more elaborate account on the similarities).

Given these strong conceptual similarities, it should not be surprising that a number of studies have shown dispositional NFC to be strongly related to a wide range of prejudiced attitudes, including blatant, subtle, modern, and implicit forms of racism (e.g., Cunningham, Nezlek, & Banaji, 2004; Onraet, et al., 2011; Roets & Van Hiel, 2006, 2011a; Van Hiel, Pandelaere, & Duriez, 2004), as well as prejudice based on sexual orientation or identity (Tebbe & Moradi, 2012; Brandt & Reyna, 2010), and sexism toward both women and men among both male and female respondents (Roets, Van Hiel, & Dhont, 2012).

A Means versus Goal Perspective on the Relationship between NFC and Prejudice

Although the accumulated body of research leaves no doubt that high NFC makes people more likely to be prejudiced, there are, however, different possible perspectives on the nature of this link, with considerably different implications. A first possibility is to consider prejudice as an integral part of NFC. In this perspective, prejudice is inevitably associated with closure pursuits, and as such, a high NFC individual is indeed the embodiment of Allport's (1954) prejudiced personality in a strict sense. This position is by and large reflective of the ideas of Allport himself, who was rather pessimistic about the possibilities to change the attitudes of people with this "prejudiced personality," claiming that exactly because of their rigid nature, change would be near impossible (see, Dhont, Roets & Van Hiel, 2011). The implication of this perspective would be that the only way to reduce prejudice in these individuals is to find ways to permanently reduce their NFC, something that may prove a very difficult undertaking. Indeed, although NFC levels can be influenced, as demonstrated by experimental research using situational manipulations of NFC (see e.g., Kruglanski & Freund, 1983; Roets, Van Hiel, Cornelis, & Soetens, 2008), the transient nature of these effects offers little opportunity for an enduring change. Recent research by Tadmor, Hong, Chao, Wiruchnipawan, and Wang (2012) showed that in some instances, exposure to multiculturalism may in a more lasting way lower NFC, and consequentially prejudice. Yet, other research has shown that such exposure may sometimes also heighten individuals' levels of NFC (Morris, Mok, & Mor, 2011), making this a rather fickle strategy.

Fortunately, a second possible perspective on NFC and prejudice allows for a more optimistic view. Although Allport (1954) described a motivated way of thinking as characteristic for the prejudiced personality, bigotry can hardly be considered a *goal* in itself. Instead, one may consider prejudice as a by-product of the means people high in NFC routinely employ in their attempts to satisfy their closure needs (i.e., their desire for quick, easy, firm, and stable knowledge about the social world). Intervening on, or acting through these means, may then be a more feasible and effective way to reduce prejudice in people high in NFC.

Roets and Van Hiel (2011a; see also Roets et al., 2015) described two key mediating processes (i.e. means) through which NFC is connected to prejudice: socio-ideological attitudes (i.e. authoritarian-conservative ideologies [see Chapter 4 of this volume]), and essentialist thinking. Here, I will focus on the latter process, for it is the one that is not only the most "epistemic" in nature, but also the least studied and documented of the two when it comes to its role in the link between NFC and prejudice. In particular, I will illustrate how essentialist categorization serves as a means to satisfy the desire for closure, yielding prejudice as a by-product. Additionally however, I will also argue and demonstrate that, similar to the "stick or switch" mechanism described earlier, essentialist categorization could be instrumental in reducing prejudice in NFC individuals as well.

Essentialist Categorizing as a Means to Achieve Closure, and a Source of Prejudice

Categorization is a crucial aspect in the construction and organization of (social) knowledge because it allows people to bring structure to the (social) world and cope with its complexity. Moreover, for social categories to be useful in everyday life, people have to believe that these social categories are not artificial or arbitrary, but meaningful because they capture a collective "essence" of some sort, shared by all members, making them what they are (see, Medin, 1989). Therefore, essentialist categorization inevitably comes with stereotyping, because stereotypes are exactly what gives content to the presumed "essence" of the category. Moreover, regardless of whether someone agrees with the dominant stereotypes (cf. essence) assigned to a particular social category, they are common "knowledge," or as Devine (1989) put it: "stereotypes are part of the social heritage of a society and no one can escape learning the prevailing attitudes and stereotypes assigned to the major ethnic groups" (p. 5).

From a NFC perspective, allocation of individuals to essentialized social categories (cf. stereotyping) is especially appealing because of its inductive potential. In particular, such categorization provides a most useful means to draw quick, easy, and stable inferences about people, making it a very convenient and intuitive way to reach closure in these situations. Indeed, previous research by Kruglanski and colleagues has shown that NFC increases the perception of group homogeneity (e.g., Dijksterhuis, Van Knippenberg, Kruglanski, & Schaper, 1996), as well as reliance on inferences based on group membership to judge individuals (e.g., Kruglanski & Mayseless, 1988). Recently, more direct evidence for the relationship between NFC and essentialism was provided in a series of studies by Roets and Van Hiel (2011b), who revealed strong correlations between dispositional NFC and essentialist thinking about ethnicity in various samples, especially with regard to beliefs about inductive potential. Moreover, the study also demonstrated that experimental manipulations of NFC increase essentialist thinking, even for fictitious ethnic groups. Finally, endorsement of essentialist (i.e., inductive potential) ideas about racial groups was shown to be responsible for a substantial part of the relation between NFC and racial prejudice in various student and adult samples.

Using Essentialist Categorizing to Lower Prejudice in High NFC Individuals through Positive Intergroup Contact

Stereotypes, or at least knowledge about them, are widespread (Devine, 1989; Devine & Elliot, 1995), making them a very common source of information. Theoretically, these essentialized characteristics of a group can be positive, negative or neutral. Yet, in practice they are predominately negative, especially when it comes to stereotypes towards outgroups, and this yields prejudice as the logical consequence. However, from an epistemic perspective, the informational value (i.e., the inductive potential) of the stereotype is most important to the high-NFC individual, not its valence per se. People high in NFC are inclined to rely on stereotypes not because of their specific content, but because they often provide the most direct and immediately available information that allows quick and easy judgment, and hence closure. However, if other information is more salient or directly accessible in the individual's mind, one can expect high NFC individuals to seize on that information instead. The findings of Dhont, Roets, and Van Hiel (2011) regarding the interaction between NFC and positive inter-group contact on outgroup attitudes suggest that this may indeed be the case. In particular, in a series of studies, these authors showed that not only was inter-group contact effective for high NFC individuals to reduce prejudice (in contrast to Allport's assertion), people high in dispositional NFC were actually even *more* susceptible to the positive effects of intergroup contact than their low NFC counterparts. This effect emerged in the various cross-sectional studies, as well as in a field experiment (Study 3) with high school students who went on a one-week, intense-contact school trip to Morocco. Dhont et al. (2011) proposed that the reduction of intergroup anxiety is an important mediator through which the effect of intergroup contact on prejudice in high-NFC individuals operates. Indeed, intergroup contact has been shown to diminish intergroup anxiety, which consequently reduces prejudice (e.g., Brown & Hewstone, 2005; Petti-grew & Tropp, 2008). Based on the findings of Study 4 and 5, which included intergroup anxiety measures, the authors concluded that people high in NFC – who feel most averse and fearful toward the unfamiliar, the ambiguous, and the unpredictable – benefit the most from the anxiety-reducing effects of positive intergroup contact. No doubt, this is indeed a principal mechanism through which intergroup contact is especially effective, not only for people high in NFC, but also for those high in ideologies that are partly driven by NFC, such as Right-Wing authoritarianism (e.g., Dhont & Van Hiel, 2009).

However, whereas the reduction in anxiety and uncertainty plays a role in the substantial drop in prejudice among individuals high (vs. low) in NFC, it seems unable to account for "reversal effects." Indeed, in several of the individual studies of Dhont et al. (2011), and most notably in the field study, the combination of high NFC and high levels of intergroup contact actually yielded the *lowest* levels of prejudice. Whereas reduced anxiety by increased familiarity with the outgroup cannot explain this "switch," a means perspective on NFC effects can. In particular, personal interaction provides the individual with most salient and highly accessible information. Importantly, this positive information, then, may replace negative information from earlier socialization (i.e., cultural stereotypes) as the paramount information in people's minds. High-NFC individuals in particular will rely (i.e., seize) upon this most salient information and exactly because of their stronger essentialist thinking about groups, they may be more inclined to consider this positive information about one group member as meaningful for the whole group (i.e., considering a likable outgroup member to be exemplary of a likable outgroup).

Although further studies are needed to fully understand these mechanisms, the rationale as well as the empirical evidence so far is supportive for a perspective on prejudice as a product of the means employed to reach closure, rather than prejudice being an inevitable, intrinsic part of need for closure as a goal. Incidentally, this perspective also provides a much more hopeful and less fatalistic view on Allport's (1954) "Prejudiced Personality."

Conclusion

Based on Arie Kruglanski's original conceptualization of NFC, and illustrated with empirical studies in various domains, I aimed to demonstrate throughout this chapter that NFC is not merely about limited or heuristic information processing and resistance to new information. Instead, it truly is about motivation and goal pursuit, in particular the pursuit of epistemic security, in which the end justifies the means. For example, new information may be eagerly embraced rather than resisted when it trumps the original information in terms of salience, directness, and opportunities for achieving cognitive closure (cf. the persuasion and prejudice reduction studies). Moreover, in situations where a particular means does not provide the desired gratification of their NFC anymore, rather than being rigid or apathetic, people will actively look for other means that suit their goal of closure better (cf. increased information sampling investment when the heuristic approach does not provide closure, or switching cultural or political frameworks if the original framework becomes unsatisfying).

On NFC and Match Quest

In addition to being consistent with Arie Kruglanski's original writings, the idea of NFC involving somewhat flexible means to a fixed end also fits with his recent theory on "Motivational Readiness" (Kruglanski, Chernikova, Rosenzweig, & Kopetz, 2014) outlining the major parameters of people's willingness to act in the service of a desire. Although Kruglanski's new Motiviational Readiness framework is a general theory, developed with no obvious connections to Lay Epistemic Theory or NFC theory (in fact, they are only mentioned most casually), one specific aspect directly relates to the core message of this chapter on the nature of NFC:

> According to the present theory, in the absence of a current Match between a Want and the perceived situational affordance, a *Match quest* will be initiated in which the individual will search for Match-affording situations in order to satisfy her or his desire. An individual who is strongly motivated in some regard, that is, has an appreciable degree of the Want factor, would likely seek a situation that contained relevant affordances ...
>
> *(Kruglanski et al., 2014, p. 381)*

In the Motivational Readiness framework this idea of *Match Quest* is primarily focused on how individuals select their (physical) environment so that it enables a match between their desires and situational affordances (e.g., person–job fit). Yet, the general principle may be applied more broadly. For example, high NFC individuals have been shown to adopt (i.e., select) conservative ideologies because these usually afford the most gratification of their desire for closure (see, Jost, Glaser, Kruglanski, & Sulloway, 2003). However, when these ideologies fall short in situations of uncertainty, the principle of Match Quest would predict that they will actively look for alternative "ideological environments" that provide more affordance. Indeed, as argued before, they may find such a match in extremist ideologies or populist movements, or in the case of immigrants, in full assimilation of the new host culture. Moreover, the Match Quest principle could be further expanded when considering that also within a particular (inescapable) situation, different means are available, providing different affordances. Then, if the default means (e.g., limited information sampling) does not afford gratification of the closure desire in that particular situation, people seek other means that are more fulfilling of their need (e.g., extensive information sampling) to achieve "Match" within that situation.

Concluding Remarks: Where Do We Go from Here?

The introduction and development of the Need for Closure construct has undoubtedly been one of Arie Kruglanski's biggest contributions to the scientific literature, as evidenced by nearly four decades of continuing research by dozens of researchers in basic and applied fields of psychology and beyond. Research on NFC has greatly advanced our insight into how epistemic motivation is central to human knowledge formation, influencing a broad spectrum of phenomena, ranging from basic primacy and anchoring effects, to complex social issues such as prejudice and extremism. Yet, as Roets and colleagues (2015) pointed out, research within the NFC framework is far from complete. For example, a more complete understanding of NFC's interplay with cognitive abilities and its developmental trajectories seem to be most relevant issues for future research, and so are the questions about the potential role of both genetic and environmental influences. However, at least as important is further research that brings NFC to the "real world," aiming to understand and explain how it contributes to the dynamics of, for example, voting behavior, organizational and societal transitions, intergroup relations, and extremism. Importantly, when studying NFC within these most relevant domains, one may want to keep in mind the core message of this chapter: it's about the goal, not the means. Indeed, compared with low NFC individuals, high NFC individuals are more committed to achieving and maintaining the desired closure, and consequentially they are committed to the means that provide it. However, if these "traditional" means fail to deliver, high NFC individuals should also be especially dedicated to finding alternative means towards the closure end (cf. Match Quest). Hence, although NFC is usually a force of "conservation," under particular conditions, it may turn into a force of "change," as indicated by the findings about i.e. extremism, acculturation, and prejudice reduction. Such a more intricate perspective on NFC, in my opinion, will be a most promising direction for future research, ensuring that the NFC branch continues to be fruitful for another few decades.

Note

1   It can be noted that some of the most commonly used NFC manipulations may also tax or deplete cognitive capacity. For an account on the relationships between NFC, cognitive load and depletion, I would like to refer the reader to Roets, Kruglanski, Kossowska, Pierro, and Hong (2015).

References

Allport, G. (1954). *The nature of prejudice*. Reading, MA: Addison-Wesley.

Brandt, M. J., & Reyna, C. (2010). The role of prejudice and need for closure in religious fundamentalism. *Personality and Social Psychology Bulletin*, 36, 715–725.

Brown, R., & Hewstone, M. (2005). An integrative theory of intergroup contact. *Advances in Experimental Social Psychology*, 37, 255–343.

Cacioppo, J. T., & Petty, R. E. (1982). The need for cognition. *Journal of Personality and Social Psychology*, 42, 116–131.

Chirumbolo, A., Mannetti, L., Pierro, A., Arieni, A., & Kruglanski, A. W. (2005). Motivated closed-mindedness and creativity in small groups. *Small Group Research*, 36, 59–82.

Cunningham, W. A., Nezlek, J. B., & Banaji, M. R. (2004). Implicit and explicit ethnocentrism. Revisiting the ideologies of prejudice. *Personality and Social Psychology Bulletin*, 30, 1338–1346.

DeDreu, C. K. W., Koole, S. L., & Oldersma, F. L. (1999). On the seizing and freezing of negotiator inferences: Need for cognitive closure moderates the use of heuristics in negotiation. *Personality and Social Psychology Bulletin*, 25, 348–362.

De Grada, E., Kruglanski, A. W., Mannetti, L., & Pierro, A. (1999). Motivated cognition and group interaction: Need for closure affects the contents and processes of collective negotiations. *Journal of Experimental Social Psychology*, 35, 346–365.

Devine, P. G. (1989). Stereotypes and prejudice: Their automatic and controlled components. *Journal of Personality and Social Psychology*, 56, 4–18.

Devine, P. G., & Elliot, A. J. (1995). Are racial stereotypes really fading? The Princeton Trilogy revisited. *Personality and Social Psychology Bulletin*, 21, 1139–1150.

Dhont, K. & Van Hiel, A. (2009). We must not be enemies: Interracial contact and the reduction of prejudice among authoritarians. *Personality and Individual Differences*, 46, 172–177.

Dhont, K., Roets, A., & Van Hiel, A. (2011). Opening closed minds: The combined effects of intergroup contact and need for closure on prejudice. *Personality and Social Psychology Bulletin*, 37, 514–528.

Dijksterhuis, A., van Knippenberg, A., Kruglanski, A. W., & Schaper, C. (1996). Motivated social cognition: Need for closure effects on memory and judgement. *Journal of Experimental and Social Psychology*, 32, 254–270.

Disatnik, D., & Steinhart, Y. (2015). Need for cognitive closure, risk aversion, uncertainty changes, and their effects on investment decisions. *Journal of Marketing Research*, 52, 349–359.

Ford, T. E., & Kruglanski, A. W. (1995). Effects of epistemic motivations on the use of accessible constructs in social judgment. *Personality and Social Psychology Bulletin*, 21, 950–962.

Freund, T., Kruglanski, A. W., & Shpitzajzen, A. (1985). The freezing and unfreezing of impressional primacy: Effects of the need for structure and the fear of invalidity. *Personality and Social Psychology Bulletin*, 11, 479–487.

Heaton, A. W., & Kruglanski, A. W. (1991). Person perception by introverts and extroverts under time pressure: Effects of need for closure. *Personality and Social Psychology Bulletin*, 17, 161–165.

Houghton, D., & Grewal, R. (2000). Let's get an answer – any answer: Need for consumer cognitive closure. *Psychology and Marketing*, 17, 911–934.

Jost, J. T., Glaser, J., Kruglanski, A. W., & Sulloway, F. J. (2003). Political conservatism as motivated social cognition. *Psychological Bulletin*, 129, 339–375.

Kim, H. (2013). How variety-seeking versus inertial tendency influences the effectiveness of immediate versus delayed promotions. *Journal of Marketing Research*, 50, 416–426.

Kosic, A., Kruglanski, A. W., Pierro, A., & Mannetti, L. (2004). The social cognition of immigrants' acculturation: Effects of the need for closure and the reference group at entry. *Journal of Personality and Social Psychology*, 86(6), 796–813.

Kruglanski, A. W. (1980). Lay epistemologic processes and contents. Another look at attribution theory. *Psychological Review*, 87, 70–78.

Kruglanski, A. W. (1989). *Lay epistemic and human knowledge: Cognitive and motivational bases*. New York: Plenum.

Kruglanski, A. W., & Freund, T. (1983). The freezing and un-freezing of lay-inferences: Effects of impressional primacy, ethnic stereotyping and numerical anchoring. *Journal of Experimental Social Psychology*, 19, 448–468.

Kruglanski, A. W., & Mayseless, O. (1988). Contextual effects in hypothesis testing: The role of competing alternatives and epistemic motivations. *Social Cognition*, 6, 1–21.

Kruglanski, A. W., & Webster, D. M. (1991). Group members' reactions to opinion deviates and conformists at varying degrees of proximity to decision deadline and environmental noise. *Journal of Personality and Social Psychology*, 61, 212–225.

Kruglanski, A. W., & Webster, D. M. (1996). Motivated closing of the mind: "Seizing" and "freezing". *Psychological Review*, 103, 263–283.

Kruglanski, A. W., Bélanger, J. J., Gelfand, M.J., Gunaratna, R., Hettiarachchi, M., Reinares, F., Orehek, E., Sasota, J., & Sharvit, K. (2013) Terrorism: A (self) love story: Redirecting the quest for significance can end violence. *American Psychologist*, 68, 559–575.

Kruglanski, A. W., Chernikova, M., Rosenzweig, E., & Kopetz, C. (2014). On motivational readiness. *Psychological Review*, 121, 367–388.

Kruglanski, A. W., Dechesne, M., Orehek, E., & Pierro, A. (2009). Three decades of lay epistemics: The why, how and who of knowledge formation. *European Review of Social Psychology*, 20, 146–191.

Kruglanski, A. W., Gelfand, M. J., Belanger, J. J., Schori-Eyal, N., Moyano, E., Trujillo, X., Gunaratna, R., & Hetiarachchi, M. (2014). *On the psychology of extremism: Effects of humiliation and need for closure in three vulnerable populations.* Manuscript submitted for publication. University of Maryland.

Kruglanski, A. W., Peri, N., & Zakai, D. (1991). Interactive effects of need for closure and initial confidence on social information seeking. *Social Cognition*, 9, 127–148.

Kruglanski, A. W., Pierro, A., Mannetti, L., & De Grada, E. (2006) Groups as epistemic providers: Need for closure and the unfolding of group-centrism. *Psychological Review*, 113, 84–100.

Kruglanski, A. W., Webster, D. M., & Klem, A. (1993). Motivated resistance and openness to persuasion in the presence or absence of prior information. *Journal of Personality and Social Psychology*, 65, 861–877.

Mayseless, O., & Kruglanski, A. W. (1987). What makes you so sure? Effects of epistemic motivations on judgmental confidence. *Organizational Behavior and Human Decision Processes*, 39, 162–183.

Medin, D. L. (1989). Concepts and conceptual structure. *American Psychologist*, 44, 1469–1481.

Morris, M. W., Mok, A., & Mor, S. (2011). Cultural identity threat: The role of cultural identifications in moderating closure responses to a foreign cultural inflow. *Journal of Social Issues*, 67, 760–773.

Onraet, E., Van Hiel, A., Roets, A., & Cornelis, I. (2011). The closed mind: 'Experience' and 'cognition' aspects of openness to experience and need for closure as psychological bases for right-wing attitudes. *European Journal of Personality*, 25, 184–197.

Pettigrew, T. F., & Tropp, L. R. (2008). How does intergroup contact reduce prejudice? Meta-analytic tests of three mediators. *European Journal of Social Psychology*, 38, 922–934.

Pierro, A., Mannetti, L., De Grada, E., Livi, S., & Kruglanski, A. W. (2003). Autocracy bias in informal groups under need for closure. *Personality and Social Psychology Bulletin*, 29, 405–417.

Richter, M., Baeriswyl, E., & Roets, A. (2012). Personality effects on cardiovascular reactivity: Need for closure moderates the impact of task difficulty on engagement-related myocardial beta-adrenergic activity. *Psychophysiology*, 49, 704–707

Roets, A., Kruglanski, A. W., Kossowska, M., Pierro, A., & Hong, Y. (2015). The motivated gatekeeper of our minds: New directions in need for closure. *Advances in Experimental Social Psychology*, 52, 221–283.

Roets, A., Raman, E., Heytens, S., & Avonds, D. (2014). Effects of dispositional need for closure and training on medical decision making. *Medical Decision Making*, 34, 144–146.

Roets, A., & Van Hiel, A. (2006). Need for closure relations with authoritarianism, conservative beliefs and racism: The impact of urgency and permanence tendencies. *Psychologica Belgica*, 46, 235–252.

Roets, A., & Van Hiel, A. (2007). Separating ability from need: Clarifying the dimensional structure of the need for closure scale. *Personality and Social Psychology Bulletin*, 33, 266–280.

Roets, A., & Van Hiel, A. (2008). Why some hate to dillydally and others do not: The arousal-invoking capacity of decision-making for low and high-scoring need for closure individuals. *Social Cognition*, 26, 333–346.

Roets, A., & Van Hiel, A. (2011a). Allport's prejudiced personality today: Need for closure as the motivated cognitive basis of prejudice. *Current Directions in Psychological Science*, 26, 349–354.

Roets, A., & Van Hiel, A. (2011b). The role of need for closure in essentialist entitativity beliefs and prejudice: An epistemic needs approach to racial categorization. *British Journal of Social Psychology*, 50, 52–73.

Roets, A., Van Hiel, A., Cornelis, I., & Soetens, B. (2008). Determinants of task performance and invested effort: A need for closure by ability interaction analysis. *Personality and Social Psychology Bulletin*, 34, 779–792.

Roets, A., Van Hiel, A., & Dhont, K. (2012). Is sexism a gender issue? A motivated social cognition perspective on men's and women's sexist attitudes toward the own and other gender. *European Journal of Personality*, 26, 350–359.

Shah, J. Y., Kruglanski, A. W., & Thompson, E. P. (1998). Membership has its (epistemic) rewards: Need for closure effects on ingroup bias. *Journal of Personality and Social Psychology*, 75, 383–393.

Tadmor, C. T., Hong, Y., Chao, M. M., Wiruchnipawan, F., & Wang, W. (2012). Multicultural experiences reduce intergroup bias through epistemic unfreezing. *Journal of Personality and Social Psychology*, 103, 750–772.

Tebbe, E. N., & Moradi, B. (2012). Anti-transgender prejudice: a structural equation model of associated constructs. *Journal of Counseling Psychology*, 59(2), 251–261.

Van Hiel, A., Pandelaere, M., & Duriez, B. (2004). The impact of need for closure on conservative beliefs and racism: Differential mediation by authoritarian submission and authoritarian dominance. *Personality and Social Psychology Bulletin*, 30, 824–837.

Vermeir, I., Van Kenhove, P., & Hendrickx, H. (2002). The influence of need for closure on consumer choice behaviour. *Journal of Economic Psychology*, 23, 703–727.

Webster, D. M. (1993a). Motivated augmentation and reduction of the overattribution bias. *Journal of Personality and Social Psychology*, 65, 261–271.

Webster, D. M. (1993b). *Groups under the influence: Need for closure effects on information sharing in decision making groups*. Unpublished doctoral dissertation. University of Maryland, College Park.

Webster, D. M., & Kruglanski, A. W. (1994). Individual differences in need for cognitive closure. *Journal of Personality and Social Psychology*, 67, 1049–1062.

Webster, D. M., Richter, L., & Kruglanski, A. W. (1996). On leaping to conclusions when feeling tired: Mental fatigue effects on impressional primacy. *Journal of Experimental Social Psychology*, 32, 181–195.

4

GETTING CLOSURE ON CONSERVATISM, OR THE POLITICS OF EPISTEMIC AND EXISTENTIAL MOTIVATION

John T. Jost, Joanna Sterling and Chadly Stern

Prologue by John T. Jost

> For the last time psychology!
> *(Franz Kafka)*

When I was 20 years old, I was pretentious enough to keep a cork-bound journal to record all of my thoughts and influences. Much of what I preserved in those notebooks were the writings of others, which I aspired to commit to memory or at least to assimilate in some inchoate fashion. One of my favorite inspirations at that time was Franz Kafka, which is a little mystifying. Unlike Arie Kruglanski, I did not hail from Eastern Europe, I was not Jewish, and I had not been falsely detained by an evil or indifferent bureaucracy (other than the Department of Motor Vehicles). I was just a kid from Cincinnati – a high school soccer player with a haircut from Supercuts. So it's a little obscure why the writings of Kafka would have left such an indelible mark on me back in the 1980s, but they did. Perhaps the mystery subsides a bit if I mention that my father was a philosopher and my mother was a professor of literature. Most of my friends grew up with *Sports Illustrated* or *Vogue* lying around; our house was littered with the *New York Review of Books*.

Here is one passage from Kafka that I copied into my journal. It moved me for reasons that I am only slightly better poised than you to understand:

> All human error is impatience, a premature renunciation of method, a delusive pinning down of a delusion.
> *(Franz Kafka, "Reflections on Sin, Pain, Hope, and the True Way," 1946a, p. 278)*

I suppose that one of the main things I knew at 20 was that most people – most adults, I mean – were deluded and impatient, full of stereotypes and prejudices, quick judgments and easy answers, always in a hurry, never in doubt – and I didn't want to be that way.

But at age 20 I did not yet understand much about why most people were in error, why they were impatient, or why they were deluded. For that, I first needed to commit myself to a career in social psychology and to prepare for an apprenticeship with Arie Kruglanski, the world's foremost expert on the psychology of impatience. Arie is, after all, the researcher who is famous for identifying the hastiest of epistemic goals: one that prompts "activities aimed at the attainment of closure" and biases "the individual's choices and preferences toward closure-bound pursuits" (Kruglanski & Webster, 1996, p. 264). When "the epistemic process is 'frozen'" in this way, Kruglanski (1990) pointed out, "hypothesis generation is arrested, and the individual becomes generally insensitive to relevant stimulus information" (p. 182). A "premature renunciation of method" indeed.

While I was waiting, not for Godot but for Kruglanski, who very definitely *did* show up (and still does), I carefully recorded my observations in a cork-bound journal. And I matriculated as an undergraduate student at Duke University. I was promptly assigned a faculty advisor from the Department of Psychology based on the first initial of my last name. (Another "premature renunciation of method.") Fortunately for me, that advisor turned out to be the personality psychologist Irving Alexander. Alexander had been a student – and later a best friend – of Silvan Tomkins, who is best remembered as a psychologist of emotion, but he was equally insightful and proficient as a political psychologist.

In 1965, more than a decade before the founding of the International Society of Political Psychology, Tomkins made this ambitious claim on behalf of a field that was just barely coming into existence:

> If we know a person's general emotional posture, I believe we can predict what ideologies he would choose if he were exposed to them – and whether they will be toward the left pole or the right.
>
> *(Tomkins, 1965, p. 27)*

What he meant is that some people – through a complex interaction of dispositional, perhaps even genetic, and situational, contextual factors – are drawn to worldviews that emphasize humanistic concerns about dignity, respect, and equality. Others are drawn instead to normative concerns about rules, standards, and achievements – what Tory Higgins might call "oughts" as opposed to "ideals" (e.g., Higgins, Roney, Crowe, & Hymes, 1994). According to Tomkins, these humanistic and normative orientations anchor, respectively, the left and right poles in politics, art, science, mathematics, philosophy, sex, and just about every other domain of life.

In Tomkins' (1987) view, the left–right conflict is an ancient one insofar as it is "a sublimated derivative of social stratification and exploitation" (p. 173). Most social systems throughout human history have been based on social stratification and exploitation, and they have had their share of defenders and challengers. Writing about the European Enlightenment, Tomkins noted that "The left represented, then as now, the oppressed and exploited against their warrior oppressors" (p. 173), whereas "The right is [and was] … apologist of primarily masculine, adversarial stratification, buttressed by 'tradition'" (p. 177). Tomkins characterized conservative, right-wing ideologies as "defensive ideologies [that] vary as a function of the nature of the society they defend" and "place the blame for [problems in society] squarely upon those who suffer and complain," like "the welfare 'cheats' who are to blame for their own problems" (p. 176). By contrast, Tomkins suggested that liberal and left-wing ideologies – for better or worse – "place the blame … on the established normative authority, which must then change itself or be changed by those who suffer" (p. 177).

When I arrived at Yale University as a doctoral student in the early 1990s, I was drawn almost immediately into the zeitgeist of theory and research on social cognition by two other extraordinary mentors, Mahzarin Banaji and Bill McGuire. I turned away – at least for the moment – from the writings of Silvan Tomkins on left-wing and right-wing personality types, and focused instead on stereotyping and nonconscious bias and the structure and functions of attitudes. It took me years to appreciate the extent to which Tomkins' work had influenced me, but those writings must have informed my ideas about system justification theory (Jost & Banaji, 1994), including the notion that some attitudes serve the ideological function of defending society – including the defense of societal arrangements and practices that may be considered exploitative or oppressive.

I also see now that Tomkins' (1965, 1987) work on left-right differences with respect to affect, cognition, and motivation must have contributed in essential ways to the theory of political ideology as "motivated social cognition" that Arie and I eventually developed, in collaboration with Jack Glaser and Frank Sulloway (Jost, Glaser, Kruglanski, & Sulloway, 2003b, 2003c). I am thinking especially of the idea that liberals and leftists are motivated by (humanistic) concerns for equality (and social justice), and this leads them to embrace social change, whereas conservatives and rightists are motivated by the (normative) desire to preserve tradition (and social order), and this is what leads them to defend and justify inequalities in the social system (see also Jost, Nosek, & Gosling, 2008).

This project of understanding political ideology as a form of motivated social cognition began soon after I arrived in College Park as one of Arie's postdocs in 1995. Arie had hired me – over the telephone, at the very end of a fascinating conversation, which always struck me as a debonair move on his part – and asked me to be one of four postdocs in his lab (a "dream team," he called us at the time). Arie recognized my interest in political psychology and therefore pitched the most exciting and excitable (read controversial) project that I have ever had the intellectual pleasure of working on. Arie wanted to know, quite simply, if *psychological* conservatism – including the "need for cognitive closure," the cognitive-motivational tendency to "seize and freeze" on information that is highly salient, familiar, accessible, preliminary, or convenient (Kruglanski & Webster, 1996; see also Roets, Chapter 3, this volume) – would be associated with *political* conservatism – the ideological tendency to defend and justify aspects of the traditional status quo, with its attendant degree of hierarchy, inequality, and structure (e.g., Mannheim, 1936, 1986).

I reckoned that the answer to this question was "yes," and I set about trying to find every study from the 1950s on – following the landmark publication of *The Authoritarian Personality* by Adorno, Frenkel-Brunswik, Levinson, and Sanford (1950) – that could be useful for addressing this question. We took it as a clue that Webster and Kruglanski (1994) had obtained a correlation of .26 between the need for cognitive closure and authoritarianism, as measured with the F- (or Fascism) Scale developed by Adorno and his colleagues. In my literature search, I may have missed a few pertinent studies – these were the days before the Internet was even remotely useful as a bibliographical search machine. But, in addition to a very useful book on *The Psychology of Conservatism* edited by Glenn Wilson (1973), I identified several dozen studies carried out between 1958 and 2002. Arie and I met weekly to discuss the theoretical and empirical fruits of my investigations. Those were inspiring meetings; Arie was invariably enthusiastic, curious, and constructive, and his cognitive style – then as now – was eager, integrative, and complex.

At that time, Arie and his friends were fomenting a "motivational revolution" that was soon to alter psychologists' understanding of social cognition from the level of automatic associations to individual judgments and even full-fledged belief systems and ideologies. Our work on political conservatism took several years to execute, but it was facilitated by the year that Arie spent (1998–1999) at the Center for Advanced Studies in Social and Behavioral Sciences (CASBS) at Stanford University, where I had taken an assistant professorship. It was then that we decided to invite Frank Sulloway, another fellow at the CASBS, and Jack Glaser, an assistant professor at the University of California at Berkeley, to collaborate with us on the project. By that point, the editorial review process had metamorphosed our narrative review into a quantitative, meta-analytic synthesis. We published our results in *Psychological Bulletin* in 2003 under the title of "Political Conservatism as Motivated Social Cognition," and the rest, as they say, is contested history. According to Google Scholar, this article has been cited well over 2,500 times, which (at the time of writing) makes it not only my most highly cited paper, but also Arie's most highly cited paper!

Political Conservatism as Motivated Social Cognition

The article by Jost, Glaser, Kruglanski, and Sulloway (2003b) reviewed 88 studies carried out by research teams from 12 different countries involving more than

22,000 individual participants and cases. The results indicated that a variety of epistemic motives and tendencies to reduce and manage uncertainty were indeed correlated with political orientation. Specifically, intolerance of ambiguity and stronger personal needs for order, structure, and closure were positively associated with the endorsement of conservative attitudes. Integrative complexity, openness to new experiences, and tolerance for uncertainty were negatively associated with conservative attitudes – or positively associated with liberal attitudes. Existential motives to reduce threat were also correlated with political orientation. The meta-analytic review indicated that stronger feelings of threat, death anxiety, and exposure to system threat were positively associated with conservatism.

Whether it was intended to or not, the article by Jost et al. (2003b) – and the accompanying exchange between Greenberg and Jonas (2003) and Jost et al. (2003c) – reignited once vigorous debates about authoritarianism, dogmatism, cognitive rigidity, and the covariation of psychological characteristics and ideological beliefs, opinions, and values (e.g., Adorno et al., 1950; Brown, 1965; Eysenck, 1999; McClosky, 1958; Rokeach, 1960; Sidanius, 1978). Tetlock (2007) summarized the dispute as follows:

> A recent meta-analysis of the literature has sparked controversy by concluding that right-wing conservatism is related to dogmatism and intolerance of ambiguity; uncertainty avoidance; fear of threat, loss, and death; system instability; and epistemic needs to achieve order, structure, and closure as well as negatively related to openness to experience, integrative complexity, and (to a lesser extent) self-esteem (Jost, Glaser, Kruglanski, & Sulloway, 2003b). The authors do, though, add a critical caveat: This does not mean that liberals crave uncertainty and risk. There can be rigidity of the left as well as of the right. Their claim is simply that rigidity of the left is markedly less common than that on the right....
>
> Neither the explanans (cognitive style) nor the explanandum (ideology) in the dispute between Jost et al. (2003b, 2003c) and Greenberg and Jonas (2003) is a static trait entity. Each has a dynamic component that permits it to vary across contexts, issues, and time. There are settings in which the linkages between cognitive style and ideology are powerful and in the direction posited by Jost and colleagues ... and other settings in which the relationships vanish.
>
> All that said, it is noteworthy that although the main effect revealed in the Jost and colleagues (2003b, 2003c) meta-analysis can be neutralized, it never seems to reverse direction so that, across issues, conservatives as a group score as more flexible and multidimensional than liberals ... In this author's view, political psychology needs more disagreements of the sort represented in the exchange between Jost and colleagues and Greenberg and Jonas. The net result was clarification.

(pp. 905–906)

In subsequent years, researchers have explored implications of the theory of political ideology as motivated social cognition in a number of stimulating directions, including (but not limited to): the influences of genetic heritability and assortative mating strategies on resistance to change and acceptance of inequality; the continuity between childhood temperament and political orientation in adulthood; interpersonal attachment styles and their implications for the adoption of right-wing ideology; ideological differences in fundamental motivational orientations, such as approach and avoidance; exploratory behavior in novel, potentially risky situations; perceptual vigilance and physiological reactivity in response to negative and threatening stimuli; happiness and subjective well-being; and the study of brain structure and function. In political science, too, the theory of political ideology as motivated social cognition has been applied to core topics of the discipline, including domestic and foreign policy, voting behavior, and political preferences (Gries, 2014; Hibbing, Smith, & Alford, 2014; Rathbun, 2014). All of this work seems to have stoked popular interest in the subject matter of political psychology, as indicated by the number of trade books devoted to the topic in the subsequent decade (*inter alia*, Dean, 2006; Haidt, 2012; Lakoff, 2008; Mooney, 2012; Tuschman, 2013; Westen, 2007).

Kruglanski and Webster (1996) once wrote: "That knowledge construction has a motivational base should come as no particular surprise" (p. 263). Nevertheless, at least one of the authors of "Political Conservatism as Motivated Social Cognition" was unprepared for the backlash he encountered, first in conservative media outlets, then in his email inbox, and eventually from opportunistic professional rivals and upstarts. But, as Kafka wrote: "From a certain point onward there is no longer any turning back. That is the point that must be reached." Some of the angriest, most telling responses came from pundits who exhibited such a high need for cognitive closure that they failed to read beyond the title of the article. Ann Coulter, for instance, weighed in on the research so fast and furiously that she completely misinterpreted a press release, concluding that liberals had a "powerful need for closure." This was precisely the opposite of the finding, so she confused herself mightily – but went to press anyway, accusing the four psychologists of "treason":

> The report described "liberal" traits as including a powerful "need for closure." (I believe conservatives just want closure on the word "closure.") But in the press release, one of the researchers, Jack Glaser, said the study suggested that Bush had "ignored intelligence information" about Iraq because of the conservative "need for closure." So I guess another liberal trait is "making no sense."
>
> The study also explained that "conservatives don't feel the need to jump through complex, intellectual hoops in order to understand or justify some of their positions … Whenever you have backed a liberal into a corner – if he doesn't start crying – he says, "It's a complicated issue." Loving America is

too simple an emotion. To be nuanced you have to hate it a little. Conservatives may not grasp "nuance," but we're pretty good at grasping treason.

Another right-wing pundit, Jonah Goldberg, fumed about the meta-analysis in the online edition of the *Wall Street Journal* before indulging in happy reminiscences of violent police crackdowns on campus radicals during the 1960s:

> Now that I've calmed down a bit (read: I've put the shotgun down, and put my car keys back on the table), I thought I'd include a "relaxation aid" at the end of this post to help calm down people who read that whole thing. Here's a photo from when Governor Ronald Reagan ordered a tear gas airstrike on UC Berkeley's Sproul Plaza during an anti-war demonstration…. The best part is that we don't have to pine for an "idealized past." In the real past, lefty nutjobs at Berkeley really were heavily sprayed with teargas.

These reactions and many others (e.g., see Dean, 2006, pp. 28–31, 211–212, for a description) appear to satisfy Kafka's criteria for "impatience," "a premature renunciation of method," and "a delusive pinning down of a delusion." Ironically, the defensiveness and aggression on display served to illustrate rather vividly the phenomenon of political conservatism as *motivated* social cognition.

Another unlikely media controversy erupted in 2010 when a few libertarians on the right floated the possibility that the conservative movement had a genuine problem with respect to "epistemic closure" (Sanchez, 2010). In essence, they warned that "closed-mindedness" and "ideological intolerance and misinformation" risked jeopardizing "modern conservatism's proud intellectual history" (Cohen, 2010; Friedersdorf, 2012). Intense denial and mutual recrimination followed. Most conservatives decided that the movement was doing just fine, thank you very much. Nevertheless, when U.S. adults were asked in a Gallup Poll conducted in 2013 to name one or two things they disliked most about each of the major political parties, 21% stated that the Republican Party was "too inflexible" or "unwilling to compromise"; this was the most common complaint, and it was shared by Democratic, Independent, and Republican respondents alike (Saad, 2013). Only 8% of respondents felt that Democrats were inflexible or unwilling to compromise.

A few years later, Donald Trump won the American presidency on the strength of a campaign that was widely decried – even by conservatives such as Andrew Sullivan (2016) – as prejudicial, irrational, intolerant, and authoritarian. In an opinion editorial published by the *Guardian*, Kruglanski (2015) conjectured that fear was contributing to Trump's popularity, at least in part because "existential anxieties … spawn yearnings for order and predictability" that "privilege simplistic concepts that lack nuance and lend significant edge to leaders who talk tough and offer what psychologists call 'closure.'"

One of the major goals of the article by Jost et al. (2003b) was to stimulate more empirical research on the psychology of left–right (or liberal–conservative) ideology; it ended with a "Plea for Future Research." In this respect, at least, the article succeeded beyond the wildest of expectations. For a variety of reasons – certainly not just the publication of a single article – there have been far more studies conducted on this topic in the last 14 years than in the preceding 50 years. As part of a broader effort to synthesize all of the newer studies and to conduct ever more comprehensive reviews of the literature, we have identified 181 studies linking political ideology to epistemic motivation and another 100 or so studies linking political ideology to existential motivation. The majority of these were conducted after 2003, and several were conducted in post-Communist societies, which are of especially great interest when it comes to understanding the generalizability of ideological differences in epistemic and existential motivation (e.g., Greenberg & Jonas, 2003; Thórisdóttir, Jost, Liviatan, & Shrout, 2007). Next, we turn to a summary of the results, beginning with studies of epistemic motivation before turning to studies of existential motivation.[1]

The Politics of Epistemic Motivation: State of the Evidence

We collected studies for the present meta-analysis using several different means, including academic search engines, "snowball" techniques based on citations of major articles, and listserv requests for unpublished data. Using these methods, we obtained data from 181 distinct samples and a total of 133,796 individual participants. To calculate effect sizes, we sorted studies (or samples) into nine categories: uncertainty tolerance, tolerance of ambiguity, need for cognitive closure, needs for order and structure, integrative complexity, need for cognition, cognitive rigidity, dogmatism, and cognitive reflection. We conducted separate analyses of the relations between each of these categories and political ideology. For all political variables, higher values reflect greater conservatism and lower values reflect greater liberalism. Point estimates are listed in online tables archived here: osf.io/6hkec.[2] Overall results are summarized in Figure 4.1, which ranks the distributions of average effect sizes, along with 95% confidence intervals.

To assess the role of publication bias – also known as the "file-drawer" problem – on the size of the average effect, we estimated Egger's regression to measure the deviation from the assumption of no bias (Egger, Smith, Schneider, & Minder, 1997). We mapped the effect sizes using funnel plots and imputed potentially missing effect sizes using Duval and Tweedie's (2000) trim-and-fill procedure. Because Egger's regression is suboptimal when it comes to small sample sizes, we also calculated an effect size fail-safe N using the equation provided by Orwin (1983). This indicates the number of unpublished studies averaging a null effect size that would be needed to reduce the reported effect size to a preselected "trivial" value. We selected this value to

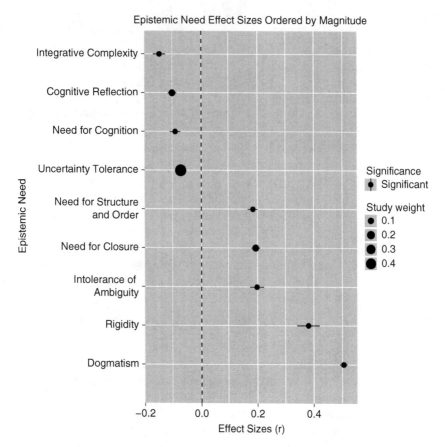

FIGURE 4.1 Summary of meta-analytic results: the distribution of average effect sizes across variables of epistemic motivation

be $r = |.10|$, because Cohen (1988) considered this to be the lower bound of a "small" effect in the population.

There have been 16 tests of the hypothesis that "uncertainty tolerance" would be greater among liberals than conservatives; seven of these tests were conducted after the publication of Jost et al. (2003b, 2003c). Uncertainty tolerance has been measured in several different ways, including aesthetic preferences for complex art and poetry and disagreement with items such as, "I can't stand being taken by surprise." In 13 of 16 cases a significant effect in the hypothesized direction was observed.[3] The unweighted ($r = -.35$) and weighted ($r = -.07$, 95% CI [−.08, −.06]) average effect sizes were negative and statistically significant, but varied dramatically in magnitude. Because the sample size for the study by Malka et al. (2014) was so large (accounting for 99% of the total [unique] n) and the psychometric properties of the measures used to gauge epistemic (and existential) motivation were problematic,[4] it diluted the

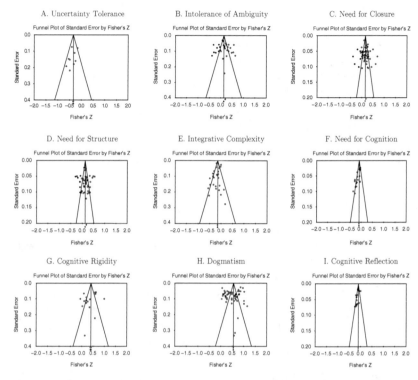

FIGURE 4.2 Funnel plots of actual (open circles) and imputed (filled circles) effect sizes for studies examining the relationship between epistemic motivation and political conservatism

weighted effect size to a disproportionate extent. When this study was excluded from calculations, the unweighted ($r = -.35$) and weighted ($r = -.33$, 95% CI [−.40, −.26]) average effect sizes were both quite strong. Furthermore, Egger's regression did not exhibit evidence of publication bias, $B_0 = -1.49$, $SE = 1.04$, $t(7) = 1.44$, $p = .19$, and the resulting funnel plot indicated that no additional missing studies would be needed to attain a symmetrical distribution of effects (Figure 4.2, Panel A). The effect size fail-safe N indicated that 22 studies averaging a null effect would be needed to reduce the average effect size to $r = -.10$. Thus, our analysis indicates liberals were more tolerant of uncertainty than conservatives in the U.S., Canada, and Scotland.

Although Jost et al. (2003b, 2003c) had identified only a handful of studies on "intolerance of ambiguity," there have now been 44 tests of the hypothesis that conservatives would be less tolerant of ambiguity than liberals conducted in eight different countries. Intolerance of ambiguity has been measured in several different ways, including the administration of questionnaires that include statements such as, "A good job is one where what is to be done and how it is to be done are always clear." In 33 of 44 cases, a significant positive association between intolerance of ambiguity and right-wing orientation was observed; in nine other cases, the effect was not statistically significant but in the predicted direction. The unweighted (r = .26) and weighted (r = .20, 95% CI [.17, .22]) average effect sizes were positive and significant. At the same time, Egger's regression showed evidence of publication bias, B_0 = 2.66, SE = 0.98, t (22) = 2.71, p = .01. A trim-and-fill funnel plot indicated that nine additional studies would be needed to attain a symmetrical distribution of effects (Figure 4.2, Panel B). The effect size fail-safe N indicated that 25 studies averaging a null effect would be needed to reduce the average effect size to r = .10. In conclusion, conservatives and rightists were found to be more intolerant of ambiguity than liberals and leftists in the U.S., Canada, England, Belgium, Sweden, Hungary, and Israel.

Jost et al. (2003b) identified nine studies that had used Arie's favorite scale, the "need for cognitive closure," which includes items like: "I usually make important decisions quickly and confidently." There have now been 100 tests of the hypothesis that conservatives would score higher than liberals on the need for cognitive closure conducted in seven different countries. In 79 of 100 cases, a positive and significant relationship was indeed obtained. The unweighted (r = .23) and weighted (r = .19, 95% CI [.18, .21]) average effect sizes were positive and significant. Egger's regression exhibited evidence of bias, B_0 = 2.21, SE = 0.88, t(39) = 2.51, p = .02, and the funnel plot supported this, indicating that 12 additional missing studies would be needed to attain a symmetrical distribution of effects (Figure 4.2, Panel C). The effect size fail-safe N indicated that 40 studies averaging a null effect would be needed to reduce the average effect size to r = .10. Conservatives and rightists were found to score higher than liberals and leftists on the need for closure in the U.S., Germany, Italy, Belgium, Sweden, Netherlands, Poland, and Turkey.

Although Jost et al. (2003b) had only identified a few studies focusing on "needs for order and structure," there have now been 77 tests of the hypothesis – carried out in six different countries – that conservatives would score higher than liberals on personal needs for order and structure. This variable is typically measured using a questionnaire that includes items such as "It upsets me to go into a situation without knowing what I can expect from it." In 51 of 78 cases a positive and significant association was observed between needs for order/structure and right-wing orientation. The unweighted (r = .20) and weighted (r = .18, 95% CI [.17, .20]) average effect sizes were positive and significant. Egger's regression showed no evidence of bias, B_0 = 0.98, SE = 0.98, t(34) = 1.00, p = .33, but the funnel plot indicated that nine additional studies would be needed to attain a symmetrical distribution of effects (Figure 4.2, Panel D). The effect size fail-safe N indicated that 31 studies averaging a null effect would be needed to reduce the average effect size to r = .10. Conservatives and rightists were found to score higher than liberals and leftists on personal needs for order and structure in the U.S., Canada, Belgium, and New Zealand – as well as two formerly Communist countries, Hungary and Poland.

On the basis of 11 studies that had explored ideological differences in "integrative complexity" – which is typically measured objectively in terms of content coding of speeches, decisions, and other forms of text – Jost et al. (2003b, 2003c) concluded that liberals generally scored higher than conservatives on integrative complexity (see also Tetlock, 2007). This conclusion was challenged by Conway et al. (2016), who failed to observe consistent ideological differences across four studies. There have now been 40 tests of the hypothesis conducted in four different countries. In 20 cases, a significant negative relationship was observed between integrative complexity and right-wing orientation; in only two cases – both reported by Conway et al. (2016) – was a significant positive relationship observed. Overall, the unweighted ($r = -.19$) and weighted ($r = -.15$, 95% CI [$-.17, -.13$]) average effect sizes were negative and significant. Egger's regression exhibited no evidence of bias, $B_0 = -0.67$, $SE = 0.57$, $t(24) = 1.17$, $p = .25$, and the funnel plot supported this, indicating that no additional missing studies would be needed to attain a symmetrical distribution of effects (Figure 4.2, Panel E). The effect size fail-safe N indicated that 13 studies averaging a null effect would be needed to reduce the average effect size to $r = -.10$. Thus, in the U.S. and England, conservatives and rightists tend to score lower than liberals on integrative complexity, even after accounting for null and contradictory results reported by Conway et al. (2016). The evidence was inconclusive in Sweden and Belgium.

To our knowledge, there were no studies of ideological differences in "need for cognition" conducted prior to the Jost et al. (2003b) review, but there have now been 40 tests of the hypothesis that liberals would score higher than conservatives on the need for cognition, which is measured with the use of a scale that includes items such as, "I find satisfaction in deliberating hard and for long hours" (Cacioppo & Petty, 1982). In 25 of 40 cases, a significant, negative association was observed between need for cognition and right-wing orientation; in all but three of the other cases, the association was negative but nonsignificant. The unweighted ($r = -.16$) and weighted ($r = -.09$, 95% CI [$-.11, -.07$]) average effect sizes were negative and statistically significant but small in terms of magnitude. Egger's regression showed evidence of bias, $B_0 = -3.45$, $SE = 0.55$, $t(17) = 6.30$, $p < .001$, although the funnel plot indicated that no additional studies would be needed to attain a symmetrical distribution of effects (Figure 4.2, Panel F).

Because Rokeach, McGovney, and Denny (1955) distinguished between dogmatic and rigid forms of thinking, we computed separate effect sizes for these two variables. We identified 23 tests of the hypothesis that conservatives would score higher than liberals on tests of perceptual or cognitive rigidity; typically, the tasks measure behaviors such as the tendency to exclude non-prototypical examples from category classification. In 14 of 23 cases, a significant positive association was observed between rigidity and right-wing orientation, and in seven other cases a positive but nonsignificant association was observed. The unweighted

(r = .32) and weighted (r = .38, 95% CI [.34, .42]) average effect sizes were strong and statistically significant. Egger's regression showed no evidence of bias, B_0 = −2.59, SE = 1.99, $t(14)$ = 1.30, p = .21, and the funnel plot supported this, indicating that no additional missing studies would be needed to attain a symmetrical distribution of effects (Figure 4.2, Panel G). The effect size fail-safe N indicated that 48 studies averaging a null effect would be needed to reduce the average effect size to r = .10. In studies conducted in the U.S., Canada, and England, conservatives and rightists exhibited greater perceptual and cognitive rigidity than liberals and leftists.

Finally, there have been 77 tests of the hypothesis (conducted in 7 different countries) that "dogmatism" – which entails, among other things, the assumption that "There are two kinds of people in this world: those who are for the truth and those who are against the truth" – would be stronger on the political right than the left. In 68 of 77 cases a significant positive relationship was observed between dogmatism and right-wing orientation; in only one case was a significant negative relationship observed. The unweighted (r = .48) and weighted (r = .51, 95% CI [.49,.52]) average effect sizes were positive and quite large. Egger's regression showed no evidence of bias, B_0 = −1.87, SE = 1.64, $t(48)$ = 1.14, p = .26, and the funnel plot suggested that no additional missing studies would be needed to attain a symmetrical distribution of effects (Figure 4.2, Panel H). The effect size fail-safe N indicated that 227 studies averaging a null effect would be needed to reduce the average effect size to r = .10. In the U.S., England, Netherlands, Poland, and New Zealand conservatives and rightists were consistently more dogmatic than liberals and leftists. The evidence was mixed or inconclusive in Belgium and Hungary.

In summary, then, an updated, more comprehensive meta-analysis reproduces all of the effect sizes estimated by Jost et al. (2003b, 2003c) concerning ideological differences in epistemic motivation. That is, aggregating across 181 studies involving over 130,000 research participants from 14 different countries, we confirmed that political conservatism was positively associated with intolerance of ambiguity, need for cognitive closure, personal needs for order and structure, cognitive rigidity, and dogmatism. In addition, conservatism was negatively associated (or liberalism was positively associated) with uncertainty tolerance, integrative complexity, and need for cognition. All average effect sizes attained statistical significance. In terms of magnitude, most of the average effect sizes would be considered moderate, but some were quite large (e.g., cognitive rigidity, dogmatism). Importantly, most (but not all) of the results were robust to concerns about publication bias (i.e., the "file drawer" problem).

Kahan (2012a, 2012b) rejected evidence based on self-report measures of cognitive style and/or epistemic motivation and argued that ideological differences should be demonstrated on "objective measures," such as the "cognitive reflection test" (CRT), which measures "the disposition to check intuition with conscious analytical reasoning." We have now identified 29 tests of the hypothesis – including four unpublished studies conducted by Kahan following his initial assessment – that there would be ideological differences in "cognitive reflection" or intuitive vs. analytic thinking. We observed that the unweighted ($r = -.13$) and weighted ($r = -.10$, 95% CI [$-.12$, $-.09$]) average effect sizes were indeed negative and statistically significant. Egger's regression suggested slight evidence of bias, $B_0 = -1.64$, $SE = 0.90$, $t(14) = 1.81$, $p = .09$, but the funnel plot suggested that no additional missing studies would be needed to attain a symmetrical distribution of effects (Figure 4.2, Panel I). In general, liberals and leftists exhibited thinking styles that were more reflective, deliberative, and analytic than conservatives and rightists, although the effect size was a relatively small one, at least in comparison with other epistemic variables.

In terms of "dual process" theories popularized by Kahneman (2011), this evidence suggests that conservatives engage in more heuristic, automatic, stereo-typical (i.e., "System 1") thinking, whereas liberals engage in more systematic, controlled, effortful (i.e., "System 2") thinking. This suggestion is consistent with the finding that liberals scored higher than conservatives on the "need for cognition." It is also consistent with the results of experiments described by Jost and Krochik (2014), which indicated that liberals were more persuaded by strong (vs. weak) arguments, whereas conservatives were not, and conservatives were more persuaded by peripheral source cues, such as similarity, whereas liberals were not.

Pennycook, Cheyne, Barr, Koehler, and Fugelsang (2015) reported that intuitive (vs. analytic) thinking styles, faith in intuition, low need for cognition, and low cognitive ability were all associated with acceptance of statements that were extremely vague or meaningless and yet seemingly profound. Following Frankfurt (2005), they dubbed this variable "bullshit receptivity," and measured it in terms of suggestibility to items such as these: "We are in the midst of a self-aware blossoming of being that will align us with the nexus itself'; "Your movement transforms universal observations"; and "Consciousness is the growth of coherence, and of us." In a re-analysis of data from one of the original studies, Sterling, Jost, and Pennycook (2016) found that individuals who endorsed neoliberal, free market ideology (see also Jost, Blount, Pfeffer, & Hunyady, 2003a) – demonstrated a stronger reliance on intuitive (or heuristic-based) cognitive processing, scored lower on the need for cognition, expressed more faith in intuition, and scored lower on measures of verbal and fluid intelligence. Individuals who endorsed free market ideology were also significantly more receptive to bullshit, and the relationship between free market ideology and bullshit receptivity appeared to be mediated by cognitive style and cognitive ability. That is, economic conservatives' greater susceptibility to bullshit was at least partially explained by their reliance on heuristic processing and lower verbal intelligence. Another study carried out by Pfattheicher and Schindler (2016) produced highly similar results: those who identified themselves as conservative and expressed favorable evaluations of Donald Trump, Ted Cruz, and Marco Rubio (the three Republican frontrunners in the 2016 presidential primary race) were more receptive to pseudo-profound bullshit than those who did not. The study revealed no significant relationship between evaluations of Hillary Clinton, Bernie Sanders, and Martin O'Malley (the Democratic candidates) and bullshit receptivity.

Because of its epistemic consequences, which may well include bullshit receptivity and the "delusive pinning down of a delusion," we would be remiss if we failed to discuss ideological differences in the variable of self-deception (see Kruglanski & Meinholdt, 1990). There are now at least three studies based on very large samples (totaling 95,000 participants) documenting a significant linear relationship between political conservatism and self-deception (Jost & Krochik, 2014; Jost, Liviatan, van der Toorn, Ledgerwood, Mandisodza, & Nosek, 2010; Wojcik et al., 2015). This relationship, in turn, may help to explain why conservatives report greater attitudinal stability, certainty, self-confidence, and self-reported happiness – and why liberals report more deliberative thought, greater ambivalence, and lesser happiness (Jost & Krochik, 2014).

There is, in summary, a great deal of evidence linking various forms of epistemic motivation – including uncertainty avoidance, intolerance of ambiguity, perceptual and cognitive rigidity, personal needs for order and structure, need for cognitive closure, dogmatism, bullshit receptivity, and self-deception – to the endorsement of conservative ideology. Most of the studies we have described so far are correlational in nature, and so the direction of causality is ambiguous. However, several experiments have triggered (or activated) epistemic needs to reduce uncertainty or to achieve cognitive closure through inductions of cognitive load, distraction, time pressure, threat, or alcohol intoxication. These manipulations have been shown to increase the individual's affinity for hierarchy and/or conservative, right-wing opinions and labels (Eidelman, Crandall, Goodman, & Blanchar, 2012; Friesen, Kay, Eibach, & Galinsky, 2014; Hansson, Keating, & Terry, 1974; Lammers & Proulx, 2013; Rock & Janoff-Bulman, 2010; Rutjens & Loseman, 2010; Skitka, Mullen, Griffin, Hutchinson, & Chamberlin, 2002; Thórisdóttir & Jost, 2011; Van Berkel, Crandall, Eidelman, & Blanchar, 2015). Experiments of this kind are especially valuable because they establish a causal link between epistemic motivation and specific political attitudes and orientations.

The Politics of Existential Motivation: State of the Evidence

Because of renewed empirical interest in political ideology as motivated social cognition, we are now also in a position to review more than 200 tests of the hypothesis that heightened existential motives are associated with politically conservative (as opposed to liberal) outcomes and orientations. Jost, Stern, Rule, and Sterling (in press) reviewed evidence from approximately 100 samples and 350,000 participants from at least 15 different countries. Figure 4.3 ranks the distributions of average effect sizes across existential variables, along with 95% confidence

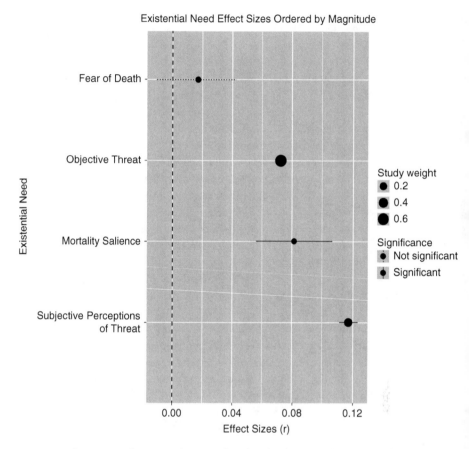

FIGURE 4.3 Summary of meta-analytic results: the distribution of average effect sizes across variables of existential motivation

intervals. Although, contrary to expectations, the association between fear of death and conservatism was not reliable, results revealed that perceptions of dangerous and competitive worlds were not only associated with right-wing authoritarianism and social dominance orientation but also with ideological self-placement, implicit conservatism, and economic system justification. Overall, the unweighted (r = .29) and weighted (r = .12, 95% CI [.11, .12]) average effect sizes between subjective perceptions of threat and conservative ideology were positive and statistically significant, although they were small to moderate in terms of magnitude.

The evidence also demonstrates that exposure to objectively threatening circumstances – such as terrorist attacks, governmental warnings, and seismic shifts in racial demography – is associated with "conservative shift" (Bonanno & Jost, 2006). All of these studies were carried out after the publication of

Jost et al.'s (2003b, 2003c) meta-analysis. There was no evidence that exposure to objectively threatening events precipitated a liberal (or left-wing) shift in any of the countries investigated, but there was clear evidence of conservative (or right-wing) shifts in the U.S., U.K., Spain, Germany, and Israel. Overall, there is a relatively small but statistically significant effect of exposure to objectively threatening circumstances, such as terrorist attacks, on conservative preferences.

It is fairly easy to see how some of these ideological differences in existential motivation play out when it comes to public opinion and the dynamics of political campaigns. A nationally representative survey conducted by Ipsos and Reuters in 2015 revealed that Republicans were far more likely than Democrats to perceive a wide variety of nations, leaders, organizations, movements, and phenomena as "highly threatening to the United States" (see Rampton, 2015). For instance, Republicans were more likely to regard Iran, China, Russia, Yemen, Syria, and Cuba and their leaders as highly threatening. They were also more likely to regard Al Qaeda, ISIS, terrorism, Islam, atheism, gay rights, illegal immigration, drug trafficking, and cyber-attacks as highly threatening, in comparison with Democrats.

Thórisdóttir and Jost (2011) homed in on a major theme emphasized by Kruglanski (2015) in his opinion editorial about Donald Trump, namely that existential motivation increases epistemic motivation and that both affect political preferences. Specifically, they investigated the hypothesis that closed-mindedness would mediate the effect of threat on political conservatism. Coincidentally, perhaps, the article began with a parable from Kafka about a mouse who could not change directions and therefore rushed headlong into the mouth of a ravenous cat:

> "Alas," said the mouse, "the whole world is growing narrower every day. At the beginning it was so big that I was afraid, I kept running and running, and I was glad when I saw walls far away to the right and left, but these long walls have narrowed so quickly that I am in the last chamber already, and there in the corner stands the trap that I must run into."
>
> "You only need to change your direction," said the cat, and ate it up.

Thórisdóttir and Jost (2011) manipulated a subjective sense of high (vs. low) threat by asking people to indicate their level of agreement with questions about terrorism – such as "I worry that terrorists might strike anytime anywhere in the United States" – on a scale that had endpoint labels ranging either from "somewhat" to "a great extent" (in the high threat condition) or from "not at all" to "somewhat" (in the low threat condition). Results revealed that completing the terrorism questionnaire with high (vs. low) threat labels caused participants to (a) score higher on the "motivated closed-

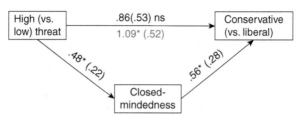

Indirect effect of threat on ideological
self-placement = .267, p < .05

FIGURE 4.4 The effect of threat exposure on political conservatism as mediated by
motivated closed-mindedness (a subscale of the need for cognitive closure
scale)
Source: Thórisdóttir and Jóst (2011)

mindedness" facet of the need for closure, and (b) identify themselves as more
conservative (or less liberal) on the ideological self-placement item. The effect
of threat on ideological self-placement was mediated by motivated closed-
mindedness, providing evidence that short-term (as well as long-term) epistemic and existential motives can affect ideological outcomes, even if those
outcomes are only temporary (see Figure 4.4).

Getting Closure

Since 2003, the theory of political conservatism as motivated social cognition has
received a great deal of corroborating evidence, and in this chapter we have
sought to provide an economical summary of this evidence. We are now in a
position to review many, many more studies than Jost et al. (2003b, 2003c) did,
and the substantive conclusions are essentially the same: the endorsement of
politically conservative or rightist (as opposed to liberal or leftist) ideology is
positively associated with numerous forms of epistemic motivation – including
uncertainty avoidance, intolerance of ambiguity, perceptual and cognitive rigidity,
personal needs for order and structure, need for cognitive closure, and dogmatism. It is also associated with low need for cognition, high self-deception, intuitive thinking, and bullshit receptivity. The endorsement of conservative ideology
is also positively associated with various forms of existential motivation – including subjective perceptions of danger and threat, and objective exposure to threatening circumstances such as terrorist attacks. These programs of research evolved,
in large part, because of Arie's leadership in the scientific movement to bring
motivation back into the study of social (and political) psychology. Consequently,
we are closer than ever to "getting closure" on the phenomenon of political
conservatism from a psychological point of view.

At the same time, there have been reasonable – as well as unreasonable – critiques
of our theoretical framework. Let us consider a few of them, at least briefly, again for

the sake of closure. First, it has been suggested that, given similar levels of intensity or extremity, leftists and rightists should be equally motivated by needs to reduce uncertainty and threat (e.g., Greenberg & Jonas, 2003). To address this possibility Jost et al. (2003c) highlighted 13 studies in which the data were presented in such a way that one could distinguish between linear effects of conservatism and quadratic effects of ideological extremity. No support was found for the "extremity" or "ideologue" hypothesis that there would be a symmetrical increase in motivated closed-mindedness as one moves farther away from the center in *either* direction. On the other hand, there was clear support for the hypothesis that closed-mindedness would increase in a linear fashion as one moves from left to right and, in some studies, both linear and quadratic effects present in combination. Follow-up studies by Jost, Napier, Thórisdóttir, Gosling, Palfai, and Ostafin (2007) likewise provided support for the notion that epistemic and existential motives were positively associated with conservatism in particular rather than ideological extremity in general (see also Jost & Krochik, 2014).

Second, it was suggested by some that leftists would be more rigid and authoritarian than rightists in formerly Communist societies (Greenberg & Jonas, 2003). There was some evidence that this was the case immediately following the changes that took place in Central and Eastern Europe in the early 1990s, when leftists were committed to defending the status quo (McFarland, Ageyev, & Djintcharadze 1996). However, the theory of political conservatism as motivated social cognition would suggest that needs to reduce uncertainty and threat would predict rightist rather than leftist orientation once the transition to a democratic, capitalist system was established. Unfortunately, the world has witnessed the rise of right-wing authoritarianism in Austria, Hungary, Poland, Germany, Bulgaria, Turkey, and other countries, and research now indicates that rightists in Central and Eastern Europe do indeed exhibit stronger needs for order and closure, intolerance of ambiguity, and closed-mindedness (e.g., Golec De Zavala et al., 2010; Kelemen et al., 2014).

A third concern, which is not actually a scientific concern at all, is that some of the descriptions of conservatives "sound" more pejorative than those of liberals (e.g., Haidt, 2012; Shermer, 2011). This may be the case, but it is not necessarily so. Not everyone believes that it is bad to desire order or structure, or even that it is a good thing to be open-minded. Some claim that "an open mind is an empty mind" and that fear of crime and terrorism is more than reasonable. In any case, it seems to us that the job of the social scientist is not to flatter people – nor to be equally flattering to the left and the right. Perhaps it is worth pointing out that research psychologists developed scales to measure cognitive and perceptual rigidity, intolerance of ambiguity, cognitive complexity, and personal needs for order, structure, and closure long before anyone knew that there would be differences between liberals and conservatives in these characteristics. It would be a strange kind of political correctness to insist that researchers change the names of variables to make them sound better simply because they have observed ideological differences in them.

Fourth, some have suggested that ideological asymmetries emerge primarily or exclusively on subjective, self-report measures, implying that the differences are superficial or purely self-presentational (Jussim et al., 2016; Kahan, 2012b; Van Hiel et al., 2010). But this is clearly not the case. In this chapter we have taken note of ideological differences on objective, behavioral measures of integrative complexity, perceptual and cognitive rigidity, cognitive reflection, and bullshit receptivity. Other studies have demonstrated that liberals and conservatives differ in terms of objective measures of intelligence or cognitive ability (Deary, Batty, & Gale, 2008; Heaven, Ciarrochi, & Leeson, 2011; Hodson & Busseri, 2012) as well as exploratory and approach-orientated behavior (Janoff-Bulman, 2009; Rock & Janoff-Bulman, 2010; Shook & Fazio, 2009), nonverbal gestures and room décor (Carney et al., 2008), perceptual attention to potentially threatening stimuli (Carraro, Castelli, & Macchiella, 2011; Vigil, 2010), language usage (Cichocka et al., 2016), and many other characteristics. Finally, there are ideological differences in uncontrollable physiological activity such as galvanic skin responses (Oxley et al., 2008), neurocognitive functioning (Amodio et al., 2007), and grey matter volume in the amygdala and anterior cingulate cortex (Kanai et al., 2011). These differences are consistent with the theory of political conservatism as motivated social cognition (see also, Jost & Amodio, 2012; Jost et al., 2014).

If, after considering all of this evidence, skeptics continue to doubt the theoretical or practical significance of ideological differences in epistemic and existential motivation, they would do well to consult a book entitled *Engineers of Jihad*, in which two of the most societally relevant research programs in Arie Kruglanski's illustrious career are brought together, namely the analysis of political ideology as motivated social cognition and the study of terrorism. In this work, Gambetta and Hertog (2016) detail the curious connection between having an educational or professional background in engineering and participating in right-wing (but not left-wing) terrorism. The common denominator they stress is the need for cognitive closure (NFC):

> The general personality traits and aspects of right-wing ideology on which engineers score highly fit the profile of Islamist ideology … remarkably well: a desire to keep society clean or purify it, a preference for social order, and rigid in-group/out-group distinctions. Our data are not fine-grained enough to weigh the relative importance of disgust, need for closure, in-group preferences, or simplism. Although we believe that all play a role, on balance the evidence for NFC is strongest.
>
> *(Gambetta & Hertog, 2016, p. 156)*

But is there a way out of Kafka's nightmare – an escape from error, impatience, and delusion, not only the traps we set for ourselves but also those set by others who wish us harm? For the most part, psychology has precious little to offer. Again and again we encounter scathing indictments of the human capacity for reasoning.

One author declares that human beings simply "sort through the facts and select those that confirm what we already believe and ignore or rationalize away those that contradict our beliefs" (Shermer, 2011, p. 36). Another claims that:

> Conscious reasoning functions like a press secretary who automatically justifies any position taken by the president. With the help of our press secretary, we are able to lie and cheat often, and then cover it up so effectively that we even fool ourselves. Reasoning can take us to almost any conclusion we want to reach.
>
> *(Haidt, 2012, p. 91)*

The work of Arie Kruglanski, like the man behind it, projects a more complex, nuanced, and optimistic image, without ever drifting into Pollyannaism. He writes, for instance:

> We cross a busy city street without being hit even once by the many passing cars. What made our judgment accurate in this case? Well, we think we know what had helped. We first looked around to see what the traffic was like. We took into account the distance we had to travel and the time this might take … . More generally, we took care to inspect as much of the relevant information as possible and apply to it as much of our relevant background knowledge as we could.
>
> *(Kruglanski, 1992, pp. 465–466)*

> Most successful judgments … [do not] represent mere lucky guesses but rather *painstakingly derived inferences from considerable information*.
>
> *(Kruglanski, 1992, p. 466, emphasis added)*

> If confronted with irrefutable evidence that a conclusion was based upon wishful thinking, the individual would presumably lose faith in the proposition. After all, congruence with wishes is hardly considered a *legitimate* basis for believing a particular conclusion.
>
> *(Kruglanski & Meinholdt, 1990, p. 272)*

We are fortunate that some people – in science and in society – continue to think this way. The work we have reviewed in this chapter suggests that there are meaningful individual (and, yes, ideological) differences in the extent to which people succumb to "a premature renunciation of method," as Kafka put it. The "fear of invalidity" can be useful, and so can the motivation to prolong closure (Kruglanski, 1990; see also Calogero & Jost, 2011).

We conclude by reminding ourselves – optimistically, in the spirit of Kruglanski's life and work – that self-deception may be common, but it is partial rather than absolute, and it is a psychological variable, not a constant. When taken in its entirety, the scientific evidence does not warrant "unmitigated nihilism about the epistemic value of the mental activity of an entire species – even ours" (Jost, 2011, p. 1222). As in so many other domains of life, people are doing the best they can, and some people seem to be doing better than others. Arie once wrote that: "our good judgment guide amounts to little more than an injunction to practice effectively the 'art of the possible,' *to do the best one can under the circumstances*" (Kruglanksi, 1992, p. 466, emphasis in original). This may be all that human beings are capable of achieving, but it may be just enough.

Acknowledgement

We thank David Dunning, Ayelet Fishbach, György Hunyady, Catalina Kopetz, Melanie Langer, H. Hannah Nam, Mitchell Rabinowitz, and Benjamin Saunders for extremely helpful comments on an earlier draft. We also wish to express our gratitude to Sara Ilyas, Ramya Jayanthi, Melissa Lobel, Alana Mayer, and Angela Wang for their work on identifying studies for the meta-analyses described in this chapter. Some of the ideas contained herein were presented at the *Festschrift* conference in honor of Arie W. Kruglanski at the University of Maryland, College Park and, very shortly thereafter, the 39th annual meeting of the International Society of Political Psychology (ISPP) in Warsaw, Poland.

Notes

1 Since 2003, there has also been an explosion of research on ideological differences in "Big Five" personality traits (e.g., see Carney, Jost, Gosling, & Potter, 2008; Gerber, Huber, Doherty, Dowling, & Ha, 2010; Hirsh, DeYoung, Xu, & Peterson, 2010; Mondak, 2010). Although Jost et al. (2003b) discussed findings pertaining to Openness to Experience and Neuroticism and "need for order" is one facet of Conscientiousness, we exclude Big Five studies from the present meta-analysis in order to focus more specifically on measures of epistemic and existential motivation (but see Sibley, Osborne, & Duckitt, 2012).

2 Several samples included multiple effect size estimates. In these situations, we averaged the estimates to create a single independent effect size estimate for each sample (and for each variable) prior to statistical aggregation

3 For the present (but not the 2003) meta-analysis, we excluded the study by Fay and Frese (2000) because, as Greenberg and Jonas (2003, p. 380) pointed out, the measure of political orientation they administered was ambiguous in terms of left-right ideology.

4 Differences between the results of Malka et al.'s (2014) research and those of other studies may be attributable to the fact that these researchers estimated the "need for certainty and security" using responses to a subset of five items that, according to the authors, "contrasted motivations for security, tradition, and conformity with motivations for self-direction and stimulation." Inter-item correlations and scale reliability for these five items were extremely low, and the items appear to have been taken from five different subscales of Schwartz's (1992) Value Priorities Scale, which typically includes a total of 56–57 items in order to measure ten value priorities that differ substantially across individuals and cultures.

References

References marked with an asterisk indicate studies included in the meta-analysis.

Adorno, T. W., Frenkel-Brunswik, E., Levinson, D. J., & Sanford, R. N. (1950). *The authoritarian personality*. New York: Harper.

★Altemeyer, R. A. (1998). The other "authoritarian personality." *Advances in Experimental Social Psychology*, 30, 47–91.

Amodio, D. M., Jost, J. T., Master, S. L., & Yee, C. M. (2007). Neurocognitive correlates of liberalism and conservatism. *Nature Neuroscience*, 10, 1246–1247.

★Atieh, J. M., Brief, A. P., & Vollrath, D. A. (1987). The Protestant work ethic conservatism paradox: Beliefs and values in work and life. *Personality and Individual Differences*, 8, 577–580.

★Barron, F. (1953). Complexity-simplicity as a personality dimension. *Journal of Abnormal and Social Psychology*, 48, 163–172.

★Benjamin Jr, A. J. (2014). Chasing the elusive left-wing authoritarian: An examination of Altemeyer's right-wing authoritarianism and left-wing authoritarianism scales. *National Social Science Journal*, 43, 7–13.

★Bizer, G. Y., Krosnick, J. A., Holbrook, A. L., Wheeler, S. C., Rucker, D. D., & Petty, R. E. (2004). The impact of personality on cognitive, behavioral, and affective political processes: The effects of need to evaluate. *Journal of Personality*, 72, 995–1028.

★Block, J., & Block, J. H. (2006). Nursery school personality and political orientation two decades later. *Journal of Research in Personality*, 40, 734–749.

Bonanno, G. A., & Jost, J. T. (2006). Conservative shift among high-exposure survivors of the September 11th terrorist attacks. *Basic and Applied Social Psychology*, 28, 311–323.

★Brandt, M. J., Chambers, J. R., Crawford, J. T., Wetherell, G., & Reyna, C. (2015b). Bounded openness: The effect of openness to experience on intolerance is moderated by target group conventionality. *Journal of Personality and Social Psychology*, 109, 549–568.

★Brandt, M. J., & Crawford, J. (unpublished data).

★Brandt, M. J., & Crawford, J. (2013). Replication-extension of 'Not for all the tea in China!' Political ideology and the avoidance of dissonance-arousing situations (Nam, H., Jost, J. & Van Bavel, J. (2013), *Plos One*, 18(4), e59837).

★Brandt, M. J., Evans, A. M., & Crawford, J. T. (2015a). The unthinking or confident extremist? Political extremists are more likely than moderates to reject experimenter-generated anchors. *Psychological Science*, 26, 189–202.

★Brandt, M. J., & Reyna, C. (2010). The role of prejudice and the need for closure in religious fundamentalism. *Personality and Social Psychology Bulletin*, 36, 715–725.

Brown, R. (1965). *Social psychology*. New York: Free Press.

★Brundidge, J., Reid, S. A., Choi, S., & Muddiman, A. (2014). The "deliberative digital divide": Opinion leadership and integrative complexity in the US political blogosphere. *Political Psychology*, 35, 741–755.

★Burke, S. (unpublished data).

★Burke, S., Dovidio, J. F., Przedworski, J. M., Hardeman, R. R., Perry, S. P., Phelan, S. M., Nelson, D. B., Burgess, D. J., Yeazel, M. W., & van Ryn, M. (2015). Do contact and empathy mitigate bias against gay and lesbian people among heterosexual first-year medical students? A report from the Medical Student CHANGE Study. *Academic Medicine*, 90, 645–651.

★Burke, S., & LaFrance, M. (unpublished data).

★Burke, S., Perry, S. P., & Dovidio, J. F. (unpublished data).

Cacioppo, J.T., & Petty, R.E. (1982). The need for cognition. *Journal of Personality and Social Psychology*, 42, 116–131.

Calogero, R. M., & Jost, J. T. (2011). Self-subjugation among women: Exposure to sexist ideology, self-objectification, and the protective function of the need to avoid closure. *Journal of Personality and Social Psychology*, 100, 211–228.

★Caparos, S., Fortier-St-Pierre, S., Gosselin, J., Blanchette, I., & Brisson, B. (2015). The tree to the left, the forest to the right: Political attitude and perceptual bias. *Cognition*, 134, 155–164.

Carney, D. R., Jost, J. T., Gosling, S. D., & Potter, J. (2008). The secret lives of liberals and conservatives: Personality profiles, interaction styles, and the things they leave behind. *Political Psychology*, *29*, 807–840.

Carraro, L., Castelli, L., & Macchiella, C. (2011). The automatic conservative: Ideology-based attentional asymmetries in the processing of valenced information. *PLoS ONE*, 6, e26456.

★Choma, B. L., Hafer, C. L., Dywan, J., Segalowitz, S. J., & Busseri, M. A. (2012). Political liberalism and political conservatism: Functionally independent? *Personality and Individual Differences*, 53, 431–436.

★Chirumbolo, A. (2002). The relationship between need for cognitive closure and political orientation: The mediating role of authoritarianism. *Personality and Individual Differences*, 32, 603–610.

★Chirumbolo, A., Areni, A., & Sensales, G. (2004). Need for cognitive closure and politics: Voting, political attitudes and attributional style. *International Journal of Psychology*, 39, 245–253.

★Cichocka, A., Bilewicz, M., Jost, J. T., Marroush, N., & Witkowska, M. (2016). On the grammar of politics – or why conservatives prefer nouns. *Political Psychology*. doi:10.1111/pops.12327.

Cohen, J. (1988). *Statistical power analysis for the behavioral sciences* (2nd Ed.). Hillsdale, NJ: Erlbaum.

Cohen, P. (2010). 'Epistemic closure'? Those are fighting words. Retrieved from http://www.nytimes.com/2010/04/28/books/28conserv.html?_r=0

★Conway, L. G., Gornick, L. J., Houck, S. C., Anderson, C., Stockert, J., Sessoms, D., & McCue, K. (2016). Are conservatives really more simple-minded than liberals? The domain specificity of complex thinking. *Political Psychology*. *37*, 777–798.

★Cornelis, I., & Van Hiel, A. (2006). The impact of cognitive styles on authoritarianism based conservatism and racism. *Basic and Applied Social Psychology*, *28*, 37–50.

★Crowson, H. M. (2009). Are all conservatives alike? A study of the psychological correlates of cultural and economic conservatism. *Journal of Psychology*, *143*, 449–463.

★Crowson, H. M., Thoma, S. J., & Hestevold, N. (2005). Is political conservatism synonymous with authoritarianism? *Journal of Social Psychology*, *145*, 571–592.

★Davids, A. (1955). Some personality and intellectual correlates of intolerance of ambiguity. *Journal of Abnormal and Social Psychology*, *51*, 415–420.

★Davids, A., & Eriksen, C. W. (1957). Some social and cultural factors determining relations between authoritarianism and measures of neuroticism. *Journal of Consulting Psychology*, *21*, 155–159.

Dean, J. W. (2006). *Conservatives without conscience*. New York: Penguin.

Deary, I. J., Batty, G. D., & Gale, C. R. (2008). Bright children become enlightened adults. *Psychological Science*, *19*, 1–6.

★Deppe, K. D., Gonzalez, F. J., Neiman, J. L., Jacobs, C., Pahlke, J., Smith, K. B., & Hibbing, J. R. (2015). Reflective liberals and intuitive conservatives: A look at the Cognitive Reflection Test and ideology. *Judgment and Decision Making*, 10, 314–331.

Dollinger, S. J. (2007). Creativity and conservatism. *Personality and Individual Differences*, *43*, 1025–1035.

★Duriez, B., & Soenens, B. (2006). Personality, identity styles and authoritarianism: An integrative study among late adolescents. *European Journal of Personality*, 20, 397–417.

Duval, S., & Tweedie, R. (2000). Trim and fill: A simple funnel-plot-based method of testing and adjusting for publication bias in meta-analysis. *Biometrics*, 56, 455–463.

Egger, M., Smith, G. D., Schneider, M., & Minder, C. (1997). Bias in meta-analysis detected by a simple, graphical test. *BMJ Clinical Research*, 315, 629–634.

Eidelman, S., Crandall, C. S., Goodman, J. A., & Blanchar, J. C. (2012). Low-effort thought promotes political conservatism. *Personality and Social Psychology Bulletin*, 38, 808–820.

★Everett, J. A. (2013). The 12 item social and economic conservatism scale (SECS). *PLoS ONE*, 8(12), e82131. doi:10.1371/journal.pone.0082131.

Eysenck, H. J. (1999). *The psychology of politics*. London: Routledge & Kegan Paul. (Original work published 1954.)

Fay, D., & Frese, M. (2000). Conservatives' approach to work: Less prepared for future work demands? *Journal of Applied Social Psychology*, 30, 171–195.

★Federico, C. M., Deason, G., & Fisher, E. L. (2012). Ideological asymmetry in the relationship between epistemic motivation and political attitudes. *Journal of Personality and Social Psychology*, 103, 381–398.

★Fibert, Z., & Ressler, W. H. (1998). Intolerance of ambiguity and political orientation among Israeli university students. *Journal of Social Psychology*, 138, 33–40.

Frankfurt, H. G. (2005) *On bullshit*. New York: Cambridge University Press.

★French, E. G. (1955). Interrelation among some measures of rigidity under stress and non-stress conditions. *Journal of Abnormal and Social Psychology*, 51, 114–118.

Friedersdorf, C. (2012). A textbook example of the right's epistemic closure. Retrieved from http://www.theatlantic.com/politics/archive/2012/05/a-textbook-example-of-the-rights-epistemic-closure/257192/

Friesen, J. P., Kay, A. C., Eibach, R. P., & Galinsky, A. D. (2014). Seeking structure in social organization: Compensatory control and the psychological advantages of hierarchy. *Journal of Personality and Social Psychology*, 106, 590–609.

Gambetta, D., & Hertog, S. (2016). *Engineers of Jihad: The curious connection between violent extremism and education*. Princeton, NJ: Princeton University Press.

Gerber, A. S., Huber, G. A., Doherty, D., Dowling, C. M., & Ha, S. E. (2010). Personality and political attitudes: Relationships across issue domains and political contexts. *American Political Science Review*, 104, 111–133.

★Gillies, J., & Campbell, S. (1985). Conservatism and poetry preferences. *British Journal of Social Psychology*, 24, 223–227.

★Glasgow, M. R., & Cartier, A. M. (1985). Conservatism, sensation-seeking, and music preferences. *Personality and Individual Differences*, 6, 393–395.

★Golec de Zavala, A., & Van Bergh, A. (2007). Need for cognitive closure and conservative political beliefs: Differential mediation by personal worldviews. *Political Psychology*, 28, 587–608.

★Golec de Zavala, A., Cislak, A., & Wesolowska, E. (2010). Political conservatism, need for cognitive closure, and intergroup hostility. *Political Psychology*, 31, 521–541.

Greenberg, J., & Jonas, E. (2003). Psychological and political orientation–the left, the right, and the rigid: Comment on Jost et al. (2003). *Psychological Bulletin*, 129, 376–382.

Gries, P. (2014). *The politics of American foreign policy: How ideology divides liberals and conservatives over foreign affairs.* Stanford, CA: Stanford University Press.

*Gruenfeld, D. H. (1995). Status, ideology, and integrative ideology on the U.S. Supreme Court: Rethinking the politics of political decision making. *Journal of Personality and Social Psychology, 68,* 5–20.

Haidt, J. (2012). *The righteous mind: Why good people are divided by politics and religion.* New York: Random House.

Hansson, R. O., Keating, J. P., & Terry, C. (1974). The effects of mandatory time limits in the voting booth on liberal-conservative voting patterns. *Journal of Applied Social Psychology, 4,* 336–342.

Heaven, P. C. L., Ciarrochi, J., & Leeson, P. (2011). Cognitive ability, right-wing authoritarianism, and social dominance orientation: A five-year longitudinal study amongst adolescents. *Intelligence, 39,* 15–21.

*Hellkamp, D. T., & Marr, J. N. (1965). Dogmatism and field-dependency. *Perceptual and Motor Skills, 20,* 1046–1048.

*Hennes, E. P., Nam, H. H., Stern, C., & Jost, J. T. (2012). Not all ideologies are created equal: Epistemic, existential, and relational needs predict system-justifying attitudes. *Social Cognition, 30,* 669–688.

*Hession, E., & McCarthy, E. (1975). Human performance in assessing subjective probability distributions. *The Irish Journal of Psychology, 3,* 31–46.

Hibbing, J. R., Smith, K. B., & Alford, J. R. (2014). Differences in negativity bias underlie variations in political ideology. *Behavioral and Brain Sciences, 37,* 297–307.

Higgins, E. T., Roney, C. J., Crowe, E., & Hymes, C. (1994). Ideal versus ought predilections for approach and avoidance distinct self-regulatory systems. *Journal of Personality and Social Psychology, 66,* 276–286.

*Hinze, T., Doster, J., & Joe, V. C. (1997). The relationship of conservatism and cognitive-complexity. *Personality and Individual Differences, 22,* 297–298.

Hirsh, J. B., DeYoung, C. G., Xu, X., & Peterson, J. B. (2010). Compassionate liberals and polite conservatives: Associations of agreeableness with political ideology and moral values. *Personality and Social Psychology Bulletin, 36,* 655–664.

Hodson, G., & Busseri, M. A. (2012). Bright minds and dark attitudes: Lower cognitive ability predicts greater prejudice through right-wing ideology and low intergroup contact. *Psychological Science, 23,* 187–195.

Janoff-Bulman, R. (2009). To provide or protect: Motivational bases of political liberalism and conservatism. *Psychological Inquiry, 20,* 120–128.

*Johnston, C. D., Newman, B. J., & Velez, Y. (2015). Ethnic change, personality, and polarization over immigration in the American public. *Public Opinion Quarterly, 79,* 662–686.

*Johnston, C. D., & Wronski, J. (2015). Personality dispositions and political preferences across hard and easy issues. *Political Psychology, 36,* 35–53.

Jost, J. T. (2011). That's incredible! *Science, 333,* 1222–1223.

Jost, J. T., & Amodio, D. (2012). Political ideology as motivated social cognition: Behavioral and neuroscientific evidence. *Motivation and Emotion, 36,* 55–64.

Jost, J. T., & Banaji (1994). The role of stereotyping in system-justification and the production of false consciousness. *British Journal of Social Psychology, 33,* 1–27.

Jost, J. T., Blount, S., Pfeffer, J., & Hunyady, G. (2003a). Fair market ideology: Its cognitive-motivational underpinnings. *Research in Organizational Behavior, 25,* 53–91.

Jost, J. T., Glaser, J., Kruglanski, A. W., & Sulloway, F. J. (2003b). Political conservatism as motivated social cognition. *Psychological Bulletin*, 129, 339–375.

Jost, J.T., Glaser, J., Kruglanski, A.W., & Sulloway, F. (2003c). Exceptions that prove the rule – Using a theory of motivated social cognition to account for ideological incongruities and political anomalies: Reply to Greenberg & Jonas (2003). *Psychological Bulletin*, 129, 383–393.

Jost, J. T., & Krochik, M. (2014). Ideological differences in epistemic motivation: Implications for attitude structure, depth of information processing, susceptibility to persuasion, and stereotyping. *Advances in Motivation Science*, 1, 181–231.

*Jost, J. T., Kruglanski, A. W., & Simon, L. (1999). Effects of epistemic motivation on conservatism, intolerance, and other system justifying attitudes. In L. Thompson, D. M. Messick, & J. M. Levine (Eds.), *Shared cognition in organizations: The management of knowledge* (pp. 91–116). Mahwah, NJ: Erlbaum.

Jost, J. T., Liviatan, I., van der Toorn, J., Ledgerwood, A., Mandisodza, A., & Nosek, B. A. (2010). System justification: How do we know it's motivated. In *The psychology of justice and legitimacy: The Ontario symposium* (Vol. 11, pp. 173–203). Hillsdale, NJ: Erlbaum.

Jost, J. T., Nam, H. H., Amodio, D. M., & Van Bavel, J. J. (2014). Political neuroscience: The beginning of a beautiful friendship. *Advances in Political Psychology* (Vol. 35, Supplement 1, pp. 3–42). doi:10.1111/pops.12162.

*Jost, J. T., Napier, J. L., Thórisdóttir, H., Gosling, S. D., Palfai, T. P., & Ostafin, B. (2007). Are needs to manage uncertainty and threat associated with political conservatism or ideological extremity? *Personality and Social Psychology Bulletin*, 33, 989–1007.

Jost, J. T., Nosek, B. A., & Gosling, S. D. (2008). Ideology: Its resurgence in social, personality, and political psychology. *Perspectives on Psychological Science*, 3, 126–136.

Jost, J. T., Stern, C., Rule, N. O., & Sterling, J. (in press). The politics of fear: Is there an ideological asymmetry in existential motivation? *Social Cognition*.

*Jugert, P., Cohrs, J. C., & Duckitt, J. (2009). Inter- and intrapersonal processes underlying authoritarianism: The role of social conformity and personal need for structure. *European Journal of Personality*, 23, 607–621.

Jussim, L., Crawford, J. T., Anglin, S. M., Stevens, S. T., & Duarte, J. L. (2016). Interpretations and methods: Towards a more effectively self-correcting social psychology. *Journal of Experimental Social Psychology*, 66, 116–133.

Kafka, F. (1946a). Reflections on sin, pain, hope, and the true way. In W. Muir & E. Muir (Trans.), *The great wall of China: Stories and reflections*. New York: Schocken.

Kafka, F. (1946b). *The great wall of China: Stories and reflections* (Vol. 2). New York: Schocken Books.

*Kahan, D. M. (2012a). Ideology, motivated reasoning, and cognitive reflection: an experimental study. *Judgment and Decision Making*, 8, 407–424.

Kahan, D. M. (2012b). What do I think of Mooney's "Republican Brain"? *The Cultural Cognition Project*. Retrieved from: http://www.culturalcognition.net/blog/2012/7/27/what-do-i-think-of-mooneys- republican-brain.html

Kahneman, D. (2011). *Thinking, fast and slow*. New York: Farrar, Strauss & Giroux.

*Kahoe, R. D. (1974). Personality and achievement correlates of intrinsic and extrinsic religious orientations. *Journal of Personality and Social Psychology*, 29, 812–818.

Kanai, R., Feilden, T., Firth, C., & Rees, G. (2011). Political orientations are correlated with brain structure in young adults. *Current Biology*, 21, 677–680.

*Kelemen, L., Szabó, Z. P., Mészáros, N. Z., László, J., & Forgas, J. P. (2014). Social cognition and democracy: The relationship between system justification, just world beliefs, authoritarianism, need for closure, and need for cognition in Hungary. *Journal of Social and Political Psychology*, 2, 197–219.

*Kemmelmeier, M. (1997). Need for closure and political orientation among German university students. *The Journal of Social Psychology*, 137, 787–789.

*Kemmelmeier, M. (2007). Political conservatism, rigidity, and dogmatism in American foreign policy officials: The 1966 Mennis data. *The Journal of Psychology*, 141, 77–90.

*Kemmelmeier, M. (2010). Authoritarianism and its relationship with intuitive-experiential cognitive style and heuristic processing. *Personality and Individual Differences*, 48, 44–48.

*Kerlinger, F., & Rokeach, M. (1966). The factorial nature of the F and D scales. *Journal of Personality and Social Psychology*, 4, 391–399.

*Kidd, A. H., & Kidd, R. M. (1972). Relation of F-test scores to rigidity. *Perceptual and Motor Skills*, 34, 239–243.

*Kirton, M. J. (1978). Wilson and Patterson's conservatism scale: A shortened alternative form. *British Journal of Social and Clinical Psychology*, 17, 319–323.

*Kohn, P. M. (1974). Authoritarianism, rebelliousness, and their correlates among British undergraduates. *British Journal of Social and Clinical Psychology*, 13, 245–255.

*Kossowska, M., & Van Hiel, A. (2003). The relationship between need for closure and conservative beliefs in Western and Eastern Europe. *Political Psychology*, 24, 501–518.

*Krosch, A. R., Berntsen, L., Amodio, D. M., Jost, J. T., & Van Bavel, J. J. (2013). On the ideology of hypodescent: Political conservatism predicts categorization of racially ambiguous faces as Black. *Journal of Experimental Social Psychology*, 49, 1196–1203.

Kruglanski, A. W. (1990). Lay epistemic theory in social-cognitive psychology. *Psychological Inquiry*, 1, 181–197.

Kruglanski, A. W. (1992). On methods of good judgment: Political decisions and the art of the possible. *Political Psychology*, 13, 455–475.

Kruglanski, A. W. (2015). Donald Trump and Isis both benefit from a powerful fuel: Our fear. Retrieved from http://www.theguardian.com/commentisfree/2015/dec/23/dona ld-trump-isis-benefit-from-powerful-fuel-fear

Kruglanski, A. W., & Meinholdt, C. (1990). Cognitive and motivational bases of judgmental bias: Toward a synthesis. *Polish Psychological Bulletin*, 21, 291–305.

Kruglanski, A. W., & Webster, D. M. (1996). Motivated closing of the mind: "Seizing" and "freezing." *Psychological Review*, 103, 263–283.

*Ksiazkiewicz, A., Ludeke, S., & Krueger, R. (2016). The role of cognitive style in the link between genes and political ideology. *Political Psychology*. doi:10.1111/pops.12318.

Lakoff, G. (2008). *The political mind: A cognitive scientist's guide to your brain and its politics*. New York: Penguin.

Lammers, J., & Proulx, T. (2013). Writing autobiographical narratives increases political conservatism. *Journal of Experimental Social Psychology*, 49, 684–691.

*Leone, L., & Chirumbolo, A. (2008). Conservatism as motivated avoidance of affect: Need for affect scales predict conservatism measures. *Journal of Research in Personality*, 42, 755–762.

*Lytwyn, T. (2012). The personality of policy preferences: Analyzing the relationship between Myers-Briggs personality types and political views. *Res Publica: Journal of Undergraduate Research*, 17, 99–119.

*Malka, A., Soto, C. J., Inzlicht, M., & Lelkes, Y. (2014). Do needs for security and certainty predict cultural and economic conservatism? A cross-national analysis. *Journal of Personality and Social Psychology*, 106, 1031–1051.

Mannheim, K. (1936). *Ideology and utopia*. New York: Harcourt, Brace.

Mannheim, K. (1986). *Conservatism: A contribution to the sociology of knowledge* (D. Kettler, V. Meja, & N. Stehr, Trans.). New York: Routledge & Kegan Paul. (Original work published 1927.)

★McAllister, P., & Anderson, A. (1991). Conservatism and the comprehension of implausible texts. *European Journal of Social Psychology*, 21, 147–164.

McClosky, H. (1958). Conservatism and personality. *American Political Science Review*, 52, 27–45.

McFarland, S. G., Ageyev, V. S., & Djintcharadze, N. (1996). Russian authoritarianism two years after communism. *Personality and Social Psychology Bulletin*, 22, 210–217.

★Meirick, P. C., & Bessarabova, E. (2015). Epistemic factors in selective exposure and political misperceptions on the right and left. *Analyses of Social Issues and Public Policy*. doi:10.1111/asap.12101

★Mendoza, J. I. (2011). *Intolerance of ambiguity and gender differences between humanists and normativists*. Doctoral dissertation, University of Central Florida Orlando, Florida.

Mondak, J. J. (2010). *Personality and the foundations of political behavior*. New York: Cambridge University Press.

Mooney, C. (2012). *The Republican Brain: The science of why they deny science – and reality*. New York: Wiley.

★Neuringer, C. (1964). The relationship between authoritarianism, rigidity, and anxiety. *Journal of General Psychology*, 71, 169–175.

★Nilsson, A., & Jost, J. T. (2016). *Rediscovering Tomkins' polarity theory: Humanism, normativism, and the bipolar structure of left-right ideology in the U.S. and Sweden*. Manuscript submitted for publication.

★Okimoto, T. G., & Gromet, D. M. (2015). Differences in sensitivity to deviance partly explain ideological divides in social policy support. *Journal of Personality and Social Psychology*, 111, 98–117.

★Onraet, E., Van Hiel, A., Roets, A., & Cornelis, I. (2011). The closed mind: 'Experience' and 'cognition' aspects of openness to experience and need for closure as psychological bases for right-wing attitudes. *European Journal of Personality*, 25, 184–197.

Orwin, R. G. (1983). A fail-safe N for effect size in meta-analysis. *Journal of Educational Statistics*, 8, 157–159.

Oxley, D. R., Smith, K. B., Alford, J. R., Hibbing, M. V., Miller, J. L., Scalora, M., Hatemi, P. K., & Hibbing, J. R. (2008). Political attitudes vary with physiological traits. *Science*, 321, 1667–1670.

Pennycook, G., Cheyne, J. A., Barr, N., Koehler, D. J., & Fugelsang, J. A. (2015). On the reception and detection of pseudo-profound bullshit. *Judgment and Decision Making*, 10, 549–563.

★Pettigrew, T. F. (1958). The measurement and correlates of category width as a cognitive variable. *Journal of Personality*, 26, 532–544.

Pfattheicher, S., & Schindler, S. (2016). Misperceiving bullshit as profound is associated with favorable views of Cruz, Rubio, Trump and conservatism. *PloS ONE*, 11, e0153419.

★Phelan, S. M., Burgess, D. J., Burke, S. E., Przedworski, J., Dovidio, J. F., Hardeman, R., Morris, M., & van Ryn, M. (2015). Beliefs about the causes of obesity in a national sample of 4th year medical students. *Patient Education and Counseling*, 98, 1446–1449.

★Plant, W. T. (1960). Rokeach's dogmatism scale as a measure of general authoritarianism. *Psychological Reports*, 6, 164.

*Price, E., Ottati, V., Wilson, C., & Kim, S. (2015). Open-minded cognition. *Personality and Social Psychology Bulletin*, 4, 1488–1504.

*Pyron, B. (1966). A factor-analytic study of simplicity-complexity of social ordering. *Perceptual and Motor Skills*, 22, 259–272.

Rampton, R. (2015). Republicans see Obama as more imminent threat than Putin: Reuters/Ipsos poll. Retrieved on February 15, 2016 from http://www.reuters.com/a rticle/us-usa-threats-poll-idUSKBN0MQ0AV20150330

Rathbun, B. C. (2014). *Diplomacy's value: Creating security in 1920s Europe and the contemporary Middle East*. Ithaca, NY: Cornell.

*Rock, M. S., & Janoff-Bulman, R. (2010). Where do we draw our lines? Politics, rigidity, and the role of self-regulation. *Social Psychological and Personality Science*, 1, 26–33.

*de Rojas, J. M. R. (2015). La influencia de la ideología política y la intolerancia a la ambigüedad sobre diversas expresiones actitudinales del heterosexismo. *Pensamiento Psicológico*, 13, 7–19.

*Rokeach, M. (1956). Political and religious dogmatism: An alternative to the authoritarian personality. *Psychological Monographs*, 70, 43.

*Rokeach, M. (1960). *The open and closed mind*. New York: Basic Books.

*Rokeach, M., & Fruchter, B. (1956). A factorial study of dogmatism and related concepts. *Journal of Abnormal and Social Psychology*, 53, 356–360.

Rokeach, M., McGovney, W. C., & Denny, M. R. (1955). A distinction between dogmatic and rigid thinking. *Journal of Abnormal and Social Psychology*, 51, 87–93.

*Rudin, S. A., & Stagner, R. (1958). Figure-ground phenomena in the perception of physical and social stimuli. *Journal of Psychology*, 45, 213–225.

*Rule, B. G., & Hewitt, D. (1970). Factor structure of anti-Semitism, self-concept and cognitive structure. *Personality*, 1, 319–332.

Rutjens, B. T., & Loseman, A. (2010). The society-supporting self: System justification and cultural worldview defense as different forms of self-regulation. *Group Processes & Intergroup Relations*, 13, 241–250.

Saad, L. (2013). Americans' top critique of GOP: "Unwilling to compromise." Retrieved from http://www.gallup.com/poll/161573/americans-top-critique-gop-unwilling-compromise.aspx

Sanchez, J. (2010). Epistemic closure, technology, and the end of distance. Retrieved from http://www.juliansanchez.com/2010/04/07/epistemic-closure-technology-and-the-en d-of-distance/

*Sargent, M. J. (2004). Less thought, more punishment: Need for cognition predicts support for punitive responses to crime. *Personality and Social Psychology Bulletin*, 30, 1485–1493.

*Schlenker, B. R., Chambers, J. R., & Le, B. M. (2012). Conservatives are happier than liberals, but why? Political ideology, personality, and life satisfaction. *Journal of Research in Personality*, 46, 127–146.

*Schroder, H. M., & Streufert, S. (1962). *The measurement of four systems of personality structure varying in level of abstractness: Sentence completion method*. Technical Report, Princeton University.

Schwartz, S. H. (1992). Universals in the content and structure of values: Theoretical advances and empirical tests in 20 countries. *Advances in Experimental Social Psychology*, 25, 1–65.

Shermer, M. (2011). *The believing brain: From ghosts and gods to politics and conspiracies – How we construct beliefs and reinforce them as truths*. New York: Holt.

Shook, N. J., & Fazio, R. H. (2009). Political ideology, exploration of novel stimuli, and attitude formation. *Journal of Experimental Social Psychology*, 45, 995–998.

Sibley, C. G., Osborne, D., & Duckitt, J. (2012). Personality and political orientation: Meta-analysis and test of a threat-constraint model. *Journal of Research in Personality*, 46, 664–677.

★Sidanius, J. (1978). Intolerance of ambiguity and socio-politico ideology: A multi-dimensional analysis. *European Journal of Social Psychology*, 8, 215–235.

★Sidanius, J. (1985). Cognitive functioning and sociopolitical ideology revisited. *Political Psychology*, 6, 637–661.

Skitka, L. J., Mullen, E., Griffin, T., Hutchinson, S., & Chamberlin, B. (2002). Dispositions, scripts, or motivated correction? Understanding ideological differences in explanations for social problems. *Journal of Personality and Social Psychology*, 83, 470–487.

★Smithers, A. G., & Lobley, D. M. (1978). Dogmatism, social attitudes and personality. *British Journal of Social and Clinical Psychology*, 17, 135–142.

★Soenens, B., Duriez, B., & Goossens, L. (2005). Social–psychological profiles of identity styles: Attitudinal and social-cognitive correlates in late adolescence. *Journal of Adolescence*, 28, 107–125.

★Steiner, I. D., & Johnson, H. H. (1963). Authoritarianism and "tolerance of trait incon-sistency." *Journal of Abnormal and Social Psychology*, 67, 388–391.

★Sterling, J. L., Jost, J. T., & Pennycook, G. (2016). Are neoliberals more susceptible to bullshit? *Judgment and Decision Making*, 11, 352–360.

★Stern, C., West, T. V., Jost, J. T., & Rule, N. O. (2013). The politics of gaydar: Ideological differences in the use of gendered cues in categorizing sexual orientation. *Journal of Personality and Social Psychology*, 104, 520–541.

★Streufert, S., & Driver, M. J. (1967). Impression formation as a measure of complexity of conceptual structure. *Educational and Psychological Measurement*, 27, 1025–1039.

★Stuart, I. R. (1965). Field dependency, authoritarianism, and perception of the human figure. *Journal of Social Psychology*, 66, 209–214.

Sullivan, A. (2016, May 2–15). Our democracy has never been so ripe for tyranny. *New York Magazine*. Retrieved from http://nymag.com/daily/intelligencer/2016/04/america-tyranny-donald-trump.html

★Talhelm, T., Haidt, J., Oishi, S., Zhang, X., Miao, F. F., & Chen, S. (2015). Liberals think more analytically (more "WEIRD") than conservatives. *Personality and Social Psychology Bulletin*, 41, 250–267.

★Tam, K. P., Leung, A. K. Y., & Chiu, C. Y. (2008). On being a mindful authoritarian: Is need for cognition always associated with less punitiveness? *Political Psychology*, 29, 77–91.

★Tetlock, P. E. (1983). Cognitive style and political ideology. *Journal of Personality and Social Psychology*, 45, 118–126.

★Tetlock, P. E. (1984). Cognitive style and political belief systems in the British House of Commons. *Journal of Personality and Social Psychology*, 46, 365–375.

Tetlock, P. E. (2007). Psychology and politics: The challenges of integrating levels of analysis in social science. In A. W. Kruglanski & E. T. Higgins (Eds.), *Social psychology: Handbook of basic principles* (2nd ed., pp. 888–912). New York: Guilford Press.

★Tetlock, P. E., Bernzweig, J., & Gallant, J. L. (1985). Supreme Court decision making: Cognitive style as a predictor of ideological consistency of voting. *Journal of Personality and Social Psychology*, 48, 1227–1239.

★Tetlock, P. E., Hannum, K. A., & Micheletti, P. M. (1984). Stability and change in the complexity of senatorial debate: Testing the cognitive versus rhetorical style hypotheses. *Journal of Personality and Social Psychology*, 46, 979–990.

★Thompson, R. C., & Michel, J. B. (1972). Measuring authoritarianism: A comparison of the F and D scales. *Journal of Personality*, 40, 180–190.

★Thórisdóttir, H., & Jost, J. T. (2011). Motivated closed-mindedness mediates the effect of threat on political conservatism. *Political Psychology*, 32, 785–811.

Thórisdóttir, H., Jost, J. T., Liviatan, I., & Shrout, P. E. (2007). Psychological needs and values underlying left-right political orientation: Cross-national evidence from Eastern and Western Europe. *Public Opinion Quarterly*, 71, 175–203.

Tomkins, S. S. (1965). Affect and the psychology of knowledge. In S. S. Tomkins & C. E. Izard (Eds.), *Affect, cognition, and personality: Empirical studies* (pp. 72–97). New York: Springer.

Tomkins, S. S. (1987). Script theory. In J. Aronoff & A. I. Rubin (Eds.), *The emergence of personality* (pp. 147–216). New York: Springer.

Tuschman, A. (2013). *Our political nature: The evolutionary origins of what divides us*. Amherst, NY: Prometheus.

Van Berkel, L., Crandall, C. S., Eidelman, S., & Blanchar, J. C. (2015). Hierarchy, dominance, and deliberation egalitarian values require mental effort. *Personality and Social Psychology Bulletin*, 41, 1207–1222.

★Van Hiel, A., & Mervielde, I. (2003). The measurement of cognitive complexity and its relationship with political extremism. *Political Psychology*, 24, 781–801.

Van Hiel, A., Onraet, E., & De Pauw, S. (2010). The relationship between social-cultural attitudes and behavioral measures of cognitive style: A meta-analytic integration of studies. *Journal of Personality*, 78, 1765–1800.

★Van Hiel, A., Pandelaere, M., & Duriez, B. (2004). The impact of need for closure on conservative beliefs and racism: Differential mediation by authoritarian submission and authoritarian dominance. *Personality and Social Psychology Bulletin*, 30, 824–837.

★Vannoy, J. S. (1965). Generality of cognitive complexity-simplicity as a personality construct. *Journal of Personality and Social Psychology*, 2, 385–396.

Vigil, J. M. (2010). Political leanings vary with facial expression processing and psychosocial functioning. *Group Processes & Intergroup Relations*, 13, 547–558.

★Webster, A. C., & Stewart, R. A. (1973). Theological conservatism. In G. D. Wilson (Ed.), *The psychology of conservatism* (pp. 129–147). New York: Academic Press.

★Webster, D. M., & Kruglanski, A. W. (1994). Individual differences in need for cognitive closure. *Journal of Personality and Social Psychology*, 67, 1049–1062.

Westen, D. (2007). *The political brain*. New York: Public Affairs.

Wilson, G. D. (Ed.). (1973). *The psychology of conservatism*. London: Academic Press.

★Wilson, G. D., Ausman, J., & Mathews, T. R. (1973). Conservatism and art preferences. *Journal of Personality and Social Psychology*, 25, 286–288.

Wojcik, S. P., Hovasapian, A., Graham, J., Motyl, M., & Ditto, P. H. (2015). Conservatives report, but liberals display, greater happiness. *Science*, 347, 1243–1246.

★Yilmaz, O., & Saribay, S. A. (2016). An attempt to clarify the link between cognitive style and political ideology: A non-Western replication and extension. *Judgment and Decision Making*, 11, 287–300.

★Zacker, J. (1973). Authoritarian avoidance of ambiguity. *Psychological Reports*, 33, 901–902.

★Zelen, S. Y. (1955). Goal-setting rigidity in an ambiguous situation. *Journal of Consulting Psychology*, 19, 395–399.

★Zippel, B., & Norman, R. D. (1966). Party switching, authoritarianism, and dogmatism in the 1964 election. *Psychological Reports*, 19, 667–670.

5

GOING IN THE RIGHT DIRECTION

Locomotion Control and Assessment Truth, *Working Together*

E. Tory Higgins

> The good life is a process, not a state of being. It is a direction not a destination.
>
> *(Carl Rogers)*

> Life is a journey, not a destination.
>
> *(Ralph Waldo Emerson)*

> The great thing in the world is not so much where we stand, as in what direction we are moving.
>
> *(Oliver Wendell Holmes)*

> Leaders establish the vision for the future and set the strategy for getting there; they cause change. They motivate and inspire others to go in the right direction.
>
> *(John Kotter)*

The message in these "words of wisdom" is that what matters in human motivation is not just having desired outcomes, not just ending goal pursuits by maximizing pleasure and minimizing pain. There is more to life than that. The process of goal pursuit, the journey, also matters. What matters is that we go in the right direction. And this is also the message in the Genesis story of Adam and Eve in the Garden of Eden – the beginning of the beginning for humans, according to the *Bible*.

The story is as follows:

> And out of the ground made the Lord God to grow every tree that is pleasant to the sight, and good for food; the tree of life also in the midst of the garden, and the tree of knowledge of good and evil....And the Lord God commanded the man, saying, Of every tree of the garden thou mayest freely

eat: But of the tree of the knowledge of good and evil, thou shalt not eat of it: for in the day that thou eatest thereof thou shalt surely die.

(Genesis 2: 8–9, 16–17, King James Version)

According to the *Bible*, Adam and Eve were blessed by God in being placed in the Garden of Eden. Notably, this was not just *a* paradise. It was *the* original paradise where there was all pleasure and no pain – a place in which grew "every tree that is pleasant to the sight, and good for food." Importantly, in the midst of the garden was the *tree of life*, and Adam and Eve knew, from God's command, that they had permission to eat the fruit from this tree and thereby have a life of all pleasure and no pain *forever*. This meant that all they had to do was stay in the Garden of Eden and enjoy the fruit of the *tree of life* and the other abundant pleasures in this paradise. But, as we all know, this is not what Adam and Eve chose to do. Instead, they chose to eat the forbidden fruit from the *tree of knowledge*. Notably, it is precisely because this fruit was *explicitly* forbidden by God's command that there is no ambiguity about Adam and Eve's choice to eat this forbidden fruit. They knew from God's command that by making this choice they would, at minimum, be banished from paradise, thereby losing an everlasting life of pleasure and no pain. Why would Adam and Eve make this choice if what people really want is to maximize pleasure and minimize pain?

I have argued (Higgins, 2012) that this story gives us the same basic message as the "words of wisdom" quoted above. There is more to human motivation than maximizing pleasure and minimizing pain. What else is there? As the quotes tell us, there is the journey, there is a life of *going in the right direction*. How does the story of Adam and Eve in the Garden of Eden tell us that? The answer lies in why it was the fruit of the tree of knowledge that Adam and Eve wanted to eat. There are two critical aspects of the tree of knowledge. First, the tree of *knowledge* is the tree of *truth*. A central motivation of humans is to *establish what's real*, to distinguish between truth and falsehood, between reality and fantasy (Higgins, 2012). This motivation for the truth can be as important to humans as life itself, and sharing the truth with others – *shared reality* – is, more than anything else, *what makes us human* (Echterhoff, Higgins, & Levine, 2009; Hardin & Higgins, 1996; Higgins et al., in press). And, notably, by *both* Adam and Eve eating the fruit of the tree of knowledge, they create a shared reality.

Second, the tree of knowledge is not just any knowledge – it is the *"tree of the knowledge of good and evil."* This means that eating the fruit of this tree also satisfies another central human motivation, the motivation to *manage what happens*, the motivation to *control* our lives. Only when humans have the knowledge of what is good and what is evil can they make *choices* based on competing preferences, choices that distinguish between different options that can vary in their hedonic and moral attributes; only then can they control their lives.

Thus, the tree of knowledge is not just any tree. It is the tree of truth and control. Importantly, because everything is provided for Adam and Eve in the

Garden of Eden, they have little need for truth or control. They can be effective in having all kinds of pleasure (and no pain), but having these pleasures is not due to their being effective in truth and control. It is given to them. To be effective at having truth or control, they must eat from the tree of the knowledge of good and evil – even if this means losing paradise. And, importantly, the *"tree of the knowledge of good and evil"* is not only a tree of truth and a tree of control. It combines the motivation for truth with the motivation for control. By eating the fruit of this tree, Adam and Eve can experience truth and control *working together* to direct life choices. By eating the fruit of this tree, Adam and Eve can begin the journey of being human. By eating the fruit of this tree, Adam and Eve can begin a human life of going in the right direction. And it is the journey that matters…not the destination.

This chapter is about what it means for humans to go in the right direction. I begin by distinguishing among the motivations for having desired outcomes (value), establishing what's real (truth), and managing what happens (control). I then discuss the importance for goal pursuit, for individuals and groups, that value, truth, and control work together. Finally, I illustrate this point by describing the advantages to goal pursuit when *locomotion* motivation, which is a control motivation, and *assessment* motivation, which is a truth motivation, work together.

I will review evidence that locomotion motivation and assessment motivation are complementary. Within an individual, performance is enhanced when that individual's locomotion and assessment motivations are both strong. Within teams, team performance is enhanced when the team includes members with predominant locomotion motivation and members with predominant assessment motivations. And even the individual performance of team members is enhanced when their predominant motivation is complemented by their teammates' predominant motivation (teammates' assessment for individuals with predominant locomotion; teammates' locomotion for individuals with predominant assessment). Performance is enhanced in all of these ways because locomotion motivation is a control motivation for "going" and assessment motivation is a truth motivation for "right." *Together*, they produce "going in the right direction."

Value, Truth, and Control

What is it that people really want? I believe that the best answer is: People want to be *effective*. This answer to what people really want did not originate with me. There is a long history of great scholars within and outside of psychology who have proposed this answer. In the first half of the twentieth century, both John Maynard Keynes, the renowned British economist, and Robert Woodworth, the psychologist who coined the term "drive," independently recognized the importance of the motivation to be effective. Other major contributors in the twentieth century to the notion that people want to be effective include Donald Hebb (e.g., 1955), Jean Piaget (e.g., 1952), Robert White (e.g., 1959), Albert Bandura (e.g., 1982), and Edward Deci and Richard Ryan (e.g., 1985).

I use the term "effective" because it is a common term in everyday language and its formal dictionary definitions capture well what I have in mind (see *Oxford English Dictionary*, 1971): (a) *having the power of acting upon something*; (b) *that part of a force that is instrumental in producing a result*; (c) *executing or accomplishing a notable effect*; (d) *fit for work or service*. Apart from my use of the specific term "effective," the difference between my approach and the earlier approaches that inspired me is my emphasis on the need to distinguish among three distinct ways of being effective in life pursuits – value effectiveness, control effectiveness, and truth effectiveness – and to consider how they relate to one another (for a fuller account, see Higgins, 2012).

Three Ways of Being Effective in Life Pursuits

Value Effectiveness

By "value effectiveness" I mean that actors are successful in ending ultimately with the outcomes they desire. Value effectiveness is about success with respect to outcomes, about the consequences of goal pursuit – success in ending with benefits versus costs, pleasure versus pain, biological needs satisfied versus unsatisfied. Simply put, *value effectiveness is being successful in having what is desired*. It should be emphasized that what matters for value effectiveness is ending with the desired outcomes – not how this ending came about, whether through a proxy, through collaboration with others, or through our own actions.

Value effectiveness was emphasized by drive theories (e.g., Hull, 1943, 1952) and the hedonic principle. For drive theories, it was the value derived from the benefits of satisfying primary biological needs, such as reducing hunger (e.g., finding food) or reducing fear (e.g., escaping danger). For the hedonic principle, it was the value derived from the benefits of making something pleasant happen or something painful not happen. Goal theories have also emphasized value effectiveness, with motivation constituting forces within us that are goal-directed or purposive (see Elliott & Dweck, 1988; Elliot & Fryer, 2008; Kruglanski et al., 2002; McDougall, 1914; Pervin, 1989). In social psychology, at least, a major influence on this conceptualization of motivation was Kurt Lewin's work on goal-directed action and goal striving within a field of forces where positive value relates to a force of attraction and negative valence relates to a force of repulsion (Lewin, 1935, 1951). Woodworth said it clearly: "What persists, in purposive behavior, is the tendency towards some end or goal. The purposeful person wants something he has not yet got, and is striving towards some future result" (Woodworth, 1921, p. 70).

Truth Effectiveness

By "truth effectiveness" I mean that actors are successful in knowing what is real. The root meaning of "truth" (as well as "trust") relates to "true"; "truth" is the quality of being "true." Something being "true" means being in accordance with an actual state of affairs, being consistent with the facts; conforming to or agreeing with an essential reality; being that which is the case, representing things as they are – in brief, knowing what's real, what's reality (*Oxford English Dictionary*, 1971). "True" also relates to accuracy; to being correct, right, and legitimate; to being genuine, honest, and faithful. It is contrasted with being imaginary, spurious, or counterfeit. Thus, *truth effectiveness is being successful in establishing what is real.*

The movie *The Truman Show* clearly illustrates how strongly people want to establish what's real. Truman's entire life is a reality TV show that began airing at his birth. Everyone he knows are actors playing their roles. Truman's life on the reality TV show is designed to be all pleasure and no pain. But there is one exception. He is anxious about being on the water because he believes his father drowned in a boating accident. However, like his entire life, this event was manufactured as part of the TV show. The actor who played his father was simply a victim of his character being written out of the show. When, accidentally, Truman sees him again – along with some other accidents on the show – he finally realizes that his life has been manufactured. Everyone tries to reassure him, including the executive producer of the show, who argues that there is no more truth in the real world than there is in his own artificial one. Despite everyone's reassurances and despite having a life of pleasure and no pain, Truman risks actual death by sailing across the water he fears because he needs to follow up his discovery and seek the truth.

Value effectiveness – having desired results – is critical for humans and other animals. But so is truth effectiveness – knowing what is real in the world, representing things as they are. Without truth effectiveness we would bump into walls, we would live in a world that William James ([1890] 1948, p. 462) referred to as "one great blooming, buzzing confusion." Each individual and each group is strongly motivated to know what is real – to attain truth effectiveness. This plays out in various ways, including wanting to know what is accurate, or what is correct or incorrect, right or wrong, legitimate or illegitimate, honest or deceitful, genuine or fraudulent.

The movie *The Matrix* provides another compelling example of how important knowing the truth is to people. In the movie, there is a future where the reality perceived by humans is actually a *simulated* reality – the Matrix – that provides people with a hedonically positive life to pacify them. Morpheus, the leader of the rebels, gives Neo, the hero of the tale, a choice between a blue pill that will keep him in this comfortable simulated reality or a red pill that offers only the truth. Morpheus tells Neo, "All I'm offering is the truth, nothing more." Neo chooses the red pill. Neo's motivation, like Truman's, is truth effectiveness, which trumps the hedonic principle. And, of course, it is not just movie characters who illustrate the power of truth effectiveness. Many people make life choices on the basis of their religious or political beliefs about what is right or proper. All too frequently, individuals will give up their lives for "truth," as evidenced by suicide bombers and protesters who set themselves on fire.

In the psychological literature, a classic example of the truth motive can be found in Asch's so-called "conformity" study, in which participants were situated among confederates who unanimously gave the same wrong answer when there was an objectively correct solution. What Asch found was that many students were willing to forgo the objectively correct answer for the incorrect answer provided by the unanimous group of confederates (Asch, 1956). Although many social psychologists have interpreted this research in terms of normative influence, i.e., "conformity" (Deutsch & Gérard, 1955), a closer look reveals that what happened had more to do with seeking the truth. This is because the students were much more likely to agree with the group when it was difficult to determine the correct answer than when it was easy (Asch, 1956). When the correct answer was less clear (the difficult condition), they needed the truth provided by the group more.

If students' motivation was only "going along to get along," i.e., "conformity," then it wouldn't matter if the correct answer was clear – you would still say what the group said. Indeed, one might argue that conformity would be *greater* in the easy situation where the answer is unambiguous, because then your correct response would be more obviously non-normative to the other group members' wrong answer (i.e., the difference between the answers would be clearer), and thus the risk of being rejected could be greater. But this was not what happened; in fact, the opposite occurred. Participants were less likely to conform when the answers were more obvious, consistent with a motivation to seek the truth rather than just seeking to "go along to get along" (Levine, 1999).

Given the dominant position of the hedonic principle within motivation, the difference between truth effectiveness and the hedonic principle needs to be emphasized. It is common knowledge that learning the truth about ourselves or those we care about can be painful, and yet we often seek the truth, even when we know it will be painful. When something pleasant but unexpected happens to people, they often want to know why it happened. Others will tell them to just enjoy it and not be concerned about why it happened. Yet, they still want to know the truth.

Another classic example in the psychological literature of truth motivation working above and beyond the hedonic principle is the research on cognitive dissonance (Festinger, 1957). In the original study by Festinger and Carlsmith (1959), participants were offered money to tell a future participant that a particular task they completed was fun and exciting even though it was not. Some participants received a small sum of money to provide this false information; others received a large sum. A basic hedonic satisfaction model would predict that those who received the larger sum would be most likely to later report that their lie was true. Indeed, according to the Law of Effect (Thorndike, 1911) – a law that is based on the hedonic principle – if the lie leads to a greater reward, then the lie should be more readily repeated. However, this was the *opposite* of what was found: participants who received the *small* amount of remuneration were *more likely* to later report beliefs consistent with their lie.

The well-known explanation for this result is that those who lied for only a *small* amount of money experienced "dissonance" between their belief that they were honest and their knowing that they had lied, without being able to justify that what they did was worth it for the money they received. The role of justification is important here. Although research has shown that negative affect tends to be higher among those experiencing dissonance compared to those who are not (Higgins, Rhodewalt, & Zanna, 1979), these affective experiences, at most, only partially mediate attitude change (Harmon-Jones, 1999). Thus, it wasn't simply that lying was more *aversive* for those in the low-compensation group, which resulted in an effort to reduce a painful state. Instead, lying in that condition didn't *make sense*, and shifting one's attitude restores a sensible world. As Festinger (1957) put it: the existence of nonfitting relations among cognitions is a motivating factor in its own right. That is, truth motivation – in this case, restoring consistency among cognitions – is its own independent motivation.

The experimental literature also contains many other instances of a motivation to "establish what is real" that works independently from the motivation to have desired outcomes. For example, individuals are motivated to obtain accurate information about themselves, even when that information may be painful to hear (Swann, 1990). People are also influenced by descriptive norms (i.e., norms of how people in general behave), not simply injunctive norms (i.e., norms about how people *should* behave), as descriptive norms act as a medium of information regarding how the world works (Kahneman & Miller, 1986; Cialdini, Reno, & Kallgren, 1990). Truth motives' ubiquity in the literature has given rise not only to broad research areas such as learning and cognitive development, but also to specific research programs such as the work on cognitive closure (Webster & Kruglanski, 1994) and curiosity (Loewenstein, 1994).

Control Effectiveness

By "control effectiveness," I mean actors experiencing success at managing what is required (procedures, competencies, resources) to make something happen (or not happen). Having control relates to exercising direction or restraint upon action; having power or authority to guide or manage; having influence over something (*Oxford English Dictionary*, 1971). *Control effectiveness is being successful in managing what happens.* Whereas value effectiveness relates to outcomes (benefits versus costs) and truth effectiveness relates to reality (real versus illusion), control effectiveness relates to *strength* (strong versus weak influence over something). It is very general. People can have strong versus weak muscles, intellect, character, arguments, willpower, teamwork, and so on. Managers, leaders, and administrators can be strong or weak.

Humans and other animals, beyond their desire to have good results from their actions, are motivated to have an effect on the world (Franks & Higgins, 2012; Eitam, Kennedy, & Higgins, 2013). Not only do individuals want to have good outcomes, but they want to have a hand in bringing about those good outcomes.

They also need to plan the different stages of goal pursuit effectively, including altering the plans based upon feedback they receive (an example of truth and control working together).

A classic example of control effectiveness is the epic story of Odysseus in Homer's *Odyssey*. In his voyage to return home with his men, Odysseus faced constant control challenges in managing what would happen to him and his crew. The story is clearly *not* about being effective in fulfilling the goal of safely returning home (value effectiveness) because by the end of the voyage not one member of his crew had survived. Odysseus himself did return home, but he was in bad shape. Instead, the story of Odysseus is about managing what is needed to make something happen and, especially in this story, to make something *not* happen. Perhaps the best-known episode in the story is the challenge of the Sirens.

The Sirens were enchantresses who lived on a rocky island and used their music and voices to lure mariners toward them, where they would be ship-wrecked on the rocks. To manage his sailors' temptation, Odysseus had their ears stuffed with wax so they could not hear the music. Odysseus could have used the same control tactic, but he was curious to hear the Sirens' song. It turned out that the Sirens' words were even more enticing than their beautiful voices because they promised to give great wisdom to whomever came to them – the great temptation of learning the truth about the world (truth effectiveness).

Odysseus managed his strong temptation for knowledge by having his followers lash him securely to the mast of the ship. In this way, he succeeded at controlling what happened. When people are effective at control, they manage what is required, such as managing procedures, competencies, and resources, to make something happen or not happen. Having control relates to exercising direction or restraint upon action, to having power or authority to guide or manage.

While high control effectiveness increases the likelihood of beneficial outcomes, it is separate from outcomes, as reflected in maxims such as "it's not whether you win or lose, it is how you play the game" and "in victory or defeat, you play with skill and courage – with strength." Indeed, control effectiveness can trump value effectiveness. Consider the phenomenon of *contra-freeloading* (for a review, see Osborne, 1977). As an example, take a study with rats that learned that by pressing a lever they could make a food pellet fall into a food tray where they could eat it. In one experimental condition, a food dish was placed in the cage, which meant that the rats could obtain the same food pellets for free (i.e., without having to work for them). On occasion a rat would accidentally push the free food dish in front of the food tray. Despite the fact that they could effortlessly attain the food from the free food dish in front of them, the rats actually pushed the food dish *out of the way* (not eating from it), and then pressed the lever to make a food pellet fall into the food tray, where they ate it (see Carder & Berkowitz, 1970). Such behavior is about control effectiveness and not just about value effectiveness. If it was just about value effectiveness, the rats would eat from the free food dish, thereby maximizing the benefits/costs ratio given that it would be the same beneficial food for less cost in effort. (For a human analog, see Eitam, Kennedy, & Higgins, 2013.)

As I mentioned earlier, control effectiveness is also separate from truth effectiveness. High predictability provides truth effectiveness, but it need not provide control effectiveness. And for most people high predictability, even when it is combined with high desired outcomes, is not enough if personal control is lacking. Consider again Neo in *The Matrix*. Morpheus asks Neo, "Do you believe in fate, Neo?" Neo answers, "No!" "Why not?" asks Morpheus. Neo replies, "Because I don't like the idea that I'm not in control of my life." For Neo, fate as high predictability or truth is still not enough. He also wants personal control.

Truth and Control *Working Together*

The motivations to be effective in truth and to be effective in control go beyond just the hedonic motivation of maximizing pleasure and minimizing pain. But that is not all to the story of how motivation goes beyond pleasure and pain. Motivation also involves all the relations among truth, control, and value (Higgins, 2012). Having effective *relations* among truth, control, and value can determine our well-being rather than just truth, control, and value as independent motivations. This part of the motivation story is something that ancient philosophers appreciated more than many psychologists today.

Early philosophers believed that *eudaimonia* – "flourishing" or "happiness" – was a condition of the soul. The soul was the "living-ness" or "alive-ness" of an individual's body. Hence, the Latin word for soul: *anima*. It is the means by which one experiences the world as a whole individual. Traditionally, the soul was organized into three aspects: reason (the faculty concerned with understanding the world), will (the faculty concerned with bringing about action), and affections (the faculty concerned with evaluating experiences, see Aquinas, 1274/1981). As noted by Cornwell, Franks, and Higgins (in press), in the terms of motivation science, reason maps onto truth, will onto control, and affections onto value. Virtues, according to philosophers like Plato (trans. 1992) and Aristotle (trans. 2009), are habits that arise through training each of these faculties to *work properly with each of the others* – so that one's reason, will, and affections "work together in concert" (Crombie, 1962).

According to Cornwell et al. (in press), the aim of "happiness" or "the good life" is the *integration of motives* (see also Higgins, 2012; Higgins, Cornwell, & Franks, 2014). Notably, the concept of "integration" has two meanings (*Oxford English Dictionary*, 1971). The first meaning is *"the harmonious combination of the different elements."* This captures the notion that the motives are "working together," that they sustain and support one another, just as in the regulatory fit cases of eager control motivation sustaining promotion value motivation and vigilant control motivation sustaining prevention value motivation (Higgins, 2000). The second meaning of integration is *"equal membership."* This captures the notion that no one motivational part dominates the other parts. Instead, each part is strong enough to constrain each of the other parts, thereby setting limits on the potential downside of each motivation.

A critical case of two strong motives working together is truth and control working together. It is important that both motives be strong in order that truth motivation can limit the downside of control motivation and control motivation can limit the downside of truth motivation. As two strong partners, they can "go in the right direction" (see Higgins, 2012). If truth motivation were weak, control motivation could simply go in any direction as long as it managed to make something happen – including something bad. Strong truth motivation is needed to guide control motivation in the *right* direction that makes something good happen (and something bad not happen). On the other hand, if control motivation were weak, then truth motivation could get "lost in thought" and go nowhere. To stop this, control motivation needs also to be strong to make something happen (to go).

In a sense, this formulation is contrary to what Aristotle said in that what should be aimed at is not "moderation" but motivational partners that are each strong enough – equally or almost equally strong – that they can limit the downsides of each other and enhance the upsides of one another (Higgins, 2012). No doubt the effect, i.e., the resultant, of having such strong motivations working together would be a kind of "moderation" in which no single motivation dominates either of the others. But this *observed* moderation would be the product of underlying strong motivational partners. According to this perspective, neither *moderation* nor *maximization* should be directly pursued for its own sake, but rather *integration*.

As discussed earlier, when Adam and Eve chose to eat from the *"tree of the knowledge of good and evil"* despite being explicitly forbidden to do so by God's command, they were expelled from the Garden of Eden where they could have enjoyed a life of all pleasure and no pain *forever*. From a hedonic perspective, their choice makes no sense. Nor does it make sense that Neo in *Matrix* and Truman in *The Truman Show* would choose to give up a guaranteed life of hedonic pleasure for a life-threatening alternative. But we intuitively know what motivates these choices. We are like Neo who, when asked if he believed in fate, said he did not, "Because I don't like the idea that I'm not in control of my life." As with Neo, Truman, and Adam and Eve, our lives are not about maximizing pleasure and minimizing pain. Truth and control are very important to us. We want to be effective in establishing what's real and in managing what happens.

The motivations of truth and control work together as a very powerful partnership. They can trump the motivation to maximize pleasure and minimize pain. How might this partnership be characterized? I believe that the epigraphs at the start of this chapter provide a good answer. Their combined message is that we have to manage to move in some direction, which is *control*. But to have a good life we cannot move just anywhere. We need to move in the *right* direction. And to know which direction is right, we need to have *truth* as well. Indeed, the strength of the truth-control partnership is so great that, according to the Oxford English dictionary, "direction" is defined as *putting or keeping in the right way or course*. That is, "direction" is defined in terms of both control (*putting or keeping* the way or course) and truth (the *right* way or course).

What needs to be emphasized is that going in the right direction does *not* necessarily mean that we will end with having desired results. For Adam and Eve, eating the fruit from the *"tree of the knowledge of good and evil"* meant that they had direction for the first time. When they were in a state of paradise, they had neither truth nor control. Now they had direction but this led, at least initially, to the undesired result of being banished by God. Neo and Truman also had direction for the first time when they chose truth and control over hedonic pleasure, but again this led initially to a dangerous situation for them. As Carl Rogers said, the good life is a direction and not a destination.

Historically, the psychological relations that have received the most attention in the literature are those where value plays the central role. This traditional emphasis on value is consistent with the predominance of pleasure and pain in theories of motivation. In contrast, this paper considers truth-control relations where value does not play the central role. This is not to say that these relations have nothing to do with value. Motivation is typically a story of *all three* ways of being effective working together. Normally, truth-control relations function to facilitate having desired results, to facilitate success at value. But the story is not always about value as the lead player, with truth and control only in supporting roles. Sometimes, the emphasis is on truth or control rather than on value. And again, truth and control when working together as partners can trump value motivationally.

Truth and control as partners in self-regulation have received the most attention in theories of *"control systems"* – devices or mechanisms that manage, direct or regulate how things behave. Norbert Wiener (1948), an applied mathematician and the founder of cybernetics, was a pioneer in formulating the role of feedback in control systems. They can include feedback systems that regulate in relation to some set point or reference value, as when air conditioning systems vary their output as the temperature changes in order to maintain a temperature that was set as the reference value. Such systems are often assumed to contain two functional elements: a *testing* component designed to evaluate a system's current state (truth), and an *action* component designed to move it toward the desired state (control). A thermostat, for instance, has sensors to detect whether the desired temperature has been reached (truth), and a switching mechanism to activate or deactivate the heating or the cooling process (control). Together, these two functional elements ensure that the temperature is *going in the right direction*. Similarly, bodily mechanisms detect low hydration levels to indicate that the activity of drinking is called for, or low blood glucose level to produce hunger that motivates eating.

An early psychological control system model was proposed by Miller, Galanter, and Pribram (1960) – the TOTE model (for Test-Operate-Test-Exit). TOTE units function at strategic, tactical, and behavioral levels. At the strategic planning level of hammering a nail, for example, there are the phases of lifting the hammer and striking the nail. But what tells us when to stop hammering? There needs to be feedback comparing where the head of the nail currently is in relation to the reference value of being flush with the surface of the work. We stop our hammering, i.e., exit, when the operation of hammering is followed by a test of the current state of the nail head in relation to the reference value of the work surface, and the test informs us that the nail head is flush with the surface.

According to the TOTE model, then, effective hammering requires a truth-control partnership. Effective truth involves establishing the current reality of the relation between the nail head and the work surface. Effective control involves managing to carry out the strategic plan at the tactical and behavioral levels, such as lifting the hammer and striking the nail. Working together, truth and control arrive at the stopping or exit point where the nail head is flush with the surface – thereby having the desired result (value).

The partnership described in the TOTE model is the type of truth-control relation that has received the most attention in the motivational literature. Truth and control are working together in order to have desired results; i.e., it is *a truth-control relation in the service of value*. A similar model is the influential self-regulation model of Carver and Scheier (1998). In their theory, there are two self-regulatory systems. One system involves a desired end-state as the reference value and an operational control function that is concerned with reducing any existing discrepancy between the current state and the desired reference value. A second self-regulatory system involves an undesired end-state as the reference value and an operational control function that is concerned with amplifying the distance between the current state and the undesired reference value. In each case there is a monitoring and feedback *truth* function that compares the current state with the reference value and provides progress information regarding the amount and rate of distance reduction or amplification – *the truth regarding "how am I doing?"* Once again, truth and control are partners in the service of value, where value is either the desired result of eliminating the discrepancy between the current state and the desired end-state, or the desired result of establishing sufficient distance between the current state and the undesired end-state.

The type of truth-control relation emphasized in Miller et al.'s (1960) TOTE model and Carver and Scheier's (1990, 1998) Control–Process model is one in which the self-regulatory functions of truth (i.e., monitoring and providing feedback about current reality) and control (i.e., managing operations) are intertwined in relation to a reference value that defines their purpose. Certainly, value, truth, and control *do* work together in this way. But, again, a desired result is not a necessary outcome of a powerful truth-control relation. My favorite example is Walt Disney's Mickey Mouse in his role as the Sorcerer's Apprentice in the movie *Fantasia*. Mickey used his apprentice-level of knowledge of magic (truth) to manage a broom (control) to do his chore of carrying buckets of water. Unfortunately for him, going in what he thought was the right direction – and clearly enjoying it – did not have desired results because he didn't know how to stop the process and the castle became flooded.

Assessment as Truth and Locomotion as Control, *Working Together*

To appreciate better how truth and control can work together as partners, it is useful to consider the distinct motivations of assessment and locomotion and how they work together. Distinguishing between assessment and locomotion modes of self-regulation began when Arie Kruglanski and I were discussing the fundamental nature of control systems. Before long, we became convinced that the test and operate functions, or the monitoring and reducing/amplifying functions, could be conceptualized more broadly as distinct and general self-regulatory functions. More important, we felt that these functions need not be conceived as inseparable parts of a self-regulation whole, as always being functionally integrated and interdependent. Instead, we hypothesized that they were two separate and independent functions of self-regulation – assessment and locomotion. These two motivational functions had wide ranges of applicability and could work together (or not) with varying degrees of emphasis on one or the other function – high emphasis on just one, high emphasis on both, or high emphasis on neither.

These ideas led to the development of regulatory mode theory. This theory posits that goal-directed activity occurs within one of two basic functions or modes: *assessment*, which is a truth motivation, is concerned with critically comparing and evaluating options to find the right one ("Get it right"); *locomotion*, which is a control motivation, is concerned with effecting and managing change without disruption ("Go for it") – the initiation and maintenance of smooth movement from a current state to another state (see Higgins, 2012; Higgins, Kruglanski, & Pierro, 2003; Kruglanski et al., 2000; Kruglanski, Pierro, Mannetti, & Higgins, 2013). Importantly, the strength of individuals' locomotion motivation or assessment motivation can vary chronically as a personality difference, and it can vary momentarily as a function of the current situation.

Individuals can be too strong in assessment or locomotion, i.e., be hyper-assessors or hyper-locomotors, and this can be maladaptive. Hyper-assessors, for example, can engage in high levels of rumination and overly critical self-assessment (Pierro et al., 2008), and such assessment for its own sake can sometimes paint a picture that is not necessarily *true* (i.e., ineffective truth). Similarly, hyper-locomotors can be overly active or driven by desire for change, which, among other potential costs, could lead to impulsive decision-making, which reflects ineffective control (see Mannetti et al., 2009). For this reason, it is important that locomotion and assessment constrain one another and work in a complementary fashion.

There is, indeed, strong evidence that when locomotion and assessment function in a complementary way, performance is better – the benefits from "going in the right direction." This is because the separate functions of locomotion control and assessment truth are jointly essential to effective action. Importantly, the advantages from complementarity can occur for both individuals and teams (see Kruglanski et al., 2013). They can exist for the motivations of an individual (defined by an individual's locomotion and assessment motivations) and for the motivations of team members (defined by the group composition of "locomotor" members and "assessor" members).

For individuals, assessment and locomotion have been found to jointly contribute to success in goal pursuit. Kruglanski et al. (2000) administered the assessment and locomotion measures to several hundred applicants for an elite combat unit in the U.S. Army prior to onset of the training period. The military training program they entered was highly selective and extremely demanding – so demanding that approximately 60% of the participants never complete the program. Stronger locomotion predicted a higher likelihood of successfully completing the course, but only when participants' assessment scores were also high (above the median of the distribution). Stronger locomotion did not predict success when participants' assessment scores were low.

This interaction between locomotion and assessment was also found for undergraduate GPA performance (controlling for participants' gender and SAT scores). Once again, stronger locomotion predicted higher GPAs, but only when the participants' assessment scores were also high (Kruglanski et al., 2000). Notably, this locomotion – assessment interaction effect was also obtained in studies by Pierro et al. (2012a) that involved different work organizations, and used different research designs (cross-sectional and longitudinal) and different work performance measures (i.e., both self-report and managerial rating measures). There is even evidence that strong locomotion combined with at least moderate assessment predicts higher retirement savings (Kim, Franks, & Higgins, 2013). Finally, there is evidence that a leader who has complementary locomotion and assessment is also more effective in motivating subordinates. Pierro et al. (2012b) conducted three field studies that examined complementarity effects of locomotion and assessment in work settings. Leaders high on both locomotion and assessment (as evaluated by the subordinates and the leaders themselves) elicited a higher level of performance from their subordinates than leaders low on one or both of these tendencies

Advantages from locomotion – assessment complementarity have also been found for teams. In a study by Mauro et al. (2009), the composition of four-member groups was experimentally manipulated by inducing either strong locomotion concerns or strong assessment concerns in the individual members prior to their becoming a group. Groups were then created that contained all high locomotors, all high assessors, or half high locomotors and half high assessors. The group task was a "homicide investigation" where different bits of evidence concerning three suspects were dispersed across the group members. After the group members read, reviewed and discussed the evidence, each group's mission was to reach a consensus on the likely culprit. The study found that the strong locomotion groups were *faster* in reaching a consensus than the strong assessment groups, whereas the strong assessment groups were more *accurate* in their final judgment than the strong locomotion groups. This sounds like the classic trade-off between speed and accuracy: a group can either be fast by having strong locomotion or it can be accurate by having strong assessment. However, the groups with an even mix of high locomotors and high assessors were *as fast* as the all locomotion groups and *as accurate* as the all assessment groups!

Perhaps most impressive of all, there is also evidence that the *individual* performance of workers in organizations is enhanced when the workers' own dominant regulatory mode (i.e., locomotion or assessment) is complemented by their *teammates'* regulatory mode (Pierro et al., 2012c). Specifically, the performance of individuals higher on locomotion (*vs.* assessment) was enhanced when their teammates' dominant mode (measured as an aggregate) was assessment. Similarly, the performance of individuals whose dominant mode was assessment was enhanced when their team members' dominant mode was locomotion.

What all these studies on locomotion-assessment complementarity show clearly is that the performance of individuals and groups is enhanced when there are locomotion motivation forces combined with assessment motivation forces. Locomotion control motivation is a force for "going" and assessment truth motivation is a force for "right." Together, they produce "going in the right direction." And "going in the right direction" benefits goal pursuit. It benefits well-being as well (Franks & Higgins, 2012; Higgins, 2012; Higgins et al., in press).

A final comment. This paper appears in a Festschrift volume honoring my very close friend and colleague, Arie Kruglanski. Our collaboration on the development and testing of regulatory mode theory, with another friend Antonio Pierro, was yet another illustration of the benefits of having locomotion – assessment complementarity. For those who know Arie well you can readily guess how he was a major force in this partnership.

References

Aquinas, T. (1981). *The Summa Theologica of St. Thomas Aquinas.* Grand Rapids, MI: Christian Classics. (Original work published c. 1274.)
Aristotle, trans. by Ross, W. D. (2009). *Nichomachean ethics.* New York: World Library Classics. (Original work published c. 350 B.C.)

Asch, S. E. (1956). Studies of independence and conformity: A minority of one against a unanimous majority. *Psychology Monographs*, 70, No. 9 (Whole No. 416).

Bandura, A. (1982). Self-efficacy mechanism in human agency. *American Psychologist*, 37, 122–147.

Carder, B., & Berkowitz, K. (1970). Rats' preference for earned in comparison with free food. *Science*, 167, 1273–1274.

Carver, C. S., & Scheier, M. F. (1990). Origins and functions of positive and negative affect: A control-process view. *Psychological Review*, 97, 19–35.

Carver, C. S., & Scheier, M. F. (1998). *On the self-regulation of behavior*. New York: Cambridge University Press.

Cialdini, R. B., Reno, R. R., & Kallgren, C. A. (1990). A focus theory of normative conduct: Recycling the concept of norms to reduce littering in public places. *Journal of Personality and Social Psychology*, 58, 1015–1026.

Cornwell, J. F. M., Franks, B., & Higgins, E. T. (2014). Truth, control, and value motivations: The 'what', 'how', and 'why' of approach and avoidance. *Frontiers in Systems Neuroscience*, 8: 192.

Crombie, I. M. (1962). *An examination of Plato's doctrines 2 Vols*. London, UK: Routledge and Kegan Paul.

Deci, E. L., & Ryan, R. M. (1985). *Intrinsic motivation and self-determination in human behavior*. New York: Plenum Press.

Deutsch, M., & Gerard, H. B. (1955). A study of normative and informational social influences upon individual judgment. *Journal of Abnormal and Social Psychology*, 51, 629–636.

Echterhoff, G., Higgins, E. T., & Levine, J. M. (2009). Shared reality: Experiencing commonality with others' inner states about the world. *Perspectives On Psychological Science*, 4, 496–521.

Eitam, B., Kennedy, P. M., & Higgins, E. T. (2013). Motivation from control. *Exp Brain Res*, 229, 475–484.

Elliot, A. J., & Fryer, J. W. (2008). The goal construct in psychology. In J. Y. Shah and W. L. Gardner (Eds.). *Handbook of motivation science* (pp. 235–250). New York: Guilford Press.

Elliott, E. S., & Dweck, C. S. (1988). Goals: An approach to motivation and achievement. *Journal of Personality and Social Psychology*, 54, 5–12.

Festinger, L. (1957). *A theory of cognitive dissonance*. Evanston, Ill.: Row, Peterson.

Festinger, L., & Carlsmith, J. M. (1959). Cognitive consequences of forced compliance. *Journal of Abnormal and Social Psychology*, 58, 203–211.

Franks, B., & Higgins, E. T. (2012). Effectiveness in humans and other animals: A common basis for well-being and welfare. In M. P. Zanna & J. M. Olson (Eds.), *Advances in experimental social psychology* (46, pp. 285–346). New York: Academic Press.

Hardin, C., & Higgins, E. T. (1996). "Shared reality": How social verification makes the subjective objective. In R. M. Sorrentino and E. T. Higgins (Eds.), *Handbook of motivation and cognition: The interpersonal context* (pp. 28–84). New York: Guilford.

Harmon-Jones, E. (1999). Toward an understanding of the motivation underlying dissonance effects: Is the production of aversive consequences necessary? In E. Harmon-Jones and J. Mills (Eds.), *Cognitive dissonance: Progress on a pivotal theory in social psychology* (pp. 71–99). Washington, DC: American Psychological Association.

Hebb, D. O. (1955). Drives and the C. N. S. (Conceptual Nervous System). *Psychological Review*, 62, 243–254.

Higgins, E. T. (2000). Making a good decision: Value from fit. *American Psychologist*, 55, 1217–1230.

Higgins, E. T. (2012). *Beyond pleasure and pain: How motivation works*. New York: Oxford University Press.

Higgins, E. T. (2016). Development of shared reality in childhood. *Perspectives on Psychological Science*, 11, 466–495.

Higgins, E. T., Cornwell, J. F. M., & Franks, B. (2014). "Happiness" and "The Good Life" as motives working together effectively. In A. J. Elliot (Ed.), *Advances in motivation science*, Volume 1 (pp. 135–180). New York: Academic Press.

Higgins, E. T., Kruglanski, A. W., & Pierro, A. (2003). Regulatory mode: Locomotion and assessment as distinct operations. In M. P. Zamma (Ed.), *Advances in experimental social psychology* (Vol. 35, pp. 293–344). San Diego, CA: Elsevier Academic Press.

Higgins, E. T., Rhodewalt, F., & Zanna, M. P. (1979). Dissonance motivation: Its nature, persistence, and reinstatement. *Journal of Experimental Social Psychology*, 15, 16–34.

Hull, C. L. (1943). *Principles of behavior*. New York: Appleton-Century-Crofts.

Hull, C. L. (1952). *A behavior system: An introduction to behavior theory concerning the individual organism*. New Haven: Yale University Press.

James, W. (1948). *The principles of psychology*. New York: The World Publishing Company. (Original publication, 1890.)

Kahneman, D., & Miller, D. T. (1986). Norm theory: Comparing reality to its alternatives. *Psychological Review*, 93, 136–153.

Keynes, J. M. (1951). *The general theory of employment, interest, and money*. (Original publication, 1936.) London: MacMillan & Co.

Kim, H., Franks, B., & Higgins, E. T. (2013). Evidence that self-regulatory mode affects retirement savings. *Journal of Aging & Social Policy*, 25, 248–263.

Kruglanski, A. W., Pierro, A., Mannetti, L., & Higgins, E. T. (2013). The distinct psychologies of "looking" and "leaping": Assessment and locomotion as the springs of action. *Personality and Social Psychology Compass*, 7, 79–92.

Kruglanski, A. W., Shah, J. Y., Fishbach, A., Friedman, R., Chun, W. Y., & Sleeth-Keppler, D. (2002). A theory of goal systems. In M. P. Zanna (Ed.), *Advances in experimental social psychology* (Vol. 34, pp. 331–378). San Diego, CA: Academic Press.

Kruglanski, A. W., Thompson, E. P., Higgins, E. T., Atash, M. N., Pierro, A., Shah, J. Y., & Spiegel, S. (2000). To "do the right thing" or to "just do it": Locomotion and assessment as distinct self-regulatory imperatives. *Journal of Personality & Social Psychology*, 79, 793–815.

Levine, J. M. (1999). Solomon Asch's legacy for group research. *Personality and Social Psychology Review*, 3, 358–364.

Lewin, K. (1935). *A dynamic theory of personality*. New York: McGraw-Hill.

Lewin, K. (1951). *Field theory in social science*. New York: Harper.

Loewenstein, G. (1994). The psychology of curiosity: A review and reinterpretation. *Psychological Bulletin*, 116(1), 75–98.

Mannetti, L., Leder, S., Insalata, L., Pierro, A., Higgins, T., & Kruglanski, A. (2009). The ant or the grasshopper in people's mind: How regulatory mode affects inter-temporal choice. *European Journal of Social Psychology*, 39, 1120–1125.

Mauro, R., Pierro, A., Mannetti, L., Higgins, E. T., & Kruglanski, A. W. (2009). The perfect mix: Regulatory complementarity and the speed-accuracy balance in group performance. *Psychological Science*, 20, 681–685.

McDougall, W. (1914). *An introduction to social psychology* (8th edition). Boston: Luce.

Miller, G. A., Galanter, E., & Pribram, K. H. (1960). *Plans and the structure of behavior*. New York: Holt, Rinehart, & Winston.

Nozick, R. (1974). *Anarchy, state, and utopia*. New York: Basic Books.

Osborne, S. R. (1977). The free food (contrafreeloading) phenomenon: A review and analysis. *Anim Learn Behav*, 5, 221–235.

Oxford English Dictionary, The Compact Edition, Volumes I & II (1971). Oxford: Oxford University Press.

Pervin, L. A. (Ed.) (1989). *Goal concepts in personality and social psychology*. Hillsdale, NJ: Erlbaum.

Piaget, J. (1952). *The origins of intelligence in children*. New York: International University Press.

Pierro, A., Leder, S., Mannetti, L., Higgins, E. T., Kruglanski, A. W., & Aiello, A. (2008). Regulatory mode effects on counterfactual thinking and regret. *Journal of Experimental Social Psychology*, 44, 321–329.

Pierro, A., Pica, G., Mauro, R., Kruglanski, A. W., & Higgins, E. T. (2012a). How regulatory modes work together: Locomotion-assessment complementarity in work performance. *TPM, Testing, Psychometry, Methodology in Applied Psychology*, 19, 247–262.

Pierro, A., Giacomantonio, M., Mannetti, L., Higgins, E. T., & Kruglanski, A. W. (2012b). Leaders as planner and movers: Supervisors' regulatory modes and subordinates' performance. *Journal of Applied Social Psychology*, 42, 2564–2582.

Pierro, A., Presaghi, F., Higgins, E. T., Klein, K. M., & Kruglanski, A. W. (2012c). Frogs and ponds: A multilevel analysis of the regulatory mode complementarity hypothesis. *Personality and Social Psychology Bulletin*, 38, 269–279.

Plato, trans. by Grube, G. M. A., revised by Reeve, C. D. C. (1992). *Republic*. Indianapolis, IN: Hackett Publishing Company. (Original work published c. 380 BC.)

Swann Jr, W. B. (1990). To be adored or to be known? The interplay of self-enhancement and self-verification. In E. T. Higgins and R. M. Sorrentino (Eds.), *Handbook of motivation and cognition: Foundations of social behavior* (Vol. 2, pp. 408–448). New York: Guilford.

Thorndike, E. L. (1911). *Animal intelligence*. New York: Macmillan.

Webster, D. M., & Kruglanski, A. W. (1994). Individual differences in need for cognitive closure. *Journal of Personality and Social Psychology*, 67, 1049–1062.

Wiener, N. (1948). *Cybernetics: Control and communication in the animal and the machine*. Cambridge, MA: M.I.T. Press.

White, R. W. (1959). Motivation reconsidered: The concept of competence. *Psychological Review*, 66, 297–333.

Woodworth, R. S. (1921). *Psychology: A study of mental life*. New York: Holt.

Woodworth, R. S. (1940). *Psychology: Fourth edition*. New York: Henry Holt & Company.

6

RISK AND SELF-DEFEATING BEHAVIORS AS GOAL PURSUIT RATHER THAN REGULATORY FAILURE

Catalina E. Kopetz

> Do you really think ... that it is weakness that yields to temptation? I tell you that there are terrible temptations that require strength, strength and courage, to yield to. To stake all one's life on a single moment, to risk everything on one throw, whether the stake be power or pleasure, I care not – there is no weakness in that.
>
> *(Oscar Wilde,* The Ideal Husband*)*

In one of his most important plays, *The Ideal Husband*, Wilde criticizes the hypocrisy of the Victorian society with its rigid sets of rules about what people *should do* and condemns what he believes to be false truth and false morality. In the paragraph above Sir Robert Chiltern responds to accusations of moral weakness and lack of willpower for not fulfilling the society expectations and for giving in to the temptation of money and power. One hundred and thirty years later and after more than one century of psychological research, the layperson and alas, the scientists as well, still judge people's behavior according to what they *should do*. Acts like substance use, overeating, overspending, driving under the influence, gambling, engagement in risky sexual behavior, and other self-defeating behaviors are treated as "irrational" and considered to be the result of lack of will power and a self-regulatory "failure" (Wagner & Heatherton, 2015). This perspective assumes that successful goal pursuit or self-regulation refers to following prescriptive norms and pursuing specific goals (e.g., health over immediate pleasures, long-term over short-term goals, etc.) and fails to take into account the function these behaviors serve (Kopetz & Orehek, 2015), in the moment, for the individual. Although they may interfere with concerns for health and safety and may appear irrational from the societal perspective, these behaviors satisfy important goals that the person may have in the moment. Indeed, as Herbert Simon argued, human behavior should be understood relative to the environment in which it evolved, as "adaptation of means to ends, of actions to goals…" (Simon, 1978) rather than to the tenets of classical rationality. People have reasons for what they do; their behavior (good or bad from an outsider's perspective) responds to their motivations and represents attempts to reach their goals. In line with this notion, I propose that individuals' self-defeating and seemingly "irrational" behavior serves as means to salient and important goals (Kopetz & Orehek, 2015; Kruglanski & Orehek, 2009) and therefore represents strategic goal pursuit rather than self-regulatory failure. To support my argument, I apply and extend Kruglanski's work on *Goals Systems* (Kruglanski et al., 2002) and *Cognitive Energetics* (Kruglanski et al., 2012) and demonstrate that self-defeating behavior is initiated and maintained according to the general principles of goal pursuit.

Risk and Self-defeating Behavior as Goal Pursuit

Human behavior is driven by goals, defined as cognitive representations of desirable end states interconnected with other goals and means of attainment (Kruglanski et al., 2002). Goal pursuit involves, but is not limited to, setting a goal, finding an appropriate means, and negotiating conflicts with other goals. This approach assumes that goal adoption, activation, and pursuit often happen in an unconscious manner (Custers & Aarts, 2010). Yet, it does not assume that successful goal pursuit or self-regulation refers to pursuing specific goals (e.g., health over immediate pleasures, long-term over short-term goals, etc.). Rather, it is concerned with the principles underlying goal pursuit in general, on a moment-to-moment basis (Kopetz & Orehek, 2015). In what follows I will briefly review these principles before I discuss their relevance for risk and self-defeating behavior.

Principles of Goal Pursuit

Goal activation and means selection

Goals can be consciously adopted or arise nonconsciously through environmental or internal cues cognitively associated with the goal (e.g., the smell of freshly brewed coffee may automatically activate the goal of having a cup thereof). Once adopted, goals are pursued through resource mobilization and selection of actions believed to advance the goal without the person being aware of the goal or its operation. Indeed, goal activation spreads to corresponding behavioral plans that are believed to be instrumental to goal attainment (e.g., through commonly shared beliefs) and stirs individuals to action (Aarts, Dijksterhuis, & DeVries, 2001; Kruglanski et al., 2002). For instance, negative affect may promote smoking as means to feel better.

Means are selected and implemented depending on their perceived instrumentality to one's goals. The stronger the association between that particular goal and the means is, the more instrumental the means is perceived and thus the higher the likelihood of selecting and implementing it when the goal becomes accessible (Kruglanski, 1996; Zhang, Fishbach, & Kruglanski, 2007). The individual's motivational map consisting of interrelated goals and means has important implications for understanding both initiation and perpetuation of self-defeating behaviors.

Counterfinality as a source of perceived instrumentality

Means are selected and implemented based on evidence that they have higher expectancy for goal attainment (e.g., previous experience, popular beliefs). However, an intriguing aspect of the relationship between goals and means refers to the fact that a means may be perceived as particularly instrumental to a focal goal to the extent to which it is counterfinal, or it undermines alternative goals (Kruglanski, Chernikova, Babush, Dugas, & Schumpe, 2015). This may be the case because people (naively) assume the association strength between a given construct (i.e., means) and other constructs in a network (i.e., goals) is a constant sum; thus a weak or even negative association between two nodes increases the strength of the remaining connections in the network and results in the means being perceived as uniquely attached to the focal goal (Kruglanski, 1996; Zhang et al., 2007).

Transfer of affect

Behaviors that are associated with successful goal pursuit acquire positive value through *transfer* of affect (Fishbach, Shah, & Kruglanski, 2004). The amount of emotional transfer from goals to means and, consequently, the emotional experience of engaging in that particular behavior, depend on the importance of the goal that they serve and the strength of the association between the behavior and the goal. Thus, behaviors that may be initially neutral, or even aversive (e.g., smoking) become desirable, or even goals in themselves capable of driving behavior in the absence of the original motivation.

Substitution

During goal pursuit, different means that serve the same goal may be substituted for one another (Kruglanski et al., 2002). For instance, one could exercise, read a book, or use alcohol to alleviate negative affect. The strength of a given means-goal association may be reduced by the simultaneous presence of alternative means. This is reminiscent of the classic "fan effect" discussed by Anderson (1974, 1983), wherein the greater the number of specific facts linked to a general mental construct, the less likely it is that any particular fact will be recalled upon the presentation of the construct. As a consequence, the higher the number of means associated with a goal, the weaker the association between any particular goal and means and the less likely that any of the means is deemed instrumental and enacted towards goal achievement (Kruglanski et al., 2002).

Goal conflict resolution

Multiple goal representations may become simultaneously activated and may produce competing behavioral tendencies (Kopetz, Hofmann, & Wiers, 2014; Orehek & Vazeou-Nieuwenhuis, 2013). In such situations, the person may try to find *multifinal* means that satisfy multiple goals at the same time (e.g., riding a bike for transportation and exercise) (Kruglanski, Kopetz et al., 2013). When one goal becomes more important than its alternatives, people may engage in *goal shielding* (Shah, Friedman, & Kruglanski, 2002) in which they inhibit the weaker alternatives in favor of the prioritized goal. Such mechanisms facilitate mobilization and allocation of the resources necessary for goal pursuit (Kruglanski, et al., 2012).

One consequence of goal shielding is *motivated distortion* whereby the information relevant to goal pursuit is actively distorted to fit with the current motivational state (Bélanger, Kruglanski, Chen, & Orehek, 2014). For instance, a smoker may be fully aware of the negative consequences associated with smoking, but may actively choose to focus his attention on the relaxing aspects of the behavior.

Mobilization of resources

Goal pursuit is dependent on resource mobilization and executive control (Botvinick & Braver, 2015; Dijksterhuis & Aarts, 2010; Kruglanski et al., 2002). Resources include, but are not limited to, physical and mental energy and various forms of executive functioning, and are generally understood to be limited and depletable (Baumeister, Bratslavsky, Muraven, & Tice, 1998; Gailliot et al., 2007; Muraven, Tice, & Baumeister, 1998; Vohs & Heatherton, 2000; but see Kruglanski et al., 2012 for a review). Resources are necessary to find and implement appropriate means, persist in the face of obstacles, and inhibit alternative goals or temptations that may thwart goal pursuit. Thus, when goals become active (consciously or unconsciously), they mobilize both physical resources (e.g., increased heart rate and systolic blood pressure, pupil dilatation) as well as mental resources (e.g. attention is directed to information relevant to goal pursuit; Brehm & Self, 1989; Bijleveld, Custers, & Aaarts, 2009; Wright, Contrada, & Patane, 1986). Resource mobilization is a function of goal importance and difficulty of pursuit. The more important a goal is, or the more difficult goal pursuit is perceived to be, the more resources are required. When the goal is of little importance, or it is easy to pursue (e.g. getting to work every morning through a series of well learned behaviors), the amount of resources necessary and therefore mobilized is minimal. On the other hand, when the goal is highly important (e.g., submitting a grant proposal), or when its pursuit cannot rely on easily available and well-learned means, or it requires persistence in a tedious task and inhibition of alternative goals (temptations and distractions), the amount of resources necessary for goal pursuit is higher. Indeed, increased goal importance (through the manipulation of rewards) enhances executive control at different levels: attenuating the influence of distractors (Padmala & Pessoa, 2011), enhancing encoding and retrieval of episodic memory (Adcock et al., 2006), and enhancing the response-inhibition (Leotti & Wager, 2010), which may in turn facilitate goal attainment. Note that according to the perspective presented here, the mobilization of resources does not vary with the content of the goals (as often assumed by popular dual-process models). In other words, smoking a cigarette may require as many resources if not more (e.g., to inhibit concerns about one's health) as resisting the temptation to eat of piece of cake when on a diet. It is the accessibility, the importance, and the difficulty of goal pursuit rather than the content that influence the extent of resource mobilization.

I propose that self-defeating behavior follows these general principles of goal pursuit and therefore does not necessarily represent irrational choice or self-regulatory failure. Specifically: 1) self-defeating behavior is enacted when perceived as instrumental to individual's goals; the instrumentality of the behavior and consequently its likelihood of being selected and enacted varies depending on the presence of alternative means (substitution) or goals that the behavior may serve (multifinality) or interfere with (counterfinality); 2) engagement in self-defeating behaviors requires goal conflict resolution and may result in the inhibition of alternative considerations for health or safety; consequently, inhibition of alternative goals may facilitate distorted beliefs about the behavior that could in turn contribute to the initiation and maintenance of that particular behavior; 3) these processes are resource-dependent such that self-defeating behavior might be enhanced rather than diminished in the presence of cognitive resources for control. This may be the case because availability of resources may allow individuals to inhibit alternative goals and/or to focus their attention on relevant information and process it in a way that enhances goal pursuit. In what follows I provide empirical evidence that risk taking in general and in particular substance use, risky sexual behavior, overeating, and self-harm, follow the principles outlined above.

Self-defeating Behavior as Means to People's Goals

Many self-defeating behaviors including substance use, drink driving, risky sexual behavior, self-harm, etc., which involve the potential for danger or harm while also providing an opportunity to obtain some form of rewards or benefits, have been studied under the umbrella of risk behaviors. Risk behavior has often been discussed in relation to social acceptance (Baumeister, 1997; Rawn & Vohs, 2011), prevention-related goals (Scholer et al., 2010), achievement goals (Atkinson, 1957; Lopes, 1987), and regulation of negative affect (Leith & Baumeister, 1996;

Tice et al., 2001). In line with the principles underlying the association between goals and means, the likelihood of engagement in risk behavior should increase to the extent to which this behavior is perceived as instrumental to relevant goals that become accessible. In line with this notion, Kopetz, Belanger, Lejuez, & Johnson (2016a) showed increased risk taking as a function of the perceived instrumentality of risk behavior to prevention versus promotion goals. Specifically, we measured participants' risk taking as a function of their regulatory focus (promotion vs. prevention) and the instrumentality of the risk behavior. Regulatory focus refers to individuals' goal to achieve positive outcomes (promotion-oriented goals) or to avoid negative outcomes (prevention-oriented goals, Higgins, 1997). Risk behavior could be perceived instrumental to both of these goals depending on whether the possibility for gains versus loses is emphasized. Thus, risk behavior will be perceived as more instrumental and enacted to achieve one's promotion-related goals if gains are emphasized. By contrast, risk behavior will be perceived as more instrumental and enacted toward prevention-orientation goals when negative consequences or potential losses are emphasized. This may be the case because in situations involving loss, risky options offer the possibility of maintaining or returning to the status quo, which is the primary motivation of prevention-focused individuals (Scholer et al., 2010). In line with these notions, participants high on promotion focus engaged in more risk taking on a behavioral task (The Balloon Analogue Risk Task, or BART; Lejuez et al., 2002) when the instructions emphasized the amount of money that participants could *make* during the task. However, participants high on prevention focus took more risk on the BART when the instructions emphasized the amount of money that they could lose during the task (Kopetz et al., 2016a).

Although this study used a lab paradigm to measure risk behavior, there is evidence that real world risk behavior such as substance use and risky sexual behavior are enacted to fulfill people's goals. For instance, drugs are often taken to socialize and fit in, to achieve a pleasant drug "high," to escape an aversive withdrawal "low," or cope with negative affect (Kopetz, Lejuez, Wiers, & Kruglanski, 2013). To give only a few examples, opiate-dependent participants were faster to respond to drug-related vs. neutral words that followed withdrawal-related sentences (Weinstein, Feldtkeller, Myles, Law, & Nutt, 2000), suggesting that drug use becomes accessible as a means to fulfill the goal of coping with negative affect associated with withdrawal. Drug use may become accessible as a means to fulfill social goals. For instance, marijuana users reported stronger motivation to use marijuana, and spent less time reading drug prevention information after being subliminally primed with social cues (i.e., the name of individuals who use marijuana), especially when such cues represented close social relationships (Leander, Shah, & Chartrand, 2009).

Risky sexual behavior (RSB) including sex with multiple partners, with casual and commercial partners, and unprotected sex may also be enacted to fulfill specific goals (e.g., need for communion, Cooper, 2010). Indeed, in several studies, across community samples, college students, and substance users, we found that women who have experienced interpersonal violence are more likely to engage in risky sexual behavior (RSB, Woerner, Kopetz, Lechner, & Lejuez, 2016; Woerner, Kopetz, & Arriaga, 2016). This may be the case because interpersonal violence potentially disrupts individual's expectations of secure relationships and may result in increased vigilance for harm in relationships, which may manifest as fear of being rejected by others (anxiety) and/or the discomfort with closeness or emotional intimacy. In such cases, RSB may become a convenient means to interpersonal connection without closeness or emotional intimacy. In line with these notions, we found that avoidant attachment mediates the relationship between interpersonal victimization and RSB. Finally, this relationship is stronger among prevention-oriented individuals, who are more likely to internalize violence as interpersonal loss and a threat to one's security in interpersonal interactions and may engage in RSB to eliminate the loss. Interestingly, these effects did not extend to other risk behaviors (i.e. substance use) supporting the notion that RSB may indeed represent a means to interpersonal connection rather than a general tendency toward risk taking.

RSB is often associated with drug use and is typically attributed to the pharmacological effects of the drugs. However, recent studies suggest that engagement in RSB occurs when it is perceived as instrumental to individuals' goals of drug obtainment. Indeed, in one study increased accessibility of the drug obtainment goal (through cocaine-related primes) resulted in faster approach tendency toward sex exchange words (crack babe, hooker, prostitute, rock star, turn a trick) in a joystick task. Notably, this effect emerged only for participants for whom sex exchange represented an instrumental means to drug obtainment despite their self-reported intentions to avoid such behavior (Kopetz, Collado, & Lejuez, 2015).

These findings challenge the self-regulatory failure approach, which suggests that most of these behaviors are not goal-directed; rather they represent the result of automatic associations or impulses (which are seen as non-motivational) coupled with weak controlled processes (e.g., Hofmann et al., 2008; Stacy & Wiers, 2010; Strack & Deutsch, 2004). Rather, they suggest that people may engage in risk behavior strategically when the behavior is perceived to be instrumental to their goals. These goals can be chronically accessible (prevention or promotion oriented goals, need for intimacy and communion) or can be momentarily activated by internal or external cues (e.g., drug obtainment) as the individual moves through his/her environment. What is important here is that enactment of risk behavior as means to one's goals follows the same principles regardless of the type of risk behavior and goal content.

Transfer of affect from goals to risk and self-defeating behavior

The association between goals and behaviors that are perceived as instrumental for goal attainment are more than cognitive associations. According to the transfer of affect principle the desirability or positive value of the goal is transferred to instrumental means. This principle may explain some of the most interesting and puzzling aspects of risk behaviors, namely engagement in risk behavior in the absence of a hedonic experience, or even when the behavior is accompanied by negative experiences. For instance, although addictive drugs can produce extremely pleasant affective states, people describe their first experience with drugs as awkward, uncomfortable, and physically unpleasant (DiFranza et al., 2002; Fallon & Rozin, 1983; Moore & Weiss, 1995). Nicotine is highly addictive, but it does not produce euphoria or other strong hedonic states. Additionally, many drugs can actually produce strong dysphoric states. Furthermore, if experienced, the subjective hedonic experience of a drug does not necessarily predict drug seeking and administration (Falk, Dews, & Schuster, 1983). For instance, opioid "postaddicts" would press a lever to get an injection of morphine, although four out of five participants would not distinguish the subjective effects of morphine from a placebo (Lamb et al., 1991). Many addicts report that they are miserable, that their life is in ruins, and that the drug is not even great anymore. Given that the negative consequences of continued drug use far outweigh the pleasurable effects, self-administration behavior should be extinguished. And yet, even if at conscious level, the addicts may be aware of all the negative consequences of continued drug use, deplore their situation, report that the drug does not provide great pleasure, drug craving persists and the addict continues to seek and use the drugs. This dissociation between "liking" and "wanting" has been typically approached as irrational (Berridge, 1999, 2003) and explained in terms of pathological neuroadaptations (e.g., Robinson & Berridge, 2004); specifically, drugs, food, or other rewarding stimuli are assumed to sensitize the neural circuits involved in reward processing and to alter the frontocortical regions that mediate the executive control such that the person becomes *incapable* to resist the temptations even when they are not associated with subjective pleasure anymore.

The principle of emotional transfer may offer insights into the psychological processes accompanying these neuroadaptations and suggests that doing something in the absence of subjective experience of pleasure is not necessarily irrational or pathological. People may start using drugs or engaging in other risk behaviors as *means* to goals (e.g., social acceptance). However, the behavior may become associated with the positive outcomes of goal attainment and may therefore become valuable (and even an end in itself as in the case of drugs) and may promote future pursuit. Indeed, studies employing measures of implicit attitudes (e.g., traditional and modified versions of the Implicit Associations Test) revealed that across different substance-use categories (e.g. drinking, cannabis, etc.), substance users evaluate their drug of choice more positively than non-substance users. Furthermore, such evaluations predict increased levels of substance use (e.g., Houben & Wiers, 2008).

Substituting alternative means for risk taking and self-defeating behavior

As outlined above, the principle of substitution suggests that the likelihood of engagement in one behavior as means to a goal decreases when alternative means that serve the same goal are present. However, this principle is rarely applied in our attempts to prevent or reduce risk behavior. Rather, numerous prevention strategies (Botvin, 1990; Cronce & Larimer, 2011; Hawkins, Catalano, & Miller, 1992; Larimer & Cronce, 2002) designed to reduce risk behavior (e.g. drink driving, smoking, etc.) are based on the economics model of rationality. Specifically, they assume that informing the public about the negative consequences of the behavior should decrease its value, or its perceived instrumentality and therefore the likelihood of engaging in the behavior. However, most of these campaigns have proved unsuccessful (e.g., Cronce & Larimer, 2011) and might sometimes have done more harm than good (Crano & Burgoon, 2002). Given that people engage in these behaviors as means to their goals, emphasizing the negative aspects of the behavior may strengthen the instrumentality of these behaviors (according to the counterfinality principle). Alternatively, risk information may simply prompt a dissonance reduction process. People may attempt to counteract the negative information with evidence regarding the instrumentality of the behavior for their goals, which may in turn provide justification to continue to engage in that particular behavior.

By contrast, the principle of substitutability (Kruglanski et al., 2002; Kruglanski et al., 2015) suggests that engagement in risk behavior may be decreased by introducing alternative means to the goals that the risk behavior serves. This may be the case because the perceived instrumentality of a means to a goal, decreases to the extent to which alternative means are available to goal pursuit.

In one study we explored risk taking in relation to sensation seeking. Sensation seeking is defined as the need for varied, novel, and complex sensations and experiences (Zuckerman, 1979). In line with the notion of substitutability, we assumed that engagement in risk taking would decrease even among high sensation seeking participants when an alternative strategy was introduced. In this study, we measured participants' sensation seeking. To manipulate instrumentality of the means, in an affective conditioning paradigm, we paired "risk" with negative adjectives (i.e. "bad") similar to the prevention campaigns emphasizing the negative aspects of risk behavior. In a second condition, we paired "caution" with positive adjectives (e.g. "good") in an attempt to introduce an alternative, caution-based strategy to pursue the goal for novel experiences (Custers & Aarts, 2005). Although the need for new and exciting experiences is typically associated with risk taking, one could achieve the same motivation in a cautions manner. For instance, when traveling to a new and exotic country one could take a risky approach and fly there without checking the appropriate means of transportation, lodging, or vaccines. Or, the person could be more cautious and prepare in advance for traveling.

Finally, participants completed the BART as a measure of risk taking. The results showed that high sensation seeking was positively related to risk taking, but only when the negative aspects of risk taking were emphasized. When an alternative means was introduced by emphasizing the positive aspects of being cautious, sensation seeking was not related to risk taking anymore; in fact, in this condition, risk taking decreased compared with the condition where risk was associated with nega-tive aspect, even among participants high on sensation seeking (Kopetz et al., 2016a). These results support the notion that the presence of alternative means (i.e., behave cautiously) to one's current motivation (i.e., sensation seeking) may decrease the likelihood that the motivation is fulfilled through engagement in risk behavior. In other words, engagement in risk behavior may be decreased by substituting it with alternative non-risky behaviors that fulfill the same goal.

Outside the lab, the principle of substitution could be applied to reduce engagement in risk and self-defeating behavior. For instance, previous studies sug-gest that social relationships may be substitutable for smoking and other addictive activities (DeGrandpre & Bickel, 1996; Fisher, 1996). In line with these notions, we attempted to reduce smoking behavior in participants with depressive symp-toms. Regulation of negative affect has long been identified as a strong motiva-tional force in initiation as well as maintenance of addictive behaviors (Baker et al., 2004), and in particular for tobacco smoking (e.g., Kassel, Stroud, & Paronis, 2003; Shiffman & Waters 2004). According to the principle of substitution, strengthening the association between alternative behaviors to smoking (alternative means) and negative affect should increase the accessibility of these activities and therefore the likelihood that the person engages in them while detracting from smoking. Parti-cipants identified as smokers with depressive symptoms were trained across four sessions in two conditions using a modified Approach Bias Modification procedure (Wiers, Eberl, Rinck, Becker, & Lindenmeyer, 2011). Negative affect was induced in both conditions. Subsequently, in the experimental condition, participants used a joystick and were trained to avoid (push away) smoking-related targets and to approach (push towards) alternative rewarding activities that were ideographically selected during a baseline assessment. In the control condition, participants pushed and pulled an equal amount of smoking and alternative activity-related targets. Compared with the participants in the control condition, those in the experimental condition showed an increase in the accessibility of the alternative activity relative to smoking and a decrease in depressive symptoms. Furthermore, participants in the experimental condition smoked less over the same period of time and took longer to relapse to smoking than participants in the control condition; however, the dif-ferences were not statistically significant (Kopetz, MacPherson, Mitchell, Huston-Ludlam, & Wiers, 2017).

Counterfinality of risk and self-defeating behaviors

One question that is rarely addressed in the literature is why people engage in risk and self-defeating behaviors as means to their goals as opposed to finding alter-native means to fulfill these goals. One intuitive answer is that they are not aware of the negative consequences of these behaviors. But there is now substantial research suggesting that, in fact, people know and understand the consequences of risk behavior. One intriguing possibility is that being aware of these consequences may actually increase the perceived instrumentality of these behaviors to various goals and motivations that people may have in the moment. This possibility is suggested by the principle of counterfinality (Kruglanski et al., 2015), whereby a means is perceived as particularly instrumental to one's goals to the extent to which it interferes with or is detrimental to alternative goals.

Research on substance use provides evidence that supports this notion. For instance, negative expectancies (i.e., expectancies of negative consequences) associated with substance use are positively related to risky substance use (i.e., binge drinking) (Li & Dingle, 2012) and dependence (Connor, Gullo, Feeney, & Young, 2011). Furthermore, substance-dependent individuals believe that substance use has greater negative consequences to a greater extent than students (Li & Dingle, 2012), but continue to use because of its instrumentality to social goals or to alleviate negative affect. In other words, substance users might perceive using drugs as a particularly effective means to one's goal to the extent to which it interferes with other goals.

To provide further support for these notions, in an exploratory study we asked participants to rate 12 behaviors (e.g., smoking, substance use, sleeping, joining a club) in terms of riskiness and interference with other goals. Perceived riskiness was positively related to perceived interference with other goals suggesting that people do perceive engagement in risk behavior as detrimental to different goals they may have. In a subsequent experimental study, we assessed participants' preference for risk behaviors (compared with non-risk behaviors) as a function of participants' regulatory orientation (assessment) and motivation for social connection. Assessment constitutes an evaluative aspect of self-regulation; thus, people high in assessment are particularly concerned with making the "right" choice and critically evaluate alternative means and goals to decide which are the best to pursue (Kruglanski et al., 2000). We reasoned that they should be particularly sensitive to the instrumentality of different means or behaviors to their current goal or motivation. In this case, the motivation was social acceptance, which was introduced through a social rejection procedure. In addition to their concern for the best option or decision, assessors are also very sensitive to the social context. Social rejection would therefore render the goal of being socially accepted more accessible. The results showed that among participants high on assessment, social rejection was associated with a preference for risk behaviors (compared with non-risk behaviors). Furthermore, social exclusion resulted in increased perceived riskiness of the behaviors, which in turn increased perceived instrumentality and preference for risk behaviors. In other words, when motivated to regain social acceptance, individuals high in assessment attempt to make the right choice and find the best means; interestingly, risk behaviors are perceived to be particularly instrumental under these circumstances, not despite their negative consequences, but because of them.

People's failure to incorporate risk information or information about the potential negative consequences into their decisions has often been treated as irrational and attributed to lack of self-control (e.g., Wagner & Heatherton, 2015) or to reasoning errors, biases, and heuristics that often characterize individuals' judgment and behavior (e.g., Kahneman, Slovic, & Tversky, 1982). Regardless of the approach, such deviation from "rationality" has been largely explained in terms of an individual's limited capacity to resist momentary temptations or to handle real-world complexity. However, the findings reviewed above suggest that people *do* incorporate risk information into their decisions, but in a way that supports their current goal pursuit rather than in a manner suggested by normative standards.

Resolution of goals in conflict with risk and self-defeating behavior

If we were to ask people what are some of their most important goals in life, they will surely mention that they want to be healthy, successful, have meaningful relationships, etc. In many cases engaging in risk or self-defeating behavior interferes with these goals. This may signal that the behavior is particularly instrumental to one's current goal (e.g., regulation of negative affect) according to the counterfinality principle. However, to engage in risk behavior as a means to one goal, the person has to forego alternative goals that are also important such as health, safety, etc. This puzzling phenomenon whereby the person seems to act in favor of short-term outcomes but against some of the most fundamental long-term motivations has often been explained by a lack of self-control (e.g., Fishbach & Trope, 2005; Fujita, Trope, Liberman, & Levin-Sagi, 2006; Mischel, 1974). However, this approach assumes that successful self-regulation refers to following prescriptive norms and pursuing specific goals (e.g., health over immediate pleasures, long-term over short-term goals, etc.). By contrast, one could argue that engagement in self-defeating or risk behavior, even to the detriment of other goals, represents the pursuit of the goal that is the most important in the moment. But how could the person "forget" goals related to safety or health? The goal that the risk behavior serves may be activated by external or internal cues (a cigarette for a "would be" quitter, negative affect). The psychological saliency and proximity of this goal reduces the saliency and importance of alternative goals through a process of goal shielding (Shah et al., 2002). Thus, although the person may value health, safety, meaningful relationships, financial security, etc., these goals may be momentarily inhibited and may fail to constrain individual's behavior. Several scholars have recently argued that self-control failure does not necessarily imply bad judgment or lack of will power, but rather people's failure to identify and experience a conflict (possibly because the long-term goals are inhibited) (e.g., Fishbach & Converse, 2011). Some have even argued that pursuing momentarily important goals through engagement in risk behavior may actually require active self-control to overcome negative experiences and to inhibit alternative concerns related to health and safety (Rawn & Vohs, 2011).

For instance, Loewenstein (1996, 2007) suggests that drug craving elicited by cues associated with substance use is similar to visceral factors such as hunger, thirst, physical pain, etc. At an intermediate level, the individual experiences a tension, or a conflict between what he/she wants to behave and how he/she should behave and may deal with such conflict in a relatively optimal manner. At high levels however, visceral factors overwhelm decision-making altogether superseding volitional control of behavior. Drug craving, just like other visceral factors, narrows individual's attention and focuses it on the highest priority goal, which is mitigating the craving. Consequently, the behavior that alleviates the craving is facilitated whereas the behavior that interferes with it is eliminated. In other words, maintenance of substance use does not necessarily reflect deficient control processes, but fulfillment of the most important current motivation. Volitional control becomes irrelevant, because there is no alternative concern other than mitigating the drug craving. Thus, once addicted, even if the individual recognizes that abstinence may be the best course of action, desire to remain abstinent dissipates when an intense drug craving is experienced.

Eating often involves balancing two goals: food enjoyment and weight control. The goal of eating enjoyment may become spontaneously activated by cues signaling palatable food (e.g., the smell of food) and may result in diet violation and unhealthy eating (Stroebe, van Koningsbruggen, Papies, & Aarts, 2013) through different processes: 1) increasing the appeal of high-caloric, fattening food through a process of transfer of affect (Fishbach et al, 2004) and 2) inhibition of the weight control goal. This is particularly relevant for restrained eaters, for whom the weight control goal is particularly important supporting the notion that inter-goal inhibition is a function of goal importance. When the eating enjoyment goal and the weight control goal are equally important, eating behavior reflects pursuit of both goals simultaneously by choosing multifinal means (foods) that are both tasty and healthy (Kopetz, Faber, Fishbach, & Kruglanski, 2011). Yet, when the weight control goal becomes prioritized over the eating enjoyment goal, people successfully and spontaneously inhibit food temptations (Fishbach, Friedman, & Kruglanski, 2003).

An interesting possibility is that goals such as abstinence, weight control, and safety do not actually get inhibited when the person decides to engage in risk or self-defeating behavior and pursue the goal that these behaviors serve. Rather, the person may "keep these goals in mind" and convince himself/herself that he/she can pursue both goals simultaneously by finding multifinal means. Imagine a driver who has been drinking and faces the dilemma of whether to drive home or call a taxi. He or she may decide that even under the influence, it could be safe to drive by "going slowly on the right lane and keeping the eyes open for police."

To summarize, understanding how one negotiates multiple, and often conflicting goals is crucial for the understanding of risk and self-defeating behavior. Engagement in these behaviors has been too often labeled as "failure" and "irrational" and has been explained in terms of lack of will power and lack of capacity to exercise self-control. However, as I am hoping the section above illustrates, the issue may not be that the person *cannot* exercise control over his/her behavior. The person may not *want* to control the behavior because in that particular moment, risk taking facilitates the pursuit of the most important goal.

Mobilization of resources

Although the idea that goal pursuit requires resources is widely accepted, most theoretical models assume that resources are mobilized for the pursuit of long-term goals such as health. When resources are lacking because people are tired, depleted, distracted, emotionally disregulated, or under the influence of alcohol and drugs, they succumb to temptations; they overeat, relapse to drug use, engage in risky sexual behavior, or become aggressive (Baumeister et al., 1998; Gailliot et al., 2007; Muraven et al., 1998; Vohs & Heatherton, 2000; Hofmann et al., 2008; Mann & Ward, 2004, 2007; Ward & Mann, 2000; Everitt & Robbins, 2005). However, in the presence of sufficient processing resources, the individual may be able to assess the relative value of the temptation compared with its alternatives and might well refrain from pursuit of the immediate goal despite the initial impulse. By contrast, I propose that in many cases, risk and self-defeating behavior as means to goal achievement requires resources: the person who decides to use drugs requires resources to overcome the obstacles associated with procuring and using the drugs (i.e. finding a drug dealer, avoiding the police, overcoming the pain associated with sticking a needle in one's arm). Similarly, the person who decides to engage in self-harm requires a tremendous amount of energy to go against his or her survival instinct and engage in mutilating and even suicidal behavior. In several studies, we obtained evidence that indeed, risk behavior is augmented rather than decreased by the presence of regulatory resources.

Risk behavior, including overeating (Heatherton & Baumeister, 1991; Tice et al., 2001), substance use (Baker et al., 2004), risky sexual behavior (Bousman et al., 2009), and self-injury (Selby & Joiner, 2013) has often been studied in the context of negative affect. Emotional distress presumably shifts an individual's priority on emotion regulation and depletes the individual of the resources necessary to consider the negative consequences and to control immediate gratification increasing the likelihood of risk behavior. However, according to my analysis, if risk behavior is actively implemented as a strategy to regulate emotional distress, the presence of cognitive resources should increase rather than decrease the likelihood of engaging in this kind of behavior. To test this possibility, we manipulated the goal of emotion regulation by engaging participants in a high-distressing (vs. low-distressing) task. The amount of cognitive resources was also manipulated by asking participants to remember an eight-digit number in the low resources condition (vs. a one-digit number in the control condition). Finally, to control for the effect of negative consequences, in one condition we emphasized the possibility to win money on the task (the positive consequences condition); in the second condition we emphasized the possibility to lose money on the task (the negative consequences condition). Risk taking was again assessed with the BART. The results showed that in the low distress condition, there was no difference in risk taking between the positive and the negative consequences

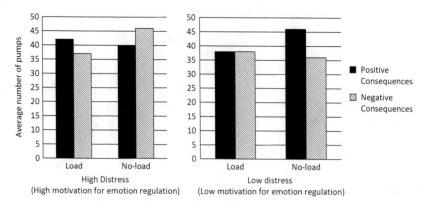

FIGURE 6.1 Engagement in risk taking as a function of motivation for emotion regulation, saliency of consequences, and cognitive resources

conditions when participants were under load. When they were not under load,
they appear to have followed the cues in the environment and risked more when
positive (vs. negative) consequences were emphasized. The picture was completely different in the distress condition, when participants presumably had the
goal to regulate their negative affect induced by the task. When they were under
load, they risked more when positive consequences were made salient than when
negative consequences were emphasized. However, in the no load condition,
when negative consequences were emphasized, participants risked *more* thanwhen
positive consequences were emphasized. The findings are presented in Figure 6.1.
The saliency of the goal of emotion regulation coupled with the availability of
cognitive resources might have allowed them to consider the negative consequences and possibly to use them as an indicator of the instrumentality of the
behavior (according to the counterfinality principle) (Kopetz. et al., 2016a).

In the real world, heightened negative emotionality and poor executive control are considered some of the most important factors of self-harm (e.g., cutting,
burning, biting), which is a symptom of Borderline Personality Disorder (BPD)
(APA, 2000), but it occurs in non-clinical populations as well (Briere & Gil,
1998; Whitlock et al., 2011). In line with the findings above, self-harm may be a
strategic response to meet emotion regulation goals. In two studies, women with
BPD showed increased risk tendency when the goal of emotion regulation
becomes important (i.e., under distress) and when the expectancy of goal attainment is high. In contrast to previous approaches, which assumed that emotional
distress impairs executive control and results in impulsive behavior, these findings
show that risk behavior under emotional distress happens when cognitive
resources are ample (Matusiewicz, Kopetz, Waverling, Ellis, & Lejuez, 2015).

Risk taking among adolescents is another phenomenon typically attributed to a
developmentally normative gap between motivational-affective processes on one
hand and cognitive control on the other hand (Somerville & Casey, 2010;

Steinberg, 2007). Early psychosocial deprivation is often believed to heighten adolescents' vulnerability to risk taking due to its deleterious effects on different processes critical for executive function such as working memory and inhibitory control (Hostinar et al., 2012; Lovallo, 2013; Lovallo et al., 2013; McDermott et al., 2012, 2013). However, recent findings from a randomized control trial of foster care present a different picture. In this study, children institutionalized at or soon after birth were randomly assigned either to be removed from institutions and placed into a family/foster care intervention or to remain in institutions receiving care as usual. These children were subsequently followed through 12 years of age and compared with a sample of children who had never been institutionalized on risk taking behavior, motivation (i.e., sensation seeking) and executive control (i.e., planning). The findings suggest that early psychosocial deprivation did indeed have deleterious effects on executive control; children who were raised in institutions performed significantly worse on planning compared with their foster care and never institutionalized counterparts. Interestingly enough, deprivation did not increase risk taking, on the contrary: institutionalized children showed significantly less risk taking than foster care and children who were never institutionalized. Furthermore, this effect was moderated by executive control and mediated by sensation seeking, an important developmental motivation (Zuckerman, 1979, p. 10). In other words, psychosocial deprivation decreased engagement in risk taking among adolescents through its impact on motivations associated with risk taking. Furthermore, the impact of early psychosocial deprivation on sensation seeking and consequently on engagement in risk taking is further reduced, rather than enhanced by its deleterious effects on executive control (Kopetz et al., 2016c).

Motivated distortion

One question that bags answers at this point is what are the resources necessary for? As suggested above, engagement in risk behavior does require the inhibition of the goals with which this behavior interferes with a process that is resource dependent (Bélanger, Lafrenière, Vallerand, & Kruglanski, 2013; Kruglanski et al., 2012). Thus, one possibility is that resources are necessary to inhibit alternative goals. Another possibility is that resources are necessary to ignore or even distort the negative consequences of the behavior, a process known as *motivated distortion* (Kunda, 1990) whereby the information relevant to goal pursuit is actively distorted to fit with the current motivational state (Bélanger, Kruglanski, Chen, & Orehek, 2014). For instance, a smoker may be fully aware of the negative consequences associated with smoking, but may actively choose to focus his attention on the relaxing aspects of the behavior. Indeed, despite known negative consequences associated with smoking, a heightened motivation to smoke (i.e., a craving) predisposes smokers to overemphasize the positive outcomes of smoking (Kirchner & Sayette, 2007) and to underestimate personal vulnerability to smoking-related disease (Windschitl, 2002).

To test these notions we conducted a study on participants' willingness to engage in drunk driving. We reasoned that people decide to drink and drive because driving is the most instrumental means to the goal of reaching one's destination quickly and conveniently. According to the theoretical analysis presented here, the decision to drink and drive may be facilitated by people's cognitive resources that would allow them to distort the consequences of the behavior in line with their motivation. Thus, we assessed participants' self-reported likelihood of drinking and driving as well as their perceived riskiness of the behavior as a function of convenience motivation and working memory capacity. To manipulate the convenience motivation we presented our participants with a hypothetical drinking and driving scenario (MacDonald, Zanna, & Fong 1995) and asked them to imagine themselves in that scenario. The scenario was designed to induce the motivation to get home conveniently as well as to present driving as an instrumental means to fulfill this motivation. Specifically, participants read about hanging out with friends and the event escalating into a party where they consumed more alcohol than anticipated. In the high motivation condition, the participant was asked to imagine feeling dead tired and simply longing to go home and go to bed. The scenario suggested the possibility of calling for a taxi but emphasized its limitations (e.g., having to wait for it to arrive). In the low motivation condition, participants were asked to imagine having a less compelling reason to drive home – they wanted to get home in time to make plans with roommates for going to brunch the next day. Again, the scenario suggested the possibility of calling for a taxi without emphasizing the limitations. To explore the role of cognitive resources, participants completed a working memory measure (OSPAN; La Pointe & Engle, 1990). They were then asked to estimate the probability that they would drive home and to rate the perceived riskiness of driving under the influence. To evaluate the extent to which the decision to drive under the influence is specific to their current motivation (i.e., convenience) rather than reflecting a general risk taking propensity, participants also completed the BART. The results showed that in the high convenience motivation participants self-reported a higher probability of driving under the influence compared with the low convenience motivation condition. Interestingly this effect was moderated by their working memory capacity, such that in the high convenience motivation, participants high in working memory capacity reported higher probability of drinking and driving compared to participants low in working memory capacity. In the low motivation condition, there was no difference in the self-reported likelihood of driving between high and low working memory capacity. Finally, the interaction between motivation and working memory capacity on risk behavior was mediated by perceived riskiness of drinking and driving, such that high motivation, coupled with high working memory reduced the perceived riskiness of the behavior, which in turn increased the self-reported likelihood of drinking and driving. These effects were specific to drinking and driving and did not extend to participants' general risk taking propensity as measured by the BART (Kopetz et al., 2016a).

The studies above further support the notion that risk and self-defeating behavior may represent strategic goal pursuit rather than self-regulatory failure. Mobilization of resources is one of the hallmarks of goal pursuit. Many models suggest that lack of resources increases the vulnerability of risk taking and other self-defeating behaviors whereas the availability of cognitive resources increases ability to resist temptation and to pursue their long-term goals. However, in line with the notions presented here, risk taking as a means to different goals that people may have in the moment is also facilitated by the availability of resources cognitive resources. These resources may allow the individual to inhibit alternative goals and/or to distort the information in line with his/her current motivation, which in turn facilitates engagement in risk and self-defeating behaviors.

Conclusions

Acting in a manner (e.g., drug use) that is inconsistent with other objectives (e.g., health) has typically been considered a case of self-regulation failure. However, what may appear to be failure with regard to some goals may represent success with regard to other goals (e.g., to fit in). In other words, people engage in self-defeating behaviors because they perceive them as instrumental means to their current goals. The instrumentality of the behavior and therefore the likelihood of engaging in it is augmented by the extent to which the behavior is perceived as detrimental to other goals and reduced by the presence of alternative means that serve the same goal. People do understand the harm that may result from these behaviors. However, activation of the goals they satisfy renders thoughts related to negative consequences momentarily irrelevant, facilitating their pursuit. Importantly, engagement in self-defeating behaviors often involves effortful processes such as inhibition of alternative goals rather than reflecting poor self-regulation. Therefore, to the extent self-defeating behaviors follow the general principles of goal pursuit, they can be portrayed as self-regulatory success rather than failure.

I do not suggest that there is no self-regulatory failure, nor that self-control is not an important principle of goal pursuit. However, approaching self-regulatory success in terms of acting according to specific goals and standards (e.g. long-term vs. short-term temptations) and overemphasizing the self-control principle without taking into account other principles of goal pursuit and the function that the behavior may have for the individual limits our capacity to understand and prevent self-defeating behaviors. Self-regulation success or failure should be evaluated by *the extent to which the person acts according to her hierarchy of goals*, or the goals that are most accessible and important in the moment, rather than to external normative standards. Furthermore, when evaluating self-regulatory success, it is important to keep in mind that goal hierarchy changes from one moment to the next. For instance, even if the person does have the long-term goal of maintaining a healthy diet, in the moment, the goal of indulging may become temporarily more important and may result in behavior that is inconsistent with the person's long-term goal. Even if the long-term goal of maintaining a healthy diet is thwarted, eating a piece of cake does not represent self-regulatory failure in general, but the result of a shift in goal hierarchy.

Much research has attempted to understand self-defeating and risk behavior by focusing on the informational content (e.g. negative consequences) or representation (e.g. abstract vs. concrete) associated with the behavior, or on increasing the capacity for executive control. However, I believe that our understanding of risk behavior and the ability to reduce the negative consequences associated with it may benefit from a better understanding of the function that these behaviors serve. Most self-defeating behaviors serve fundamental goals such as emotion regulation, the need to belong, achievement, power, etc. Although they may look problematic according to the modern societal standards, risk behaviors became part of our repertoire due to their evolutionary value (e.g. Steinberg & Belsky, 1996). The challenge for future research would be to understand the conditions under which self-defeating and risk behaviors become the preferred means to pursue important goals at the expense of other means, rather than to approach them as failures.

References

Aarts, H., Dijksterhuis, A., & De Vries, P. (2001). On the psychology of drinking: Being thirsty and perceptually ready. *British Journal of Psychology*, 92.

Adcock, R. A., Thangavel, A., Whitfield-Gabrieli, S., Knutson, B., & Gabrieli, J. D. (2006). Reward- motivated learning: Mesolimbic activation precedes memory formation. *Neuron*, 50(3), 507–517.doi:10.1016/j.neuron.2006.03.036.

Anderson, J. R. (1974). Retrieval of propositional information from long-term memory. *Cognitive Psychology*, 6(4), 451–474.

Anderson, J. R. (1983). *The architecture of cognition*. Hillsdale, NJ: Lawrence Erlbaum Associates, Inc.

APA (2000). *Diagnostic and statistical manual of mental disorders*, 4th ed., text revision. Washington, DC: American Psychiatric Association.

Atkinson, J. W. (1957). Motivational determinants of risk-taking behavior. *Psychological Review*, 64(6, Pt.1), 359–372. doi:10.1037/h0043445.

Baker, T. B., Piper, M. E., McCarthy, D. E., Majeskie, M. R., & Fiore, M. C. (2004). Addiction motivation reformulated: An affective processing model of negative reinforcement. *Psychological Review*, 111(1), 33–51. doi:10.1037/0033–295X.111.1.33.

Baumeister, R. F. (1997). Esteem threat, self-regulatory breakdown, and emotional distress as factors in self-defeating behavior. *Review of General Psychology*, 1, 145–174.

Baumeister, R. F., Bratslavsky, E., Muraven, M., & Tice, D. M. (1998). Ego depletion: Is the active self a limited resource? *Journal of Personality and Social Psychology*, 74, 1252–1265. doi:10.1037/0022–3514.74.5.1252.

Bélanger, J. J., Kruglanski, A.W., Chen, X., & Orehek, E. (2014). Bending perception to desire: Effects of task demands, motivation and cognitive resources. *Motivation and Emotion*, 38, 802–814.

Bélanger, J. J., Lafrenière, M.-A. K., Vallerand, R. J., & Kruglanski, A. W. (2013). When passion makes the heart grow colder: The role of passion in alternative goal suppression. *Journal of Personality and Social Psychology*, 104(1), 126–147. doi:10.1037/a0029679.

Berridge, K. C. (1999). Pleasure, pain, desire, and dread: Hidden core processes of emotion. In D. Kahneman, E. Diener, N. Schwarz, D. Kahneman, E. Diener, & N. Schwarz (Eds.), *Well-being: The foundations of hedonic psychology* (pp. 525–557). New York: Russell Sage Foundation.

Berridge, K. C. (2003). Irrational pursuits: Hyperincentives from a visceral brain. In I. Brocas & J. D. Carrillo (Eds.), *The Psychology of Economic Decisions* (Vol. 1, pp. 14–40). Oxford: Oxford University Press.

Bijleveld, E., Custers, R., & Aarts, H. (2009). The unconscious eye opener: Pupil dilation reveals strategic recruitment of resources upon presentation of subliminal reward cues. *Psychological Science*, 20(11), 1313–1315. doi:10.1111/j.1467–9280.2009.02443.x.

Botvin, G. J. (1990). Substance abuse prevention: Theory, practice, and effectiveness. *Criminal Justice and Behavior*, 13, 461–519.

Botvinick, M., & Braver, T. (2015). Motivation and cognitive control: From behavior to neural mechanism. *Annual Review of Psychology*, 66, 83–113. doi:10.1146/annurev-psych-010814-015044.

Bousman, C. A., Cherner, M., Ake, C., Letendre, S., Atkinson, J. H., Patterson, T. L., Grant, I., & Everall, I. P. (2009). Negative mood and sexual behavior among non-monogamous men who have sex with men in the context of methamphetamine and HIV. *Journal of Affective Disorders*, 119(1–3), 84–91. doi:10.1016/j.jad.2009.04.006.

Brehm, J. W., & Self, E. A. (1989). The intensity of motivation. *Annual Review of Psychology*, 40, 109–131. doi:10.1146/annurev.ps.40.020189.000545.

Briere, J., & Gil, E. (1998). Self-mutilation in clinical and general population samples: Prevalence, correlates, and functions. *American Journal of Orthopsychiatry*, 68, 609–620.

Connor, J. P., Gullo, M. J., Feeney, G. F. X., & Young, R. M. (2011). Validation of the Cannabis Expectancy Questionnaire (CEQ) in adult cannabis users in treatment. *Drug and Alcohol Dependence*, 115(3), 167–174. doi:10.1016/j.drugalcdep.2010.10.025.

Cooper, M. L. (2010). Toward a person × situation model of sexual risk-taking behaviors: Illuminating the conditional effects of traits across sexual situations and relationship contexts. *Journal of Personality and Social Psychology*, 98, 319–341.

Crano, W. D., & Burgoon, M. (2002). *Mass media and drug prevention: Classic and contemporary theories and research*. Mahwah, NJ: Psychology Press.

Cronce, J. M., & Larimer, M. E. (2011). Individual-focused approaches to the prevention of college student drinking. *Alcohol Research Health*, 34(2), 210–221.

Custers, R., & Aarts, H. (2005). Positive affect as implicit motivator: On the nonconscious operation of behavioral goals. *Journal of Personality and Social Psychology*, 89(2), 129–142.

Custers, R., & Aarts, H. (2010). The unconscious will: How the pursuit of goals operates outside of conscious awareness. *Science*, 329, 47–50.

DeGrandpre, R. J., & Bickel, W. K. (1996). Drug dependence as consumer demand. In L. Green, & J. H. Kagel (Eds.), *Advances in behavioral economics: Substance use and abuse* (Vol. 3, pp. 1–36). Westport, CT: Ablex Publishing.

DiFranza, J. R., Savageau, J. A., Fletcher, K., Ockene, J. K., Rigotti, N. A., McNeill, A. D., Coleman, M., & Wood, C. (2002). Measuring the loss of autonomy over nicotine use in adolescents: The DANDY (Development and Assessment of Nicotine Dependence in Youths) study. *Archives of Pediatrics and Adolescent Medicine*, 156(4), 397–403.

Dijksterhuis, A., & Aarts, H. (2010). Goals, attention, and (un)consciousness. *Annual Review of Psychology*, 61, 467–490. doi:10.1146/annurev.psych.093008.100445.

Everitt, B. J., & Robbins, T. W. (2005). Neural systems of reinforcement for drug addiction: From actions to habits to compulsion. *Nature Neuroscience*, 8(11), 1481–1489.

Falk, J. L., Dews, P. B., & Schuster, C. R. (1983). Communalities in the environmental control of behaviour. In P. K. Levison, D. R. Gerstein, & D. R. Maloff (Eds.), *Commonalities in Substance Abuse and Habitual Behavior* (pp. 47–110). Lexington, MA: D. C. Health and Co.

Fallon, A. E., & Rozin, P. (1983). The psychological bases of food rejections by humans. *Ecology of Food and Nutrition*, 13(1), 15–26.

Fishbach, A., & Converse, B. A. (2011). Identifying and battling temptation. In K. D. Vohs, R. F. Baumeister, K. D. Vohs, & R. F. Baumeister (Eds.), *Handbook of self-regulation: Research, theory, and applications, 2nd ed.* (pp. 244–260). New York: Guilford Press.

Fishbach, A., Friedman, R. S., & Kruglanski, A. W. (2003). Leading us not unto temptation: Momentary allurements elicit overriding goal activation. *Journal of Personality and Social Psychology*, 84, 296–309.

Fishbach, A., Shah, J. Y., & Kruglanski, A. W. (2004). Emotional transfer in goal systems. *Journal of Experimental Social Psychology*, 40, 723–738.

Fishbach, A., & Trope, Y. (2005). The substitutability of external control and self-control. *Journal of Experimental Social Psychology*, 41(3), 256–270.

Fisher Jr, E. B. (1996). A behavioral-economic perspective on the influence of social support on cigarette smoking. In L. Green & J. H. Kagel (Eds.), *Advances in behavioral economics: Substance use and abuse* (Vol. 3, pp. 207–236). Norwood, NJ: Ablex.

Fujita, K., Trope, Y., Liberman, N., & Levin-Sagi, M. (2006). Construal levels and self-control. *Journal of Personality and Social Psychology*, 90(3), 351–367.

Gailliot, M. T., Baumeister, R. F., DeWall, C. N., Maner, J. K., Plant, E. A., & Tice, D. M. (2007). Self-control relies on glucose as a limited energy source: Willpower is more than a metaphor. *Journal of Personality and Social Psychology*, 92(2), 325–336.

Hawkins, J. D., Catalano, R. F., & Miller, J. Y. (1992). Risk and protective factors for alcohol and other drug problems in adolescence and early adulthood: Implications for substance abuse prevention. Review. *Psychological Bulletin*, 112(1), 64–105.

Heatherton, T. F., & Baumeister, R. F. (1991). Binge eating as escape from self-awareness. *Psychological Bulletin*, 110(1), 86–108. doi:10.1037/0033-2909.110.1.86.

Higgins, E. T. (1997). Beyond pleasure and pain. *American Psychologist*, 52(12), 1280–1300.

Hofmann, W., Gschwendner, T., Friese, M., Wiers, R. W., & Schmitt, M. (2008). Working memory capacity and self-regulatory behavior: Toward an individual differences perspective on behavior determination by automatic versus controlled processes. *Journal of Personality and Social Psychology*, 95(4), 962–977. doi:10.1037/a0012705.

Hostinar, C. E., Stellern, S. A., Schaefer, C., Carlson, S. M., & Gunnar, M. R. (2012). *Associations between early life adversity and executive function in children adopted internationally from orphanages*. PNAS Proceedings of the National Academy of Sciences of the United States of America, 109(Suppl 2), 17208–17212. doi:10.1073/pnas.1121246109.

Houben, K., & Wiers, R. W. (2008). Implicitly positive about alcohol? Implicit positive associations predict drinking behavior. *Addictive Behaviors*, 33, 979–986.

Kahneman, D., Slovic, P., & Tversky, A. (1982). *Judgment under Uncertainty: Heuristics and Biases*. New York: Cambridge University Press.

Kassel, J. D., Stroud, L. R., & Paronis, C. A. (2003). Smoking, stress, and negative affect: Correlation, causation, and context across stages of smoking. *Psychological Bulletin*, 129(2), 270–304. doi:10.1037/0033-2909.129.2.270.

Kirchner, T. R., & Sayette, M. A. (2007). Effects of smoking abstinence and alcohol consumption on smoking-related outcome expectancies in heavy smokers and tobacco chippers. *Nicotine & Tobacco Research*, 9, 365–376.

Kopetz, C., Belanger, J., Lejuez, C. W., & Johnson, M. (2016a). *Risk-taking as motivated cognition and action*. Manuscript in preparation.

Kopetz, C. E., Collado, A., & Lejuez, C. W. (2015). When the end (automatically) justifies the means: Automatic tendency toward sex exchange for crack cocaine. *Motivation Science*, 1 (4), 233–243. doi:10.1037/mot0000025.

Kopetz, C., Faber, T., Fishbach, A., & Kruglanski, A. W. (2011). The multifinality constraints effect: how goal multiplicity narrows the means set to a focal end. *Journal of Personality and Social Psychology*, 100, 810–826.

Kopetz, C., Hofmann, W., & Wiers, R. W. (2014). On the selection and balancing of multiple selfish goals. Commentary. *Behavioral and Brain Sciences*, 37, 147–148.

Kopetz, C., Lejuez, C. W, Wiers, R., & Kruglanski, A. W. (2013). Motivation and self-regulation in addiction. *Perspectives in Psychological Sciences*, 8(1), 3–24.

Kopetz, C., MacPherson, L., Mitchell, A. D., Huston-Ludlam, A., Wiers, R. W. H. J. (2017). A novel alternative behavior approach bias modification intervention for smoking cessation: The relevance of implicit mechanisms. *Experimental and Clinical Psychopharmacology*, 25, 50–60.

Kopetz, C., & Orehek, E. (2015). When the end justifies the means: Self-defeating behaviors as 'rational' and 'successful' self-regulation. *Current Directions in Psychological Science*, 24(5), 386–391. doi:10.1177/0963721415589329.

Kopetz, C., Woerner, J. I., MacPherson, L., & Lejuez, C. W., Nelson, C. A., Zeanah, C. H., & Fox, N. (2016c). *Early psychosocial deprivation and adolescent risk-taking: The role of motivation and executive control*. Manuscript under review at *Psychological Science*.

Kruglanski, A. W. (1996). Goals as knowledge structures. In P. M. Gollwitzer & J. A. Bargh (Eds.), *The psychology of action: Linking cognition and motivation to behavior*. (pp. 599–618). New York: Guilford Press.

Kruglanski, A. W., Belanger, J., Chen, X., Kopetz, C., Pierro, A., & Mannetti, L. (2012). The Energetics of Motivated Cognition: A Force Field Analysis. *Psychological Review*, 119, 1–20.

Kruglanski, A. W., Chernikova, M., Babush, M., Dugas, M., & Schumpe, B. M. (2015). The architecture of goal systems: Multifinality, equifinality, and counterfinality in means-end relations. In E. J. Elliot (Ed.), *Advances in Motivation Science* (Vol. 2, pp. 69–98). Elsevier.

Kruglanski, A. W., Köpetz, C., Bélanger, J. J., Chun, W. Y., Orehek, E., & Fishbach, A. (2013). Features of multifinality. *Personality and Social Psychology Review*, 17, 22–39.

Kruglanski, A. W., & Orehek, E. (2009). Toward a relativity theory of rationality. *Social Cognition*, 27, 639–660.

Kruglanski, A. W., Shah, J. Y., Fishbach, A., Friedman, R., Chun, W. Y., & Sleeth-Keppler, D. (2002). A theory of goal systems. *Advances in Experimental Social Psychology*, 34, 331–378.

Kruglanski, A. W., Thompson, E. P., Higgins, E. T., Atash, M. N., Pierro, A., Shah, J. Y., & Spiegel, S. (2000). To "do the right thing" or to "just do it": Locomotion and assessment as distinct self-regulatory imperatives. *Journal of Personality and Social Psychology*, 79(5), 793–815. doi:10.1037/0022-3514.79.5.793.

Kunda, Z. (1990). The case for motivated reasoning. *Psychological Bulletin*, 108(3), 480–498.

Lamb, R. J., Preston, K. L., Schindler, C. W., Meisch, R. A., Davis, F., Katz, J. L., … Goldberg, S. R. (1991). The reinforcing and subjective effects of morphine in post-addicts: A dose-response study. *The Journal of Pharmacology and Experimental Therapeutics*, 259(3), 1165–1173.

La Pointe, L. B., & Engle, R. W. (1990). Simple and complex word spans as measures of working memory capacity. *Journal of Experimental Psychology: Learning, Memory, and Cognition*, 16(6), 1118–1133. doi:10.1037/0278-7393.16.6.1118.

Larimer, M. E., & Cronce, J. M. (2002). Identification, prevention and treatment: A review of individual-focused strategies to reduce problematic alcohol consumption by college students. *Journal of Studies on Alcohol*, 14(Suppl), 148–163.

Leander, N. P., Shah, J. Y., & Chartrand, T. L. (2009). Moments of weakness: The implicit context dependencies of temptations. *Personality and Social Psychology Bulletin*, 35(7), 853–866. doi:10.1177/0146167209334784.

Leith, K. P., & Baumeister, R. F. (1996). Why do bad moods increase self-defeating behavior? Emotion, risk tasking, and self-regulation. *Journal of Personality and Social Psychology*, 71(6), 1250–1267. doi:10.1037/0022–3514.71.6.1250.

Lejuez, C. W., Read, J. P., Kahler, C. W., Richards, J. B., Ramsey, S. E., Stuart, G. L., Strong, D. R., & Brown, R. A. (2002). Evaluation of a behavioral measure of risk taking: The Balloon Analogue Risk Task (BART). *Journal of Experimental Psychology: Applied*, 8(2), 75–84. doi:10.1037/1076–898X.8.2.75.

Leotti, L. A., & Wager, T. D. (2010). Motivational influences on response inhibition measures. *J Exp Psychol Hum Percept Perform*, 36(2), 430–447. doi:10.1037/a0016802.

Li, H. K., & Dingle, G. A. (2012). Using the Drinking Expectancy Questionnaire (revised scoring method) in clinical practice. *Addictive Behaviors*, 37(2), 198–204. doi:10.1016/j.addbeh.2011.10.002.

Loewenstein, G. (1996). Out of control: Visceral influences on behavior. *Organizational Behavior and Human Decision Processes*, 65(3), 272–292. doi:10.1006/obhd.1996.0028.

Loewenstein, G. (2007). *Exotic preferences: Behavioral economics and human motivation*. New York: Oxford University Press.

Lopes, L. L. (1987). Between hope and fear: The psychology of risk. In L. Berkowitz & L. Berkowitz (Eds.), *Advances in experimental social psychology, Vol. 20.* (pp. 255–295). San Diego, CA: Academic Press.

Lovallo, W. R. (2013). Early life adversity reduces stress reactivity and enhances impulsive behavior: Implications for health behaviors. *International Journal of Psychophysiology*, 90(1), 8–16. doi:10.1016/j.ijpsycho.2012.10.006.

Lovallo, W. R., Farag, N. H., Sorocco, K. H., Acheson, A., Cohoon, A. J., & Vincent, A. S. (2013). Early life adversity contributes to impaired cognition and impulsive behavior: Studies from the Oklahoma Family Health Patterns Project. *Alcoholism: Clinical and Experimental Research*, 37(4), 616–623. doi:10.1111/acer.12016.

MacDonald, T. K., Zanna, M. P., & Fong, G. T. (1995). Decision making in altered states: Effects of alcohol on attitudes toward drinking and driving. *Journal of Personality and Social Psychology*, 68(6), 973–985. doi:10.1037/0022–3514.68.6.973.

Mann, T., & Ward, A. (2004). To eat or not to eat: Implications of the attentional myopia model for restrained eaters. *Journal of Abnormal Psychology*, 113(1), 90–98. doi:10.1037/0021-843X.113. 1. 90.

Mann, T., & Ward, A. (2007). Attention, self-control, and health behaviors. *Current Directions in Psychological Science*, 16(5), 280–283. doi:10.1111/j.1467-8721.2007.00520.x.

Matusiewicz, A., Kopetz, C., Waverling, G., Ellis, J., & Lejuez, C. W. (2015). Distress and risk behavior in borderline personality disorder: Regulatory failure or goal directed behavior? Revised and resubmitted for *Personality Disorders: Research, Theory and Treatment*.

McDermott, J. M., Troller-Renfree, S., Vanderwert, R., Nelson, C. A., Zeanah, C. H., & Fox, N. A. (2013). Psychosocial deprivation, executive functions, and the emergence of socio-emotional behavior problems. *Frontiers in Human Neuroscience,* 7. doi:10.3389/fnhum.2013.00167.

McDermott, J. M., Westerlund, A., Zeanah, C. H., Nelson, C. A., & Fox, N. A. (2012). Early adversity and neural correlates of executive function: Implications for academic adjustment. *Developmental Cognitive Neuroscience,* 2(Suppl 1), S59-S66. doi:10.1016/j.dcn.2011.09.008.

Mischel, W. (1974). Processes in delay of gratification. In L. Berkowitz (Ed.), *Advances in Experimental Social Psychology* (Vol. 7, pp. 249–292). New York: Academic Press.

Moore, M., & Weiss, S. (1995). Reasons for non-drinking among Israeli adolescents of four religions. *Drug and Alcohol Dependence,* 38(1), 45–50.

Muraven, M., Tice, D. M., & Baumeister, R. E. (1998). Self-control as a limited resource: Regulatory depletion patterns. *Journal of Personality and Social Psychology,* 74(3), 774–789.

Orehek, E., & Vazeou-Nieuwenhuis, A. (2013). Sequential and concurrent strategies of multiple goal pursuit. *Review of General Psychology,* 17, 339.

Padmala, S., & Pessoa, L. (2011). Reward reduces conflict by enhancing attentional control and biasing visual cortical processing. *Journal of Cognitive Neuroscience,* 23(11), 3419–3432. doi:10.1162/jocn_a_00011.

Rawn, C. D., & Vohs, K. D. (2011). People use self-control to risk personal harm: An intra-interpersonal dilemma. *Personality and Social Psychology Review,* 15(3), 267–289. doi:10.1177/1088868310381084.

Robinson, T., & Berridge, K. (2004). Incentive-sensitization and drug 'wanting'. *Psychopharmacology,* 171, 352–353.

Scholer, A. A., Zou, X., Fujita, K., Stroessner, S. J., & Higgins, E. T. (2010). When risk seeking becomes a motivational necessity. *Journal of Personality and Social Psychology,* 99, 215–231.

Selby, E. A., & Joiner Jr, T. E. (2013). Emotional cascades as prospective predictors of dysregulated behaviors in borderline personality disorder. *Personality Disorders: Theory, Research, and Treatment,* 4(2), 168–174. doi:10.1037/a0029933.

Shah, J. Y., Friedman, R., & Kruglanski, A. W. (2002). Forgetting all else: on the antecedents and consequences of goal shielding. *Journal of Personality and Social Psychology,* 83, 1261–1280.

Shiffman, S., & Waters, A. J. (2004). Negative affect and smoking lapses: A prospective analysis. *Journal of Consulting and Clinical Psychology,* 72(2), 192–201. doi:10.1037/0022-006X.72.2.192.

Simon, A. H. (1978). Rationality as process and as product of thought. *The American Economic Review,* 68(2), 1–16.

Somerville, L. H., & Casey, B. J. (2010). Developmental neurobiology of cognitive control and motivational systems. *Current Opinion in Neurobiology,* 20(2), 236–241. doi:10.1016/j.conb.2010.01.006.

Stacy, A. W., & Wiers, R. W. (2010). Implicit cognition and addiction: A tool for explaining paradoxical behavior. *Annual Review of Clinical Psychology,* 6, 551–575. doi:10.1146/annurev.clinpsy.121208.131444.

Steinberg, L. (2007). Risk taking in adolescence: New perspectives from brain and behavioral science. *Current Directions in Psychological Science,* 16(2), 55–59. doi:10.1111/j.1467–8721.2007.00475.x.

Steinberg, L., & Belsky, J. (1996). An evolutionary perspective on psychopathology in adolescence. In D. Cicchetti, S. L. Toth, D. Cicchetti, & S. L. Toth (Eds.), *Adolescence: Opportunities and challenges.* (pp. 93–124). Rochester, NY: University of Rochester Press.

Strack, F., & Deutsch, R. (2004). Reflective and Impulsive Determinants of Social Behavior. *Personality and Social Psychology Review,* *8*(3), 220–247. doi:10.1207/s15327957pspr0803_1.

Stroebe, W., van Koningsbruggen, G. M., Papies, E. K., & Aarts, H. (2013). Why most dieters fail but some succeed: A goal conflict model of eating behavior. *Psychological Review,* 120, 110–138.

Tice, D. M., Bratslavsky, E., & Baumeister, R. F. (2001). Emotional distress regulation takes precedence over impulse control: If you feel bad, do it! *Journal of Personality and Social Psychology,* *80*(1), 53–67. doi:10.1037/0022–3514.80.1.53.

Vohs, K. D., & Heatherton, T. F. (2000). Self-regulatory failure: A resource-depletion approach. *Psychological Science,* *11*(3), 249–254. doi:10.1111/1467-9280.00250.

Wagner, D. D. and Heatherton, T. F. (2015). Self-regulation and its failure: Seven deadly threats to self-regulation. In E. Borgida, and J. Bargh (Eds.), *APA handbook of personality and social psychology: Volume 1. Attitudes and social cognition* (pp. 805–842). American Psychological Association.

Ward, A., & Mann, T. (2000). Don't mind if I do: Disinhibited eating under cognitive load. *Journal of Personality and Social Psychology,* *78*(4), 753–763. doi:10.1037/0022 3514.78.4.753.

Weinstein, A. M., Feldtkeller, B. T., Law, F., Myles, J., & Nutt, D. J. (2000). The processing of automatic thoughts of drug use and craving in opiate-dependent individuals. *Experimental and Clinical Psychopharmacology,* *8*(4), 549–553. doi:10.1037/1064–1297.8.4.549.

Whitlock, J., Muehlenkamp, J., Purington, A., Eckenrode, J., Barreira, P., Baral Abrams, G., … Knox, K. (2011). Nonsuicidal self-injury in a college population: General trends and sex differences. *Journal of American College Health,* 59(8), 691–698.

Wiers, R. W., Eberl, C., Rinck, M., Becker, E. S., & Lindenmeyer, J. (2011). Retraining automatic action tendencies changes alcoholic patients' approach bias for alcohol and improves treatment outcome. *Psychological Science,* 22(4), 490–497.

Windschitl, P. D. (2002). Judging the accuracy of a likelihood judgment: The case of smoking risk. *Journal of Behavioral Decision Making,* 15, 19–35.

Woerner, J. I., Kopetz, C., & Arriaga, X. (2016). *Interpersonal victimization and sexual risk-taking among women: The role of attachment style and regulatory focus.* Manuscript in preparation.

Woerner, J., Kopetz, C., Lechner, W. V., & Lejuez, C. (2016). History of abuse and risky sex among substance users: The role of rejection sensitivity and the need to belong. *Addictive Behaviors,* 62, 73–78. doi:10.1016/j.addbeh.2016.06.006.

Wright, R. A., Contrada, R. J., & Patane, M. J. (1986). Task difficulty, cardiovascular response, and the magnitude of goal valence. *Journal of Personality and Social Psychology,* *51*(4), 837–843. doi:10.1037/0022–3514.51.4.837.

Zhang, Y., Fishbach, A., & Kruglanski, A. W. (2007). The dilution model: How additional goals undermine the perceived instrumentality of a shared path. *Journal of Personality and Social Psychology,* 92(3), 389–401.

Zuckerman, M. (1979) Sensation seeking. *Corsini Encyclopedia of Psychology.* Hillsdale, NJ: Lawrence Erlbaum.

7

GOAL PURSUIT AND CLOSE RELATIONSHIPS

A People as Means Perspective

Edward Orehek

Consider a situation in which you travel to attend a friend's wedding. You purchase your tickets, pack your bags, travel to the airport, traverse the terminal, check into your hotel, iron your clothes, get ready, and ultimately arrive at the celebration. You may feel like you have accomplished a lot. Indeed, you have. You have engaged in forethought, exercised patience, navigated an unfamiliar environment, and even lifted some heavy bags. You can give yourself a pat on the back for all that you have accomplished. It may feel as if you have done all of this by yourself, on your own, and that you deserve the credit. On the other hand, you could not have made this trip without the help of your taxi driver, airplane pilot, hotel employees, and countless other people who assisted you along the way. Everything you do is carried out with the help of other people. This example illustrates that while we may often take credit for the actions we carry out, even the most mundane of everyday activities require the assistance of other people.

The remainder of this chapter outlines how our goals influence how we come to evaluate the people in our lives. First, I detail the intimate alignment between goals and close relationships. Second, I present a people as means approach to understanding the link between goal pursuit and close relationships. This approach uses goal systems theory (Kruglanski et al., 2002) to make predictions about close relationships. By considering people as means to goals, each of the principles that describe means-goals relations can be applied to interpersonal perception and evaluation. Next, I explain who we turn to when we want help, when we turn to others rather than work alone, and why the presence of instrumental others is beneficial in our daily lives. Finally, I consider the way people sustain their relationships with others as a way of engaging in means maintenance.

Goal pursuit and close relationships are inextricably intertwined from life's earliest moments throughout adulthood. When a person is born, she emerges kicking and screaming and embarks on her first goal pursuit. She requires warmth and nutrition, yet is unable to regulate her own body temperature or feed herself. Instead, she must rely on caregivers to help her attain these goals. Through her crying and cooing, she is able to influence the behavior of others and get what she needs. As she grows through childhood, she starts to carry out some tasks independently. When she feels secure, she freely explores her environment, and when the world overwhelms her, she returns to the safety provided by her caregivers (Ainsworth & Bell, 1970). She is able to learn from a variety of people, including parents, teachers, coaches, and peers, who function as epistemic authorities (Kruglanski et al., 2005) and provide social support (Kahn & Antonucci, 1980). She engages in goal pursuit under close guidance from others and seeks their approval. As she moves into adolescence and adulthood, she begins to rely less on authority figures, and more on peers (Furman & Buhrmester, 1992; Kruglanski, Dechesne, Orehek, & Pierro, 2009). Entering adulthood, she may establish a close partnership with a spouse. Ultimately, she develops a sense that she can work independently, but also knows that she can turn to trusted others for counsel or comfort (Kruglanski, Orehek, Dechesne, & Pierro, 2010). The intimate alignment between goal pursuit and close relationships makes it difficult to depict one without considering the other.

The present perspective investigates the intersection of goal pursuit and close relationships by considering the implications of considering people as means to goals. When people facilitate goal pursuit, they serve as means to goals because they become an important part of the way one's goal pursuit is initiated, carried out, and attained (Orehek & Forest, 2016). To consider a person as a means to a goal is to recognize his or her usefulness (i.e., instrumentality) to one or more goals. When a person serves as a means to a goal, s/he is evaluated according to his or her instrumentality. People feel close to and spend time with others who they perceive as instrumental to their goals (Converse & Fishbach, 2012; Fitzsimons & Fishbach, 2010; Fitzsimons & Shah, 2008; Slotter & Gardner, 2011).

Even (or especially) infants rely on people as means to goals. Throughout the chapter, research will be reviewed showing that adults (or college students) evaluate others according to their perceived instrumentality. Yet, if the story starts at birth, then even infants should evaluate others according to their instrumentality. In one study, six- and ten-month-old infants were presented with a story in which a character was attempting to climb a hill. A second character then either helped or hindered the first character's progress by either providing a boost or knocking the character down. After the presentation, infants preferred the helpful over the harmful character (Hamlin, Wynn, & Bloom, 2007), demonstrating that infants evaluate others according to their perceived instrumentality. The remainder of the chapter investigates the implications of evaluating other people according to their instrumentality (i.e., treating people as means to goals).

People use their social relationships to make individual goal pursuit possible. People take on a variety of roles, engage in a number of relationships, and adapt to changing norms; and they are typically able to do so relatively gracefully (Bargh & Chartrand, 1999). For instance, initiation of goal pursuit leads people to bring to mind the people who enable goal progress (Fitzsimons & Shah, 2008) and the presence of helpful others leads people to bring to mind the goals they facilitate (Fitzsimons & Bargh, 2003; Leander, Shah, & Chartrand, 2009; Shah, 2003; vanDellen & Hoyle, 2010). Every goal is supported by at least one other person, and every time a person initiates contact with someone else, she expects the other person to be instrumental to some goal pursuit (cf., Orehek & Forest, 2016).

People as Means to Goals

Relationships should thrive when partners facilitate each other's goal pursuit. Specifically, we have proposed that relationship satisfaction should be highest when partners experience mutual perceived instrumentality, depicted in Figure 7.1. **Mutual perceived instrumentality** occurs when each person in a relationship perceives both themselves and the other person as instrumental to the other's goal pursuit (Orehek & Forest, 2016). The "people as means" framework uses insights gleaned from goal systems theory (Kruglanski et al., 2002; Kruglanski et al., 2015) to understand close relationship dynamics (Orehek & Forest, 2016).

To illustrate the mutual perceived instrumentality principle, consider a relationship between Milo and Stephanie. Milo evaluates Stephanie in terms of her instrumentality to his goals. He should evaluate her more positively if she is instrumental to goals he is pursuing at the moment, and should evaluate her more positively if she serves a larger rather than smaller set of goals. In addition, Milo wants to be instrumental to Stephanie's goals. He experiences increased self-worth when he feels useful in helping other people attain their goals. In addition,

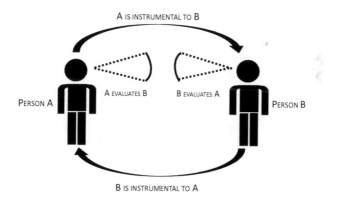

FIGURE 7.1 Depiction of mutual perceived instrumentality in a dyad

he feels best when Stephanie recognizes and appreciates his instrumentality and when her expectations of the ways in which he will be instrumental align with the ways he wants and is capable of being instrumental. Finally, relationship satisfaction will be maximized when Milo recognizes and appreciates Stephanie's instrumentality, and when she wants to be instrumental to the goals Milo would like her to support.

The foregoing example highlights the complexity of the mutual instrumentality principle. In the sections that follow, I review the research in support of each of the components of mutual perceived instrumentality. If these conditions are met, then treating people as means can be prosocial, warm, compassionate, and moral. When these conditions are violated, then the treatment of people as means can turn antisocial, cold, callous, and immoral. I return to this issue after reviewing the evidence in support of each component.

People Evaluate Others Based on their Instrumentality

The first proposition of the people as means framework postulates that people evaluate relationship partners according to their perceived instrumentality to their goals. If Stephanie is helpful toward Milo's goals, then he should draw closer to her, evaluate her positively, and experience positive affect in her presence. This prediction is derived from the transfer of the affect principle in goal systems theory, which states that the properties of goals (e.g., commitment, positivity) transfer to the means of attainment proportionally to the strength of the means-goal connection (Fishbach et al., 2004; Kruglanski et al., 2002). Research has investigated this question in a variety of ways. Some of the earliest research to consider people as means to goals experimentally manipulated whether a goal was active versus inactive in a particular moment. These studies revealed that active goals prompt individuals to bring to mind goal-instrumental others, to evaluate them positively, and to approach those individuals more readily (Fitzsimons & Shah, 2008). Consistent with these findings, research has found that people want to spend more time with potential new friends who are instrumental (vs. non-instrumental) to their current (academic achievement or fitness) goal (Slotter & Gardner, 2011). These studies provide initial support for the notion that people evaluate others based on their instrumentality to active goals.

Additional research has investigated important implications of this principle, and provides further support for the goal-dependent evaluations of relationship partners. One question that arises is whether people will evaluate others more positively prior to goal completion or following goal completion. On the one hand, it seems that a person who has been helpful toward the attainment of a goal should be evaluated positively because they have proven their instrumentality. On the other hand, once a goal has been attained, it should be deactivated (Bargh, 1990; Carver & Scheier, 1998; Kruglanski et al., 2002; Orehek, Bessarabova, Chen, & Kruglanski, 2011), and the person is no longer instrumental to an active goal. Thus, from the point-of-view of a goal pursuer, one would expect that evaluations of people should be more positive while they are helping a yet-unattained goal than after the help has been delivered and the goal has been accomplished (Fitzsimons, Friesen, Orehek, & Kruglanski, 2009).

Several studies have investigated the effects of goal progress and goal attainment on evaluations of instrumental others. In a series of studies, participants' sense of progress on their goals was manipulated, and researchers predicted that instrumental others would be more appreciated when goal progress was low rather than high. Confirming hypotheses, goal instrumental others were perceived as interpersonally closer when progress was low. When progress was high, participants rated instrumental and non-instrumental others as equally close (Fitzsimons & Fishbach, 2010). Thus, it seems that people appreciate and draw closer to people when they are instrumental to an active goal, but once sufficient progress has been made, they no longer appreciate the person's instrumentality. To investigate this effect further, researchers assessed participants' gratitude toward a person who was helpful for a task before or after the task's completion (Converse & Fishbach, 2012). Consistent with previous work, they once again found that instrumental others were appreciated more prior to goal completion than after. Thus, evaluations of people seem to track their usefulness. During times a person is instrumental, they are evaluated more positively than times in which they are not instrumental.

In each of these studies, a person was evaluated more positively while they were instrumental toward goal pursuit. Thus, appreciation for instrumental others is often fleeting. People evaluate others positively and appreciate their helpful acts while they are pursuing a goal, but appreciation wanes once the goal has been accomplished. An important challenge is to understand how to help people transform momentary experiences of appreciation into lasting relationship quality. To address this challenge, research on the way people may facilitate multiple goals may shed new light on how relationships are sustained over time.

Some authors have speculated about the consequences of having relationships in which partners serve many goals (Finkel, Hui, Carswell, & Larsen, 2014; Light & Fitzsimons, 2014). These authors focused on marriage and noted that marriage partners in modern times are more commonly expected to serve many goals than they were in previous generations, to the point that a marriage partner is expected to be one's primary support provider, closest confidante, activity partner, and best friend (Finkel et al., 2014). Because of this, modern marriages have the potential to be incredibly satisfying because they serve many of a person's needs. When means serve many goals, they accrue greater value (Chun et al., 2011; Orehek, Mauro, Kruglanski, & van der Bles, 2012; Kruglanski et al., 2013), thus marriage partners who serve more goals may be evaluated more positively than marriage partners who serve fewer goals (Light & Fitzsimons, 2014). To date, very little research has investigated whether there is a link between the number of goals partners serve and relationship evaluations. In my lab, we have conducted two studies in which participants reported on each of the people with whom they maintain regular contact. We found that relationship partners who serve more (vs. fewer) goals are evaluated as interpersonally closer, more supportive, and more responsive (Orehek, Forest, & Wingrove, 2017). More research is needed to investigate the implications of people as means to multiple goals.

Taken together, the research to date has demonstrated that people seem to be sensitive to the usefulness of their close relationship partners, and evaluate them according to their perceived instrumentality. However, more research is needed. Future research should explore the extent to which romantic relationships, friend-ships, and colleagues come to evaluate each other as interpersonally close, supportive, and whether having a partner who is instrumental fosters relationship satisfaction.

People Evaluate Themselves According to Their Own Instrumentality

People often want and like to serve as means to other's goals. People develop their own sense of self-worth based on whether they are useful or helpful to other people, and whether people accept or reject them on those grounds (Leary & Baumeister, 2000). The present perspective and mutual perceived instrumen-tality principle suggest that serving as an instrumental means is just as important as having instrumental others. Being instrumental to others should increase both the felt closeness to the person for whom one has helped and increase one's own sense of self-worth. The former suggestion was offered by Ben Franklin, who stated "He that has once done you a kindness will be more ready to do you another, than he whom you yourself have obliged."

Supporting Ben Franklin's assertion, participants who performed a favor for someone with whom they previously had a negative or neutral impression came to like that person more (Jecker & Landy, 1969). Correlational research suggests that giving affection to a romantic partner is associated with commitment to the rela-tionship (Horan & Booth-Butterfield, 2010). The tendency to provide support to members of one's social network is associated with higher self-efficacy, greater self-esteem, less depression, and less stress (Piferi & Lawler, 2006). In addition, experi-mental research has shown that giving support to others increases the felt social connection with that person (Inagaki & Eisenberger, 2012). In short, giving support to others' goal pursuit benefits the helper (Inagaki & Orehek, 2017). Consistent with the present perspective, researchers have suggested that "the motivation for helping is essentially egoistic. That is, the primary motive for helping another person is that helping improves the helper's own situation" (Penner, Dovidio, & Albrecht, 2000, p. 64). Thus, serving as an instrumental means is important to people: they want to feel valuable, useful and helpful. Doing so allows them to feel close to their relationship partners and to feel valuable.

Consistent with the foregoing analysis, research has shown that people are sensitive to times in which they should serve as a means to others' goals. People want to serve the role of caregiver to close others (Hazan & Shaver, 2004).

People in communal relationships feel decreased positive mood following failure to help their partner (Williamson, Clark, Pegalis, & Behan, 1996). In addition, newlyweds are likely to perform instrumental actions such as running errands for their partner when they feel inferior in the relationship (Murray et al., 2009). This sensitivity to opportunities to prove oneself useful highlights the value-creating aspect of giving support. When a partner serves as an instrumental means to her partner, she reaps benefits in the form of a self-worth and mood boost. Lacking or missing such opportunities, therefore, decreases mood and can lead to decreased self-esteem.

Thus, research supports the mutual perceived instrumentality principle. Research suggests that people benefit just as much (or more) from being instrumental to close others as having instrumental others. More research should investigate the consequences of perceiving oneself as instrumental to others and engaging in instrumental actions for the sake of others.

Importance of Personal Autonomy and Partner Recognition

At this point, some astute readers may be struck by a sense of unease because treating people as means to goals can feel cold and callous. To suggest that people are evaluated positively only when they are useful, and to suggest that individual productivity depends on successful exploitation of one's social network can indeed conjure images of people who have been coerced or taken advantage of. And, of course, this can happen. When women are treated as sex objects while their minds are ignored or denied (Fredrickson & Roberts, 1997; Nussbaum 1998; Orehek & Weaverling, in press), when people exchange sex for drugs (Kopetz, Collado, & Lejuez, 2015), or when people are coerced into becoming suicide terrorists (Orehek & Vazeou-Nieuwenhuis, 2014), the use of people as means is cold, careless, and callous. However, consider cases in which a person helps his or her partner eat healthy meals, serves as a source of advice during a difficult time, celebrates after s/he receives a promotion at work, or holds his or her partner's hand while s/he receives chemotherapy. Each of these instances conjures an image of a warm, caring, and compassionate exchange in which both people benefit from the support provided (Inagaki & Orehek, 2017). It is important to determine the critical ingredients of a mutually beneficial relationship.

The first two pieces of the mutual instrumentality puzzle have stated (1) people evaluate others according to their instrumentality, and (2) people want to be instrumental to other's goals because they evaluate themselves according to their own instrumentality. While the two pieces discussed above provide a starting point, they do not preclude instances in which a person would be taken advantage of. In order for a person to feel comfortable serving as a means to another's goals, and in order for that person to be treated justly, the person serving as a means must feel a sense of autonomy and recognition. Without them, the person is likely to feel taken advantage of, and disrespected. The missing ingredient in considering whether a person has been treated fairly, therefore, is a recognition of whether the person wants to serve a particular goal.

I suggest that two conditions must be met in order for an interpersonally warm interaction to occur. First, the person must feel as if they have freely chosen to serve as a means to a particular goal. Second, the person must be recognized for his or her contribution. While Milo may want to be instrumental toward some goals (perhaps he would like to be considered a great cook and good at managing finances), he may not want to be instrumental toward other goals (perhaps he does not want to plant a vegetable garden or to be handy at fixing things around the house). He is likely to experience discomfort if he is evaluated according to goals he is not attempting to serve, sometimes even if he is praised for his instrumentality in those domains. Consistent with this notion, research has found that support providers benefit when they experience the decision to help as autonomous, but not otherwise (Weinstein & Ryan, 2010).

The predictions derived from the present perspective regarding autonomy and recognition, while being supported by preliminary evidence (Weinstein & Ryan, 2010), await empirical validation. Future research should examine whether the experience of free choice in deciding whether to serve as a means and whether partner recognition for one's instrumentality are important for a person to experience the benefits of being instrumental. In addition, future research could explore the consequences of unwanted compliments from a people-as-means perspective. Such instances represent cases in which a person is praised for his or her instrumentality toward a goal for which the person did not wish to be instrumental, therefore representing a case in which they are recognized as instrumental in a domain in which they did not choose to be instrumental. The present perspective suggests that a person in this situation would not appreciate the compliment because s/he did not want to be instrumental in that domain.

Who, When, and Why of People as Means

While the foregoing sections detailed the implications of considering a person to be instrumental (or not), important questions regarding people as means remain. Evaluating someone positively does not necessarily mean that one will turn to that person for advice. Saying that someone is instrumental toward goal pursuit does not mean that they effectively rely on that person for help. A first question, therefore, concerns to whom people turn for help with their goals. A second question concerns when people turn to others for assistance. It is likely that some conditions foster a desire for self-reliance whereas others lead to support seeking. Finally, a third question concerns why people turn to others. In other words, do people benefit from turning to others, and if so, in what ways?

Who do People Turn to?

When goal pursuit is initiated, people bring to mind means that have proven to be a reliable path toward obtaining the goal (Aarts & Dijksterhuis, 2000) and adopt the means that are both perceived to be instrumental and are available to the actor (Bargh, 1990; Kruglanski et al., 2002; Ouellette & Wood, 1998). Similarly, people should seek the help of others who are instrumental and available. Indeed, people bring to mind others who are perceived to be instrumental to goal pursuit (Fitzsimons & Shah, 2008). Recently, investigators tested the features of support providers that lead participants to turn to them for help. This research found that while both a person's previous effectiveness as a support provider and the frequency with which they typically interact with the person were positively associated with seeking support from the person, frequency of contact was a stronger predictor than effectiveness of support (Armstrong, Kammrath, Iida, & Suppes, 2017). In other words, participants seemed to prioritize a person's availability over their instrumentality when deciding to whom to turn. However, when participants indicated that the issue for which they wanted support was severe, effectiveness of previous support was a stronger predictor, suggesting that people are at least sometimes sensitive to the instrumentality of the person.

Another way of investigating this question is to examine the number of support providers to which people turn and how often they turn to each helper. Research has demonstrated that it is useful to have social networks composed of a diverse array of people who serve different types of goals (Cheung, Gardner, Anderson, 2015; Cohen & Janicki-Deverts, 2009). In that way, people can turn to different people for different issues, maximizing the skills of the people in their social networks. Such an approach suggests using a larger set of people to provide support, or what has been termed a breadth tactic. A breadth tactic is employed when a person turns to many people, while a depth tactic is employed when a person turns to the same person repeatedly (Armstrong & Kammrath, 2015). Armstrong and Kammrath found individual differences in the extent to which people enact each of these tactics. On average, people seem to turn to about one to three others for each specific issue they face, with women appearing more likely than men to use a diverse set of others as support providers (Armstrong & Kammrath, 2015; see also Kiecolt-Glaser & Newton, 2001). While people benefit from having social networks composed of people with diverse skill sets, and turning to a large number of people for assistance, it appears that many people under-utilize people as means to goals.

People should receive the best help if they turn to others who are the most instrumental for the goal they are pursuing in the moment (i.e., who have proven to be effective support providers). Importantly, the instrumentality of a person is a matter of personal preference. Research has consistently demonstrated that people have unique preferences when it comes to their perception of who would make the best support provider (Lakey & Orehek, 2011; Neely et al., 2006), the best mate (Eastwick & Hunt, 2014), the best teacher (Gross, Lakey, Edinger, Orehek, & Heffron, 2009), and the best therapist (Lakey, Cohen, & Neely, 2008). In addition, people seem to be able to forecast who they will find instrumental after brief exposure to the person. For example, people can forecast who they will find uniquely supportive after a single short conversation (Veenstra et al., 2011). Similarly, students are able to forecast how effective they will find a teacher after watching a short video of the instructor teaching (Gross et al., 2015). Thus, people could improve the quality of help they receive during goal pursuit by spending more time with instrumental others, and seem to be able to determine who is most instrumental. While people seem to turn to others who are available to them, they also appear to have the tools necessary to make accurate forecasts about who they will find instrumental. Thus, increasing the prioritization of instrumentality over availability could help people be happier, healthier, and more productive. It does seem that people may naturally do this when the issue they are facing is severe (i.e., when the goal is important).

When do People Turn to Others?

Setting out alone and working closely with others each have their advantages and disadvantages. When people think of themselves as independent, they take full responsibility for successes and failures. In times of success, it means they can take full credit for positive outcomes. However, it also means that in times of failure, they must take full responsibility for negative outcomes. Working inter-dependently with others can feel empowering. It creates and bolsters one's sense of self-worth and personal significance (Kruglanski et al., 2013; Kruglanski, Chen, Dechesne, Fishman, & Orehek, 2009; Kruglanski & Orehek, 2011). The empowering nature of social interdependence fosters the willingness to serve as a means by sacrificing for the sake of others (Orehek, Sasota, Kruglanski, Dechesne, & Ridgeway, 2014). Given these advantages and disadvantages, when do people prefer to work interdependently, and when do they prefer to work independently?

We predicted that experiences of failure would prompt individuals to shift toward a preference for interdependence over independence. To investigate this possibility, we carried out a series of experiments in which we manipulated par-ticipants' experiences of success versus failure and measured the relative value they placed on interdependence versus independence (Orehek, Vazeou-Neiuwenhuis, & Kruglanski, 2017). In our first experiment, participants engaged in a videogame task said to predict their future life success. The task was rigged such that half the participants would fail and the other half would succeed. Participants in the fail-ure condition reported greater value placed on interdependence. In our second experiment, participants once again were prompted to succeed or fail. This time, they took an exam said to measure their verbal and quantitative abilities. Bogus feedback informed participants that they either scored in the top 90 percent of test-takers (success condition) or in the bottom 15 percent (failure condition). Once again, participants in the failure condition reported stronger valuation of social interdependence. In a third study, participants recalled either a time in which they failed at an important personal goal (failure condition) or a time in which they watched television (control condition). This study confirmed that feelings of failure prompted participants to increase the value placed on interdependence with others.

Why do People Turn to Others?

People have many goals and must allocate their time, energy and attention in such a way as to maximize their outcomes (Orehek & Vazeou-Nieuwenhuis, 2013). Yet, however clever one is in allocating one's personal resources, the total pool is fixed. This limitation may be circumvented by working with other people, and having them serve as means to goals, in order to expand the total possible effort. To investigate the advantages of using other people as means, research has tested whether having instrumental others increases the likelihood of goal pursuit success.

Research consistently demonstrates that having strong relationships with close partners contributes to successful goal pursuit (Fitzsimons & Finkel, 2010). Close others can serve as a secure base from which to explore one's environment when they support goal progress (Feeney, 2004; Feeney & Thrush, 2010; Orehek, Vazeou-Nieuwenhuis, Quick, & Weaverling, 2017). This support is important. Previous research has found that having social networks composed of supportive others increases the likelihood that people are successful. For example, people who experience relationship satisfaction are more likely to be successful in their goal pursuits (Hofmann, Finkel, & Fitzsimons, 2015). People who have relationships with goal-instrumental others are more likely to accomplish the goal for which they have support (Fitzsimons & Shah, 2008). People are more successful in their goal pursuits if they have social networks composed of individuals who are effective self-regulators (vanDellen et al., 2015). This is likely because people who are effective self-regulators are better equipped to provide assistance (i.e., are more instrumental). Thus, establishing a social network of people who support goal pursuit is important for the attainment of one's goals.

The people as means framework also applies to cases in which people serve emotion regulation goals. In addition to helping a person be productive, others can help a person feel good. For example, research has found that having a social network composed of people who meet specific emotion regulation needs is associated with well-being (Cheung et al., 2015). The well-known link between perceived support and experience of positive affect (Lakey & Orehek, 2011) may potentially be explained by the perceived instrumentality of the relationship partner. To rate a person as supportive may be equivalent to perceiving that person as instrumental to one's goals. Consistent with the suggestion, people experience positive affect when engaged in instrumental activities or when with instrumental people (Fishbach, Shah, & Kruglanski, 2004). Recent research in my lab has found a link between the number of goals a person serves and the perceived supportiveness of that person (Orehek, Forest, & Wingrove, 2017). More research is needed to investigate whether social support processes may be explained according to a people as means framework.

Relationship Maintenance as a Goal

Once a person is committed to a means, maintaining the means can become a subgoal in its own right. For example, a person who purchases a car as a means of transportation must fill it with gasoline, get regular oil changes, keep it clean, and repair any damage. In order for it to continue to be instrumental, it must be kept in good working order. So it goes when people serve as means. When a person commits to a relationship partner, s/he must care for the relationship and maintain interpersonal closeness with the other person. The people as means approach makes apparent two ways of doing this. First, the person can increase their own standing in their partner's eyes, thereby highlighting their instrumentality to their partner. This should lead the partner to draw closer. Second, the person can increase the partner's standing in their own eyes, thereby recognizing the instrumentality of their partner. This should lead them to move closer to the partner. The next two sections consider each of these possibilities.

Increasing Self-Standing in a Partner's Eyes

To maintain closeness to an established relationship partner, people can attempt to increase their perceived instrumentality in that person's eyes. For example, research has found that times in which a person perceives a potential instrumentality imbalance (e.g., "My partner does more for me than I do for him/her") prompt romantic partners to appear useful by performing tasks for their partner, such as taking care of a chore that is typically the partner's responsibility (Murray, Aloni, Holmes, Derrick, Stinson, & Leder, 2009; see also Overall, Fletcher, & Simpson, 2006). In order to remain important to a partner, people want to feel as if they are valuable, and even irreplaceable (Murray, Leder, MacGregor, Holmes, Pinkus, & Harris, 2009). One way of creating the sense that one is irreplaceable is to serve as the exclusive means to particular goals. In monogamous romantic relationships, partners serve as exclusive means to sex. A friend may be the only person who shares a secret. A parent may be the only person who can bask in the nostalgic glow of one's childhood memories. By remaining the exclusive (or best) means to a goal, the person maintains a privileged position in their partner's life. The desire to be irreplaceable may contribute to the desire to be evaluated as uniquely positive by one's romantic partner (Eastwick, Finkel, Mochon, & Ariely,

2007). In other words, people want to feel not just as if their partner evaluates them positively, but that their partner evaluates them more positively than they evaluate other people, and more positively than other people evaluate the self (termed a relationship effect, Eastwick & Hunt, 2014; Lakey & Orehek, 2011).

A second way to be irreplaceable is to serve multiple goals in such a way that is unlikely to be duplicated by another person. A person who serves multiple goals is said to be multifinal (Kruglanski et al., 2013; Light & Fitzsimons, 2014). People may benefit in two ways by being multifinal. First, multifinal people should be evaluated more positively because they are able to satisfy more goals (Chun et al., 2011; Orehek et al., 2012; Orehek et al., 2017). Second, the multifinality constraint effect demonstrates that the more goals that are involved, the smaller is the set of means that potentially serve the set of goals is smaller (Köpetz et al., 2011). Finding a food that is tasty is relatively easy. Finding a food that is tasty, healthy, convenient, and cheap is quite difficult. So it is with people. Finding a person who will play tennis with you may be relatively easy. Finding a person who will play tennis, bake brownies, watch avant-garde French films, make a good co-parent, is sexually appealing, and is also good with finances is another matter. Thus, a multifinal person is less likely to have an equivalent than someone who serves a smaller set of goals.

Thus, one would like to be uniquely useful in their partner's eyes, and can accomplish this by being the exclusive means to particular goals or by satisfying a large set of goals. Very little research has examined the implications of these insights. Much more research is needed on how people feel when instrumental to their partner in these various ways. More generally, much more research is needed on how people attempt to be instrumental to their partners.

Increasing a Partner's Standing in One's Own Eyes

Even if Milo is convinced that he is appreciated by Stephanie, he must maintain his own positive evaluation of Stephanie. This can lead to motivated processing of information about the partner and alternative partners in such a way that enhances one's evaluation of the relationship (Bélanger, Kruglanski, Chen, & Orehek, 2014; Bélanger, Kruglanski, Chen, Orehek, & Johnson, 2015). For example, people enhance their partner's positive attributes and minimize their partner's negative traits (Fletcher, Simpson, & Thomas, 2000; Murray & Holmes, 1999). Such motivated reasoning may have some benefits. Idealizing partners may contribute to greater relationship satisfaction. Interestingly, research has found that partner idealization has positive effects on relationship satisfaction by increasing mutual perceived instrumentality. When one partner idealizes the other (perceiving him or her as more instrumental), it can lead to the partner then seeing him- or herself as more instrumental, and ultimately leading the person to confirm these expectations and become more instrumental (Murray, Holmes, & Griffin, 1996). Thus, the idealization process increased (a) the partner's standing in one's own eyes, leading (b) the other partner to increase their own standing in their own eyes, leading to (c) behaviors that confirmed the original idealization. At the end of the day, relationship satisfaction can be higher when this process is instigated (Murray et al., 1996).

In addition, facilitating recognition of the ways a partner is instrumental should increase felt satisfaction in a relationship. It may be easy to forget all the ways a partner is helpful, especially if the goals are generally satisfied. Once a couple has successfully purchased a home, car, and navigated daily life, the comfort of that life may ironically lead to a reduction in the recognition of the other person's instrumentality. If people are aware of the ongoing nature of the relationship with the helper and the many goals the relationship partner serves, then they should be less apt to experience this reduction in appreciation following goal progress, and more likely to express the appreciation they feel. Thus, it is likely that people who are made aware of the multiplicity of goals the relationship partner serves will be more likely to exhibit enduring appreciation for their partner. This possibility could be explored in future research.

People in monogamous romantic relationships face the challenge of encountering attractive alternative partners and the expectation that they do not initiate romantic relationships with those individuals. While one may be free to have several close friends, activity partners, and so on, the expectations of monogamous relationships mean that the person is motivated to maintain the relationship by viewing alternatives as less desirable than one's current partner. A similar situation arises when people are pursuing one goal, and are reminded of an alternative goal or are faced with a temptation. Goal shielding occurs when focal goal commitment is high, such that people disengage from and devalue alternative goals (Shah, Friedman, & Kruglanski, 2002). When committed to a goal, people also inhibit and avoid temptations that may undermine goal pursuit (Fishbach, Friedman, & Kruglanski, 2003; Fishbach & Shah, 2006). Applying these principles to romantic relationships, people should direct their attention away from and devalue alternative romantic partners when they are committed to their current partner. Thus, the large body of research on alternative partner derogation represents a case of goal shielding.

Research has investigated whether people engage in relationship maintenance by devaluing and directing attention away from alternative partners, and whether they are more likely to do so when they are highly committed to their current partner. The findings consistently show a relationship shielding effect. People in a romantic relationship rate photographs of opposite sex individuals as less attractive than do single people (Karremans, Dotsch, & Corneille, 2011; Simpson, Gangestad, & Lerma, 1990). Once in a romantic relationship, individuals who report strong commitment to their current partner rate alternative romantic partners as less attractive than do those who are weakly committed to their current partner (Johnson & Rusbult, 1989; Lydon, Fitzsimons, & Naidoo, 2003; see also, Meyer, Berkman, Karremans, & Lieberman, 2011). Participants highly (vs. lowly) committed to their current partner also attend less to attractive alternatives (Linardatos & Lydon, 2011; Maner, Gailliot, & Miller, 2009). Thus, people seem to shield their relationships from potential threats.

Conclusion

When attempting to understand what people think, feel, and do, we must understand what people want (Kruglanski, Chernikova, Rosenzweig, & Kopetz, 2014) and how they go about getting it (Kruglanski et al., 2002). Almost everything people do is driven by their personal goals (Kruglanski, 1996; Kruglanski & Orehek, 2009). People want, and need, to have lasting and deep social connections with other people. Satisfaction of the need to form social relationships characterized by lasting commitment is critical for human functioning and flourishing, and therefore represents a goal that deserves special consideration (Bowlby, 1969; Baumeister & Leary, 1995; Feeney & Collins, 2015; Lakey & Orehek, 2011). Just as a person becomes committed to any other means of goal attainment, people become committed to specific relationship partners who have proven themselves to be instrumental (Rusbult, Agnew, & Arriaga, 2012). When commitment to a relationship partner is strong, relationship maintenance becomes a goal. When a person establishes a close bond with another person and relies on him or her to help pursue goals, s/he must keep in touch with the person, be responsive to his or her needs, and otherwise maintain the relationship. Thus, an important aspect of a "people as means" approach is the active process of means maintenance.

The people as means notion was developed originally to understand the way in which perceiving others as instrumental influences evaluations of the relationship with that person (Orehek & Forest, 2016). But, what role do close relationships have in moving individual goal pursuit forward? Close relationships can serve as both a catalyst and a constraint to individual ambitions. While the term catalyst typically has a positive connotation and constraint a negative connotation, each function can be beneficial or harmful, depending on the goals of the person. When a partner serves as a catalyst to individual goal pursuit, she makes it more likely that the person will attain a goal. For example, when a friend applauds your marathon training, she supports you in the endeavor and provides a morale boost that facilitates increased effort investment in the goal. However, a person can also serve as a catalyst to self-defeating behaviors. Engaging in behaviors that may typically be viewed as unwise, such as drug abuse (Kopetz, Lejuez, Wiers, & Kruglanski, 2013), prostitution (Kopetz, Collado, & Lejuez, 2015), over-eating (Orehek & Vazeou-Nieuwenhuis, 2016), joining a terrorist organization (Orehek & Vazeou-Nieuwenhuis, 2014), or martyrdom (Orehek et al., 2014) represent instances of goal pursuit (Kopetz & Orehek, 2015) in which a person who serves as an instrumental means to these goal may be considered a catalyst to risky behavior.

Social relationships also serve as a constraint when partners establish norms and set expectations. A person constrains goal pursuit when they hinder progress on that goal. When a person interferes with healthy or productive pursuit, this constraint is detrimental to positive life outcomes. Importantly, relationships can often constrain an individual in a way that prevents them from engaging in self-defeating behaviors. When one's social network members constrain behavior by communicating that drug abuse, unhealthy actions, self-harm, and violence are unacceptable; it prevents the person from engaging in such activities. Thus, in order for people to engage in self-defeating behaviors, they must establish relationships with people who support such practices and be willing to suffer strife in relationships that do not support such behaviors (Kopetz & Orehek, 2015). Thus, the constraining function of relationships is just as important as the catalytic function.

References

Aarts, H., & Dijksterhuis, A. (2000). The automatic activation of goal-directed behaviour: The case of travel habit. *Journal of Environmental Psychology*, 20(1), 75–82.

Ainsworth, M. D., & Bell, S. M. (1970). Attachment, exploration, and separation: illustrated by the behavior of one-year-olds in a strange situation. *Child Development*, 41(1), 49–67.

Armstrong, B. F., & Kammrath, L. K. (2015). Depth and breadth tactics in support seeking. *Social Psychological and Personality Science*, 6(1), 39–46.

Armstrong, B., Kammrath, L. K., Iida, M., & Suppes, L. (2017). Who you gonna call? A new theory and methodological approach to studying supporter-selection processes. Unpublished Data, Wake Forest University.

Bargh, J. A. (1990). Auto-motives: Preconscious determinants of social interaction. In E. T. Higgins & R. M. Sorrentino (Eds.), *Handbook of motivation and cognition: Foundations of social behavior, Vol. 2* (pp. 93–130). New York: Guilford Press.

Bargh, J. A., & Chartrand, T. L. (1999). The unbearable automaticity of being. *American Psychologist*, 54, 462–479.

Baumeister, R. F., & Leary, M. R. (1995). The need to belong: desire for interpersonal attachments as a fundamental human motivation. *Psychological Bulletin*, 117(3), 497–529.

Bélanger, J. J., Kruglanski, A. W., Chen, X., & Orehek, E. (2014). Bending perception to desire: Effects of task demands, motivation, and cognitive resources. *Motivation and Emotion*, 38(6), 802–814.

Bélanger, J. J., Kruglanski, A. W., Chen, X., Orehek, E., & Johnson, D. J. (2015). When Mona Lisa smiled and love was in the air: On the cognitive energetics of motivated judgments. *Social Cognition*, 33(2), 104–119.

Bowlby, J. (1969). *Attachment and loss: Vol. 1. Attachment*. New York: Basic Books.

Carver, C. S., & Scheier, M. F. (1998). *On the self-regulation of behavior*. New York: Cambridge University Press.

Cheung, E. O., Gardner, W. L., & Anderson, J. F. (2015). Emotionships examining people's emotion-regulation relationships and their consequences for well-being. *Social Psychological and Personality Science*, 6(4), 407–414.

Chun, W. Y., Kruglanski, A. W., Sleeth-Keppler, D., & Friedman, R. S. (2011). Multifinality in implicit choice. *Journal of Personality and Social Psychology*, 101, 1124–1137.

Cohen, S., & Janicki-Deverts, D. (2009). Can we improve our physical health by altering our social networks? *Perspectives on Psychological Science*, *4*(4), 375–378.

Converse, B. A., & Fishbach, A. (2012). Instrumentality boosts: Appreciation helpers are more appreciated while they are useful. *Psychological Science*, 23, 560–566.

Eastwick, P. W., Finkel, E. J., Mochon, D., & Ariely, D. (2007). Selective versus unselective romantic desire: Not all reciprocity is created equal. *Psychological Science*, *18*(4), 317–319.

Eastwick, P. W., & Hunt, L. L. (2014). Relational mate value: Consensus and uniqueness in romantic evaluations. *Journal of Personality and Social Psychology*, 106(5), 728–751.

Feeney, B. C. (2004). A secure base: Responsive support of goal strivings and exploration in adult intimate relationships. *Journal of Personality and Social Psychology*, 87(5), 631–648.

Feeney, B. C., & Collins, N. L. (2015). A new look at social support: A theoretical perspective on thriving through relationships. *Personality and Social Psychology Review*, 19, 113–147.

Feeney, B. C., & Thrush, R. L. (2010). Relationship influences on exploration in adulthood: The characteristics and function of a secure base. *Journal of Personality and Social Psychology*, 98, 57–76.

Finkel, E. J., Hui, C. M., Carswell, K. L., & Larson, G. M. (2014). The suffocation of marriage: Climbing Mount Maslow without enough oxygen. *Psychological Inquiry*, 25, 1–41

Fishbach, A., Friedman, R. S., & Kruglanski, A. W. (2003). Leading us not into temptation: Momentary allurements elicit overriding goal activation. *Journal of Personality and Social Psychology*, 84(2), 296–309.

Fishbach, A., & Shah, J. Y. (2006). Self-control in action: implicit dispositions toward goals and away from temptations. *Journal of Personality and Social Psychology*, 90(5), 820–832.

Fishbach, A., Shah, J. Y., & Kruglanski, A. W. (2004). Emotional transfer in goal systems. *Journal of Experimental Social Psychology*, 40, 723–738.

Fitzsimons, G. M., & Bargh, J. A. (2003). Thinking of you: nonconscious pursuit of interpersonal goals associated with relationship partners. *Journal of Personality and Social Psychology*, 84(1), 148–164.

Fitzsimons, G. M., & Finkel, E. J. (2010). Interpersonal influences on self-regulation. *Current Directions in Psychological Science*, 19(2), 101–105.

Fitzsimons, G. M., & Fishbach, A. (2010). Shifting closeness: Interpersonal effects of personal goal progress. *Journal of Personality and Social Psychology*, 98, 535–549.

Fitzsimons, G. M., Friesen, J., Orehek, E., & Kruglanski, A. (2009). Progress-induced goal shifting as a self-regulatory strategy. In J. P. Forgas, R. F. Baumeister, & D. M. Tice (Eds.), *Psychology of self-regulation: Cognitive, affective, and motivational processes* (pp. 181–194). New York: Psychology Press.

Fitzsimons, G. M., & Shah, J. Y. (2008). How goal instrumentality shapes relationship evaluations. *Journal of Personality and Social Psychology*, 95, 319–337.

Fletcher, G. J., Simpson, J. A., & Thomas, G. (2000). Ideals, perceptions, and evaluations in early relationship development. *Journal of Personality and Social Psychology*, 79(6), 933–940.

Fredrickson, B. L., & Roberts, T. A. (1997). Objectification theory. *Psychology of Women Quarterly*, 21(2), 173–206.

Furman, W., & Buhrmester, D. (1992). Age and sex differences in perceptions of networks of personal relationships. *Child Development*, 63(1), 103–115.

Gross, J., Lakey, B., Edinger, K., Orehek, E., & Heffron, D. (2009). Person perception in the college classroom: Accounting for taste in students' evaluations of teaching effectiveness. *Journal of Applied Social Psychology*, 39(7), 1609–1638.

Gross, J., Lakey, B., Lucas, J. L., LaCross, R., Plotkowski, A., & Winegard, B. (2015). Forecasting the student–professor matches that result in unusually effective teaching. *British Journal of Educational Psychology*, 85(1), 19–32.

Hamlin, J. K., Wynn, K., & Bloom, P. (2007). Social evaluation by preverbal infants. *Nature*, 450, 557–559.

Hazan, C., & Shaver, P. R. (2004). Attachment as an organizational framework for research on close relationships. In H. T. Reis, & C. E. Rusbult (Eds.), *Close relationships: Key readings* (pp. 153–174). Philadelphia, PA: Taylor & Francis.

Hofmann, W., Finkel, E. J., & Fitzsimons, G. M. (2015). Close relationships and self-regulation: How relationship satisfaction facilitates momentary goal pursuit. *Journal of Personality and Social Psychology*, 109(3), 434–452.

Horan, S. M., & Booth-Butterfield, M. (2010). Investing in affection: An investigation of affection exchange theory and relational qualities. *Communication Quarterly*, 58(4), 394–413.

Inagaki, T. K., & Eisenberger, N. I. (2012). Neural correlates of giving support to a loved one. *Psychosomatic Medicine*, 74(1), 3–7.

Inagaki, T. & Orehek, E. (in press). On the benefits of giving social support: When, why, and how support providers gain by caring for others. *Current Directions in Psychological Science*, 26, 109–113.

Jecker, J., & Landy, D. (1969). Liking a person as a function of doing him a favour. *Human Relations*, 22(4), 371–378.

Johnson, D. J., & Rusbult, C. E. (1989). Resisting temptation: Devaluation of alternative partners as a means of maintaining commitment in close relationships. *Journal of Personality and Social Psychology*, 57(6), 967–980.

Kahn, R. L., & Antonucci, T. C. (1980). Convoys over the life course: Attachment, roles, and social support. *Life-Span Development and Behavior*, 3, 253–286.

Karremans, J. C., Dotsch, R., & Corneille, O. (2011). Romantic relationship status biases memory of faces of attractive opposite-sex others: Evidence from a reverse-correlation paradigm. *Cognition*, 121, 422–426.

Kiecolt-Glaser, J. K., & Newton, T. L. (2001). Marriage and health: his and hers. *Psychological Bulletin*, 127(4), 472–503.

Kopetz, C. E., Collado, A., & Lejuez, C. W. (2015). When the end (automatically) justifies the means: Automatic tendency toward sex exchange for crack cocaine. *Motivation Science*, 1(4), 233.

Köpetz, C., Faber, T., Fishbach, A., & Kruglanski, A. W. (2011). The multifinality constraints effect: How goal multiplicity narrows the means set to a focal end. *Journal of Personality and Social Psychology*, 100, 810–826.

Köpetz, C. E., Lejuez, C. W., Wiers, R. W., & Kruglanski, A. W. (2013). Motivation and self-regulation in addiction a call for convergence. *Perspectives on Psychological Science*, 8 (1), 3–24.

Kopetz, C., & Orehek, E. (2015). When the end justifies the means self-defeating behaviors as "rational" and "successful" self-regulation. *Current Directions in Psychological Science*, 24(5), 386–391.

Kruglanski, A. W. (1996). Goals as knowledge structures. In P. M. Gollwitzer, & J. A. Bargh (Eds.), *The psychology of action: Linking cognition and motivation to behavior* (pp. 599–618). New York: Guilford Press.

Kruglanski, A. W., Chen, X., Dechesne, M., Fishman, S., & Orehek, E. (2009). Fully committed: Suicide bombers' motivation and the quest for personal significance. *Political Psychology*, 30, 331–557.

Kruglanski, A. W., Chernikova, M., Babush, M., Dugas, M., & Schumpe, B. (2015). The architecture of goal systems: Multifinality, equifinality, and counterfinality in means – end relations. *Advances in Motivation Science*, 2, 69–98.

Kruglanski, A. W., Chernikova, M., Rosenzweig, E., & Kopetz, C. (2014). On motivational readiness. *Psychological Review*, 121(3), 367–388.

Kruglanski, A. W., Dechesne, M., Orehek, E., & Pierro, A. (2009). Three decades of lay epistemics: The why, how, and who of knowledge formation. *European Review of Social Psychology*, 20(1), 146–191.

Kruglanski, A. W., Kopetz, C., Belanger, J. J., Chun, W. Y., Orehek, E., & Fishbach, A. (2013). Features of multifinality. *Personality and Social Psychology Review*, 17, 22–39.

Kruglanski, A. W., & Orehek, E. (2009). Toward a relativity theory of rationality. *Social Cognition*, 27(5), 639.

Kruglanski, A. W. & Orehek, E. (2011). The role of quest for significance in motivating terrorism. In J. Forgas, A. Kruglanski, & K. Williams (Eds.), *Social conflict and aggression* (pp. 153–164). New York: Psychology Press.

Kruglanski, A. W., Orehek, E., Dechesne, M., & Pierro, A. (2010). Lay epistemic theory: The motivational, cognitive, and social aspects of knowledge formation. *Social and Personality Psychology Compass*, 4(10), 939–950.

Kruglanski, A. W., Raviv, A., Bar-Tal, D., Raviv, A., Sharvit, K., Ellis, S., Bar, R., Pierro, A., & Mannetti, L. (2005). Says who?: Epistemic authority effects in social judgment. *Advances in Experimental Social Psychology*, 37, 345–392.

Kruglanski, A. W., Shah, J., Fishbach, A., Friedman, R., Chun, W., & Sleeth-Keppler, D. (2002). A theory of goal systems. In M. P. Zanna (Ed.), *Advances in experimental social psychology* (Vol. 34, pp. 331–378). San Diego, CA: Academic Press.

Lakey, B., Cohen, J. L., & Neely, L. C. (2008). Perceived support and relational effects in psychotherapy process constructs. *Journal of Counseling Psychology*, 55(2), 209–220.

Lakey, B., & Orehek, E. (2011). Relational regulation theory: A new approach to explain perceived social support's link to mental health. *Psychological Review*, 118, 482–495.

Leander, N. P., Shah, J. Y., & Chartrand, T. L. (2009). Moments of weakness: The implicit context dependencies of temptations. *Personality and Social Psychology Bulletin*, 35, 853–856.

Leary, M. R., & Baumeister, R. F. (2000). The nature and function of self-esteem: Sociometer theory. *Advances in Experimental Social Psychology*, 32, 1–62.

Light, A. E., & Fitzsimons, G. M. (2014). Contextualizing marriage as a means and a goal. *Psychological Inquiry*, 25, 88–94.

Linardatos, L., & Lydon, J. E. (2011). Relationship-specific identification and spontaneous relationship maintenance processes. *Journal of Personality and Social Psychology*, 101, 737–753.

Lydon, J. E., Fitzsimons, G. M., & Naidoo, L. (2003). Devaluation versus enhancement of attractive alternatives: A critical test using the calibration paradigm. *Personality and Social Psychology Bulletin*, 29(3), 349–359.

Maner, J. K., Gailliot, M. T., & Miller, S. L. (2009). The implicit cognition of relationship maintenance: Inattention to attractive alternatives. *Journal of Experimental Social Psychology*, 45(1), 174–179.

Meyer, M. L., Berkman, E. T., Karremans, J. C., & Lieberman, M. D. (2011). Incidental regulation of attraction: The neural basis of the derogation of attractive alternatives in romantic relationships. *Cognition and Emotion*, 25(3), 490–505.

Murray, S. L., Aloni, M., Holmes, J. G., Derrick, J. L., Stinson, D. A., & Leder, S. (2009). Fostering partner dependence as trust-insurance: The implicit contingencies of the exchange script in close relationships. *Journal of Personality and Social Psychology*, 96, 324–348.

Murray, S. L., & Holmes, J. G. (1999). The (mental) ties that bind: Cognitive structures that predict relationship resilience. *Journal of Personality and Social Psychology*, 77(6), 1228–1244.

Murray, S. L., Holmes, J. G., & Griffin, D. W. (1996). The self-fulfilling nature of positive illusions in romantic relationships: love is not blind, but prescient. *Journal of Personality and Social Psychology*, 71(6), 1155–1180.

Murray, S. L., Leder, S., MacGregor, J. C. D., Holmes, J. G., Pinkus, R. T., & Harris, B. (2009). Becoming irreplaceable: How comparisons to the partner's alternatives differentially affect low and high self-esteem people. *Journal of Experimental Social Psychology*, 45, 1180–1191.

Neely, L. C., Lakey, B., Cohen, J. L., Barry, R., Orehek, E., Abeare, C. A., & Mayer, W. (2006). Trait and social processes in the link between social support and affect: An experimental, laboratory investigation. *Journal of Personality*, 74, 1015–1046.

Nussbaum, M. C. (1998). *Sex and social justice*. Oxford: Oxford University Press.

Orehek, E., Bessarabova, E., Chen, X., & Kruglanski, A. W. (2011). Positive affect as informational feedback in goal pursuit. *Motivation and Emotion*, 35, 44–51.

Orehek, E. & Forest, A. L. (2016). When people serve as means to goals: Implications of a motivational account of close personal relationships. *Current Directions in Psychological Science*, 25, 79–84.

Orehek, E., Forest, A. L., & Wingrove, S. (2017). When people serve as means to multiple goals: Perceived instrumentality and relationship evaluations. Unpublished data, University of Pittsburgh.

Orehek, E., Mauro, R., Kruglanski, A. W., & van der Bles, A. M. (2012). Prioritizing association strength versus value: Regulatory mode and means evaluation in single and multigoal contexts. *Journal of Personality and Social Psychology*, 102, 22–31.

Orehek, E., Sasota, J. A., Kruglanski, A. W., Dechesne, M., & Ridgeway, L. (2014). Interdependent self-construals mitigate the fear of death and augment the willingness to become a martyr. *Journal of Personality and Social Psychology*, 107(2), 265–275.

Orehek, E., & Vazeou-Nieuwenhuis, A. (2013). Sequential and concurrent strategies of multiple goal pursuit. *Review of General Psychology*, 17, 339–349.

Orehek, E. & Vazeou-Nieuwenhuis, A. (2014). Understanding the terrorist threat: Policy implications of a motivational account of terrorism. *Policy Insights from the Behavioral and Brain Sciences*, 1, 248–255.

Orehek, E. & Vazeou-Nieuwenhuis, A. (2016). On the obesity problem: Policy implications of a motivational account of (un)healthy eating. *Social Issues and Policy Review*, 10, 151–180.

Orehek, E., Vazeou-Niuwenhuis, A., & Kruglanski, A. W. (2017). Failure makes society seem fonder: An inquiry into the roots of social interdependence. Unpublished data, University of Pittsburgh.

Orehek, E., Vazeou-Nieuwenhuis, A., Quick, E., & Weaverling, G. C. (2017). Attachment and self-regulation. *Personality and Social Psychology Bulletin*, 43, 365–380.

Orehek, E. & Weaverling, C. G. (in press). On the nature of objectification: Implications of considering people as means to goals. *Perspectives on Psychological Science*.

Ouellette, J. A., & Wood, W. (1998). Habit and intention in everyday life: the multiple processes by which past behavior predicts future behavior. *Psychological Bulletin*, 124(1), 54–74.

Overall, N. C., Fletcher, G. J., & Simpson, J. A. (2006). Regulation processes in intimate relationships: the role of ideal standards. *Journal of Personality and Social Psychology*, 91(4), 662–685.

Penner, L. A., Dovidio, J. F., & Albrecht, T. L. (2000). Helping victims of loss and trauma: A social psychological perspective. In J. H. Harvey, & E. D. Miller (Eds.), *Loss and trauma: General and close relationship perspectives* (pp. 62–85). New York: Brunner-Routledge.

Piferi, R. L., & Lawler, K. A. (2006). Social support and ambulatory blood pressure: An examination of both receiving and giving. *International Journal of Psychophysiology*, 62(2), 328–336.

Rusbult, C. E., Agnew, C., & Arriaga, X. (2012). The investment model of commitment processes. In P. Van Lange, A. Kruglanski, & E. Higgins (Eds.), *Handbook of theories of social psychology* (pp. 218–232). London: Sage.

Shah, J. (2003). Automatic for the people: How representations of significant others implicitly affect goal pursuit. *Journal of Personality and Social Psychology*, 84, 661–681.

Shah, J. Y., Friedman, R., & Kruglanski, A. W. (2002). Forgetting all else: On the antecedents and consequences of goal shielding. *Journal of Personality and Social Psychology*, 83, 1261–1280.

Simpson, J. A., Gangestad, S. W., & Lerma, M. (1990). Perception of physical attractiveness: Mechanisms involved in the maintenance of romantic relationships. *Journal of Personality and Social Psychology*, 59(6), 1192–1201.

Slotter, E. B., & Gardner, W. L. (2011). Can you help me become the "me" I want to be? The role of goal pursuit in friendship formation. *Self and Identity*, 10(2), 231–247.

vanDellen, M. R., & Hoyle, R. H. (2010). Regulatory accessibility and social influences on state self-control. *Personality and Social Psychology Bulletin*, 36, 251–263.

vanDellen, M. R., Shah, J. Y., Leander, N. P., Delose, J. E., & Bornstein, J. X. (2015). In good company: Managing interpersonal resources that support self-regulation. *Personality and Social Psychology Bulletin*, 41, 869–882.

Veenstra, A., Lakey, B., Cohen, J., Neely, L., Orehek, E., Barry, R., & Abeare, C. (2011). Forecasting the specific providers that recipients will perceive as unusually supportive. *Personal Relationships*, 18, 677–696.

Weinstein, N., & Ryan, R. M. (2010). When helping helps: autonomous motivation for prosocial behavior and its influence on well-being for the helper and recipient. *Journal of Personality and Social Psychology*, 98(2), 222–244.

Williamson, G. M., Clark, M. S., Pegalis, L. J., & Behan, A. (1996). Affective consequences of refusing to help in communal and exchange relationships. *Personality and Social Psychology Bulletin*, 22, 34–47.

8

THE RISE AND FALL OF VIOLENT EXTREMISM

The Science behind Community-based Interventions

Jocelyn J. Bélanger

> You can bomb the world to pieces, but you can't bomb it into peace.
>
> *(A graffito in Washington, DC)*

Despite declining rates of criminality in many parts of the world (*The Economist*, 2013), the problem of radicalization and violent extremism is a growing concern. According to the Bureau of Counterterrorism (BoC, 2014), terrorist attacks have increased 35% (13,463 incidents) worldwide over 2013, resulting in the death of at least 32,700 people. Beyond infamous Islamist groups, such as ISIS and Al-Qaeda, who are credited with the vast majority of attacks, more than 250 terrorist organizations have used or have threatened to use violence to further a wide range of ideologies, such as racial supremacy, ethno-nationalism, and environmentalism (BoC, 2014). Recently, the United Nations Security Council estimated that up to 30,000 foreign fighters have traveled to join Al-Qaeda and ISIS (Security Council, 2015).

With the world continuously on the cusp of a new terrorist attack, it is generally agreed that shedding light on how and why individuals are willing to join terrorist organizations is key to curbing the rise of violent extremism. Indeed, without basic knowledge of the main drivers of radicalization, developing effective community-based counterterrorism initiatives remains quixotic. Thousands of books have been written about terrorism and, at this point, the number of experts trying to understand violent extremism probably exceeds the number of actual terrorists (which is not entirely a bad thing). In fact, so many people have written so much on terrorism that one might truly wonder why anyone would bother to write further. Yet, the reality is that for many frontline workers and government officials, hard evidence about violent extremism is as hard to find as a needle in a haystack.

So what happened? Why is such evidence lacking? Part of the answer is that scientific rigor has given way under the urgency of finding immediate solutions to terrorism. Specifically, while important questions have been raised (e.g., risk and protection factors, how people join terrorist groups, etc.) and a number of important insights about violent extremism have been uncovered, many sweeping remarks have also been made based on second-hand analyses and shaky empirical evidence. As a result, oft-cited assertions about terrorists have been mistaken for undeniable truths among practitioners and researchers. A closer look at the evidence supporting these claims has revealed important shortcomings. For instance, the Canadian Security Intelligence Service (CSIS, 2015) recently revisited the widespread belief that terrorists do not have a distinct personality profile. In their extensive literature review, they found "only one empirical study where terrorists were administered a standardized personality test and the findings were compared to the personality traits of individuals not involved in terrorism" (p. 11). The lone study was conducted by Gottschalk and Gottschalk (2004) and the standardized test was the MMPI-2, an instrument more related to mental illness than to personality. To further complicate matters, terrorists ($N = 90$) in that study reported higher levels of psychopathic, depressive, and schizophrenic tendencies, which challenges yet another common belief that mental illness is not related to violent extremism (Corrado, 1981; Silke, 1998; cf. Corner & Gill, 2015; Gill, Horgan, & Deckert, 2014).

When it is not contradictory evidence, it is the long lists of potential root causes of terrorism that has contributed to the murkiness of the field. To the question, "Why do people become terrorists?" which has permeated research efforts since the early 1970s, researchers have generated a plethora of seemingly unrelated psychological motives (a point which I address later on) based on questionable evidence or sheer speculation. In all fairness, accessing terrorist samples is excruciatingly painstaking—a reality that impairs researchers' ability to replicate and rigorously test innovative hypotheses. Unsurprisingly, then, terrorism researchers have eschewed broad theorizing, and little effort has been made to piece together the knowledge accumulated over the years. An unintended consequence of this reluctance to theorize is that, despite years of academic research, most terrorism-related questions continue to elude us like sand through our fingers.

At least that was true until social psychologist, Arie Kruglanski, and his team, started to bring not only substantial empirical evidence to the table, but a comprehensive theoretical framework to piece this fragmented field together. In what follows, I would like to pay tribute to my mentor's impressive and growing contribution to our understanding of violent extremism. I begin by clarifying what is meant by radicalization, what are the most important risk factors and how it can be observed (a topical issue for law-enforcement agencies). Then, I introduce the Quest for Personal Significance theory to discuss what drives the radicalization process and how to turn it around to bring about deradicalization. Finally, I explain how this knowledge can be translated into concrete actions with the help of community-based organizations to prevent violent extremism.

Radicalization

Radicalization is generally defined as "the social and psychological process of incrementally experienced commitment to extremist political or religious ideology" (Horgan, 2009, p. 152). In simple words, radicalizing means adopting political or religious beliefs that are not shared by most people. Although radical ideas are often perceived as malevolent and dangerous, they are necessary for our societies to grow: They are the seeds that germinate into social movements and eventually bear fruit by changing our sociopolitical landscape. Throughout human history, there have been many examples of people inspired by radical ideas. Think of women's suffrage or the end of racial segregation, for example. Both were radical ideas that met great resistance, but today, they are no longer disputed in mainstream politics (at least in the US), they are the "new normal." To be sure, radicalization is not specific to any political or religious ideology, nor is it, per se, a risk to public safety. However, radicalization can and does become a major concern when radical ideas are expressed through violent behaviors, in which case government officials, scholars, and practitioners start talking about violent extremism. Below, I describe three real cases that provide a flavor of the different trajectories leading to violent extremism. They are discussed across the rest of the chapter to illustrate some of the key concepts.

Three Stories of Radicalization

Our first case is Audrey. She has an unconditional love for animals and she can't stand animal cruelty. She becomes interested in several local animal advocacy groups, but notices that these actions have little impact on society. The daily pang of disappointment and powerlessness kindles her desire for political action. She joins an ecologist group and falls in love with its leader. Their thinking progressively polarizes and eventually everything becomes permissible to protect wildlife from human savagery. Together with the rest of the group, Audrey sabotages government, research, and industrial facilities that she believes have violated animal rights.

Meet Vincent. From a very young age, he has been interested in philosophy and sociopolitical issues. Through friends he learns about an international social protest movement taking place in major cities around the world. He joins the local movement with friends. Weeks later, during one of the protests, Vincent and his comrades are arrested for throwing stones at police officers pushing back the wave of protesters demanding social justice.

Our last case is Abu Ali. On a sunny January morning he crossed the Turkish border into ISIS territory. He felt he was a man with nothing to lose. He had recently divorced his wife (in part because his brother-in-law was fighting with the Syrian army), and he was struggling with a severe addiction to alcohol and cigarettes. He was out of shape and definitely not fit to fight, but the prospect of a desk job with ISIS in the caliphate meant he could wipe his sinful slate clean and make himself into a good Muslim.

These real case studies illustrate, albeit succinctly, different pathways to radicalization. There are two points to be made here. First, there is a common thread of frustration, anger and vengeance that weaves through these stories—some sort of emotional upheaval that compels one to use violence to redress an injustice, a wrong committed to one's values or community. And indeed, the terrorism literature is replete with case studies supporting this perspective (e.g., Della Porta, 2013; Gurski, 2015; Horgan, 2009). Second, these stories reveal that radicalization is not an "all or nothing" psychological phenomenon; it is a continuum with different degrees of involvement in social movements, which is what we turn to next.

Fifty Shades of Radicalization

Kruglanski and colleagues (2014) recently theorized that the radicalization process may be experienced through different degrees of increasing intensity, whereby higher levels of radicalization represent greater "imbalance between the focal goal served by the extreme behavior and other common ends that people have" (p. 71). At the lower end of the spectrum, the individual may simply agree with the group's ideology (passive support). The person may then become engaged in a series of behaviors that allow him or her to show support for the group (active support), such as "liking" the group's Facebook page or sharing its messages (e.g., "tweets") on online platforms. At a higher degree of intensity, the individual becomes directly engaged in behaviors to further the cause (participation). Generally, because of the support that the group affords the individual, the person may not even be conscious of all the negative consequences his or her involvement entails. Yet, the person sacrifices several important life domains, such as family, health, education, and career. Ultimately, when an individual is radicalized at the highest level, that person becomes ready to sacrifice everything, including his or her life for the ideology (self-sacrifice).

No consensus exists on the specific stages or phases involved in the making of a violent extremist for at least two reasons. The first is methodological. Low-base-rate phenomena, such as radicalization, are intrinsically difficult to predict because of the high probability of false positives, even when tests with high specificity and sensitivity are developed (for a discussion, see Hecker & Thorpe, 2015 and Meehl & Rosen, 1955). In addition to this methodological hurdle, researchers have often tarred terrorists with the same brush, failing to consider the wide range of roles individuals may take on within the organization (Horgan, 2008). Although it remains to be empirically demonstrated, the process of radicalization is unlikely to be the same for a suicide bomber as it is for someone who provides logistical and financial support to the group.

Risk Factors

In spite of these gaps in knowledge, valuable information about radicalization is beginning to emerge. Beyond being a young male, one of the most robust risk factors associated with violent extremism is knowing someone who belongs to a radical organization. Sageman (2008) reports that for Al-Qaeda "about two thirds of the people in the sample were friends with other people who joined together or already had some connection to terrorism" (p. 66). In her research with the Brigate Rosse, Della Porta (1988) reaches similar conclusion. She reports that 69% (843/1214) of Italian left-wing militants who joined an underground group had been friends with at least one member before joining. One explanation for this phenomenon is that friends and family members share strong social bonds, which foster trust and organizational commitment (Krebs, 2002; Lin, 2001; Qin, Xu, Hu, Sageman, & Chen, 2005; Sageman, 2004), two key elements complex military operations need to succeed. This could potentially explain why terrorists have been repeatedly found to be siblings: The Tsarnaev brothers (Boston Bombings), the Kouachi brothers (Charlie Hebdo attacks), the Bakraoui brothers (Brussels attacks), not to mention that six of the nineteen 9-11 hijackers were also brothers.

Although these risk factors are crucial to our understanding of violent extremism, one key question is whether there are any early signs or "symptoms" of radicalization which could help frontline workers flag potential terrorists before it is too late.

The Checklist

Security and law-enforcement agencies love checklists. After all, they are concrete and observable indicators that enable them to detect individuals susceptible to committing violence to further an ideological cause. Checklist-based screening instruments have been devised for risk assessment of violent and mentally ill offenders (e.g., Violent Risk Appraisal Guide, Harris, Rice, & Quinsey, 1993); however, similar tools for violent extremists are still in their infancy (e.g., ERG22+, VERA-2). Nevertheless, researchers and practitioners have started to identify a series of potential behavioral indicators which, in their proper context, may help flag those that have been lured into violent extremism. For instance, in his recent book, *The Threat from Within*, former CSIS strategic analyst Phil Gurski (2015) discusses eleven indicators related to Al-Qaeda-inspired radicalization and violence, which arguably can be clustered into the following three dimensions: (1) intolerance and rejection of alternative worldviews, (2) obsession with the cause (e.g., sacrifice of other life domains, excessive violent media consumption), and (3) association with like-minded people (e.g., sudden change in the circle of friends). Similar checklists have been developed by other organizations and researchers as well (e.g., Bélanger et al., 2015a; Australian Government Attorney-General's Department, 2015). More importantly, if one concedes that these checklists share a common viewpoint of the "symptoms" associated with radicalization, then the next logical step would be to identify what causes these symptoms. And if one generally agrees that, once ignited, goals mobilize and direct attentional resources toward means serving them (Bélanger et al., 2016; Campbell & Pritchard, 1976; Kanfer & Ackerman, 1989; Kruglanski, et al., 2012; Pinder, 1984), it follows that we should take an interest in the goals that propel individuals to engage in ideological violence.

Beyond the Checklist: Why do People Radicalize?

Understanding the motivational underpinnings of terrorism has been at the top of scholars' research agenda for decades. In an analysis of this literature, Kruglanski and colleagues (2009) documented over 30 different motives associated with suicide terrorism. This laundry list, scattered enough to make anyone's head spin, includes motivations such as resistance to foreign occupation (Pape, 2005), honor, dedication to the leader, social status, pain, personal loss, feminism (Bloom, 2005), humiliation, lack of alternative prospects, the need to belong (Stern, 2003), and emotions such as revenge and resentment (Ricolfi, 2005).

Some researchers have reduced the plurality of motivations to a smaller set of dimensions, namely, *ideological reasons* and *personal causes* (e.g., Pedahzur, 2005; Taarnby, 2005). Motives aggregate around the theme of ideology include defenses of *sacred values*, defined as "nonnegotiable preferences whose defense compels actions beyond … calculable costs and consequences" (Atran, 2016, p. 2; see also Ginges et al., 2007). Sacred values include duties such as carrying out God's will and liberating one's occupied land (Atran, 2004, 2006, 2016; Pape, 2005). Motives centered on personal causes have revolved around the notion of grievances, including relative deprivation, loss of honor, pain, and trauma (Bloom, 2005; Gurr, 1970). In addition to ideological and personal motives, a third motivational category incorporating *social duties* and obligations has been suggested, based on historical records of Japanese Kamikaze pilots during World War II (e.g., Ohnuki-Tierney, 2006) and other accounts of suicide terrorism (Bloom, 2005; Gambetta, 2005).

Although this classification of motives is helpful, it is purely descriptive and, as Kruglanski and colleagues (2009) have observed, it "stops short of explicating the underlying dynamics of suicidal terrorism" (p. 334). However, if we assume that all these different approaches capture something of the truth, the question is can we reconcile the notions of grievances, ideology, and social processes under a common framework? Could the confluence of these three ingredients help better explain how and why individuals radicalize? The Quest for Personal Significance Theory articulates how this could well be the case (Kruglanski et al., 2009).

The Quest for Personal Significance

The theory proposes that there is a common human striving for *personal significance* underlying the grievances discussed in the terrorism literature. Building on the work of Victor Frankl (2000) and Abraham Maslow (1943, 1965), the quest for significance refers to people's need to "make a difference," "to matter," "to be someone." Of note, psychologists have long recognized the notion of significance and discussed it using various labels such as the need for achievement (McClelland, Atkinson, Clark, & Lowell, 1953), competence (Bandura, 1977; Deci & Ryan, 2000), self-esteem (Crocker and Wolfe, 2001), meaning and existence (e.g., Frankl, 2000; Greenberg et al., 1990; Steger, Frazier, Oishi, & Kaler, 2006). Central to all of these perspectives is the role of society in prescribing which activities are worth pursuing to gain significance.

Activating the Significance Quest

According to Kruglanski et al. (2009, 2014), three events can activate the significance quest: (1) the loss of significance (e.g., humiliation, social alienation), (2) a threat to one's significance (e.g., the possibility of being rejected), and (3) the opportunity of gaining considerable significance (e.g., becoming a hero, a martyr).

The three case studies mentioned earlier illustrate how these concepts translate into the real world. In the case of Audrey, her significance loss stemmed from feeling powerless and appalled at animal cruelty, which led her to join a group impassioned about animal rights to redress this inequality. But could this moral outrage really be sufficient to instigate her willingness to use violence (e.g., burning down research facilities) and to put herself in harm's way for the sake of the cause? There are grounds to believe so. For instance, Dugas and colleagues (2016) recently demonstrated across a variety of experiments and culturally-distinct samples, that decreases in individuals' significance (e.g., social rejection, failing an IQ test vs. fun puzzles) were associated with greater readiness to self-sacrifice for a cause (see also Bélanger, Caouette, Sharvit, & Dugas, 2014). One of their experiments also evinced that self-sacrifice for a cause was an effective means to restore significance. Similar patterns of results were obtained with a terrorist sample of 241 members of the LTTE (Liberation Tigers of Tamil Eelam): Terrorists' personal insignificance (i.e., feeling small, worthless, and hopeless) positively predicted their willingness to self-sacrifice for their group, which in turn predicted their support for armed struggle to further their ethnonationalist agenda (Bélanger, 2013).

Neuroscientific evidence also suggests that significance loss can instigate strong reactions. According to Eisenberger, Lieberman, and Williams (2003), the brain correlates associated with physical pain are the same as those associated with social pain (e.g., as when triggered by social rejection). If significance loss is indeed psychologically painful, it is conceivable that individuals would be motivated to use extreme means to mitigate it. This would also explain why the threat of losing significance is sufficient to motivate individuals to take action to prevent it. To come back to the story of Vincent, one hypothesis is that he joined a social movement and engaged in political violence to avoid receiving the cold shoulder from his friends who had already joined the movement. In other words, jumping on the bandwagon was a means to prevent his loss of significance. A slightly different dynamic can be gleaned from Abu Ali's case. He was living a miserable life, going nowhere. ISIS promised to restore his dignity and purpose, and the caliphate might have been enticing enough to convince him to travel to a conflict zone. In a way, adhering to ISIS and "basking in its glory" could have been a way of expiating his previous sins (e.g., excessive drinking and smoking), allowing him to be reborn a respectable Muslim.

Consequences of Triggering the Significance Quest

What are the consequences of activating a goal as important as the significance quest? Basic social psychology research informs us that goals are *selfish* (Bargh & Huang, 2009; Köpetz, Hofmann, & Wiers, 2014) in the sense that, "once active, goals pursue their own agendas independently of conscious control" (Bargh, Green, Fitzsimons, 2008, p. 3) and suppress alternative goals that vie for limited attentional resources—a phenomenon called *goal-shielding* (Shah, Friedman, and Kruglanski, 2002). Goal-shielding is part and parcel of effective goal-pursuit because it facilitates being on-task by inhibiting distracting information. Of note, goal-shielding is accentuated by the importance attributed to the goal. Put differently, the greater people's commitment to a goal, the greater the automatic inhibition of alternative goals. Consistent with these findings, Kruglanski and colleagues (2013a) proposed that activating the significance quest would result in the suppression and devaluation of other goals, including self-preservation, which is why, at the highest level of radicalization, terrorists are ready to sacrifice everything, including their own lives to further their ideology. Accounts provided by the Tamil Tigers in Sri Lanka support this proposition (see Hettiarachchi, 2014; Kruglanski et al., 2013a). For instance, in one interview a Tamil recalls his experience in one of the training camps that would make him a suicide bomber (i.e., a black tiger): "There they taught us to turn love into a passion for killing. All what we received and knew was hatred, murder and destruction" (Hettiarachchi, 2014, p. 10).

Furthermore, goal-shielding is more likely to occur when certain types of goals are pursued. In a series of experiments, Bélanger and colleagues (Bélanger, Lafrenière, Vallerand, & Kruglanski, 2013a) demonstrated that goals regularly in conflict with other goals (i.e., obsessive passions, see Vallerand et al., 2003; Bélanger et al., 2013b) facilitate the inhibition of alternative goals, whereas goals that are well-integrated with other life domains (i.e., harmonious passions) do not. Because it is more challenging to find means that fulfill several goals simultaneously (i.e., multifinal means, see Kruglanski et al., 2002, 2013b) as opposed to means that serve a single goal (i.e., unifinal means), an immediate consequence of inhibiting alternative goals is an expansion of the number of means suitable for goal-pursuit (see Köpetz, Faber, Fishbach, & Kruglanski, 2011). Consistent with this reasoning, in another set of experiments, Bélanger, Chamberland, Nociti, & Schumpe (2017) demonstrated that those with an obsessive passion for a cause (e.g., protecting the environment) reported greater moral disengagement and were thus supportive of radical (e.g., putting themselves in harm's way) means to further their cause. In contrast, harmonious passion was not related to moral disengagement and was associated with support for mainstream activism (e.g., peaceful protests). Similar results were found with supporters of the "Black Lives Matter" movement, which stands against violence and systematic racism toward black people (Blacks Lives Matter, n.d.). Overall, then, when people obsessively (vs harmoniously) pursue a cause, other life domains are suppressed from the mind and the pursuit of one's cause becomes unbridled—unconstrained by other considerations—as a result, violence becomes more permissible.

The Role of Social Networks and Ideology

Goal-activation and alternative-goal suppression are not enough to inspire behavior: Finding a means of achieving one's goal is also vital to energize behavior (Bélanger et al., 2016; Kruglanski et al., 2002; Kruglanski et al., 2012). In this regard, the Quest for Personal Significance proposes that joining a group is one of the fastest routes to gain significance. This is so because group membership tends to be rewarded with prestige, status, resources, and a sense of belonging (e.g., Tajfel & Turner, 1979). This propensity to turn to groups when in need of significance is called a *collectivistic shift* (Kruglanski, & Orehek, 2011; Kruglanski et al., 2013a).

Whilst defining oneself in terms of relationships with others (i.e., developing an interdependent self-construal, Markus & Kitayama, 1991) is an effective means of gaining significance, recent research shows that this psychological process could also have far-reaching implications for understanding radicalization. In a series of experiments, Orehek and colleagues (2014) demonstrated that:

> interdependent self-construals, compared to independent self-construals, attenuate death anxiety, reduce the avoidance of death, increase the approach

to death-related stimuli, induce a greater willingness to become a martyr, and induce a greater willingness to sacrifice the self for other members of important groups.

(p. 265)

As the old saying goes, there is strength in numbers: When individuals define themselves as part of a group, they feel empowered, and they become devoted to the defense of their group, even at the expense of their own lives if the group they belong to is threatened (Kruglanski et al., 2013a). Joining a group to gain recognition and significance, of course, is a normal process. It does not necessarily imply that individuals will turn to violence. As the theory suggests, choosing between violent and peaceful means critically depends on the type of ideology group members adhere to.

Loosely defined, ideologies are the ideas and beliefs through which we interpret our experiences, thereby influencing the decisions we make and the actions we take. They are "prepackaged units of interpretation that spread because of basic human motives to understand the world, avoid existential threat and maintain valued interpersonal relationships" (Jost, Ledgerwood, & Hardin, 2008, p. 1). Another fundamental characteristic of ideologies is that they are embedded in the values of one's group and thus, they provide group members with a shared sense of reality (Echterhoff, Higgins, & Levine, 2009; Hardin & Conley, 2001; Hardin & Higgins, 1996). Collectivistic ideologies thus "elucidate what a significance gain according to one's group consists of and afford a way of preventing a significance loss involving adherence to these ideological dictates" (Kruglanski et al., 2009, p. 349). In the case of terrorism-justifying ideologies, Kruglanski et al. (2014) postulate the presence of three fundamental ingredients:

> There is the element of *grievance* (injustice, harm) believed to have been suffered by one's group (religious, national, ethnic, etc.); there is a *culprit* presumed responsible for the perpetrated grievance (e.g., the United States, Israel, Christians, Crusaders, Jews), and there is a *morally warranted* and *effective* (hence, significance promoting) *method* of removing the dishonor created by the injustice, namely terrorism, for which the implementer is accorded reverence and appreciation from the group
>
> *(p. 77).*

It is also worth noting that those who defend the group are remembered long after their deaths (e.g., eulogy, songs, stories, etc.) and in joining the collective memory of the group, individuals can transcend death and live on in the memories of others (Elster, 2005). Kruglanski et al. (2009) noted this paradox: "the willingness to die in an act of suicidal terrorism may be motivated by the desire to live forever" (p. 336).

Moreover, ideologies do not have to be complex to be alluring. As a former jihadist pointed out in a recent interview with the *Guardian*:

> It's not about ideals—90% of them never subscribe to the ideals—it's other factors that are a draw. This is the new rock and roll; *jihad is sexy* (emphasis added). The kid who was not very good-looking now looks good holding a gun. He can get a bride now, he's powerful. The ISIS gun is as much a penis extension as the stockbroker with his Ferrari.
>
> *(McVeigh, 2015)*

As we will see a bit later, intervening on the morality and effectiveness of terrorism as a means of regaining significance might help people walk away from terrorism.

The Radicalization Process

In the foregoing sections, we argued that radicalization includes three key ingredients (1) a goal (i.e., the significance quest), (2) the means of achievement (i.e., the ideology), and (3) group processes which binds the first two ingredients together. But how does the radicalization process unfold to the point where one becomes compelled to harm others and even oneself for the sake of a cause? The case studies discussed across this chapter illustrate how this is possible. Importantly, they also reveal that the ingredients of radicalization may come in different temporal orders (Kruglanski et al., 2014); yet the cocktail, more often than not, results in accentuated radicalization to further a specific ideology.

In the case of Audrey, her grievance led her to join a group, and she progressively espoused its violent ideology through social interactions (especially with the leader of the organization, whom she was madly in love with). But Vincent's case is a bit different. Although he was already sensitive to social inequalities, it was through his friends that he learned about the social movement, and came to share its grievances. Abu Ali, on the other hand, originally had a grievance (i.e., a life going nowhere) and after learning about ISIS's ideology (probably through the media), he joined this group in the hope of restoring his sense of self.

In sum then, the Quest for Personal Significance explains the process of radicalization and integrates insights from a number of perspectives. It also does something that few other theories have attempted by explaining the different pathways that lead to violence. In the next section, I introduce another major contribution of this theoretical framework by discussing the topic of deradicalization. Currently, the Quest for Personal Significance is the only empirically-supported theory that describes the psychological mechanisms through which people abandon violence, while proposing concrete interventions oriented toward countering violent extremism.

Deradicalization

Kruglanski and colleagues (2014) define deradicalization as reversing the process of radicalization. Whereas "radicalization reflects increased commitment to the ideological quest for significance and to the violent means of its pursuit, coupled with reduced commitment to alternative, incompatible pursuits", the process of "deradicalization constitutes a decreased commitment to the ideological goal, accompanied by a resurgence of alternative pursuits and objectives" (p. 87).

Often, the reversal of this process is somewhat fortuitous. Recall the story of Abu Ali. Despite his best attempt to get a desk job with ISIS, his commanders kept using him as cannon fodder. After witnessing extreme amounts of wanton cruelty in Syria, a text message from his former wife (which he eventually remarried), spurred him into coordinating with smugglers to leave ISIS' territory. In the case of Vincent, after being arrested, he was ordered by the court to avoid participating in further protests. To stay in the movement, he became involved with a support group, created by and for militants, where he offered counseling. He realized that helping others made a bigger difference. When the movement fell apart, Vincent went back to school and completed a degree in social work to help fight inequalities. In the case of Audrey, she eventually realized that committing arson did not have much impact on animal rights. She left the movement and became an assistant veterinarian.

What transpires in these stories is that, at some point, all the protagonists became disillusioned with the use of violence; they recognized it was immoral and/or ineffective to further their cause. Also apparent, is how finding alternative ways of achieving significance seems to have contributed to their disengagement from violent groups. What is puzzling, however, is the extent to which the process they underwent could have been anticipated. It seems that it was mostly beyond anyone's control, including their own. Thus, inevitably, a pressing question for researchers and practitioners is whether deradicalization can be engineered: Can we devise interventions to re-channel the quest for significance toward peaceful means, reconciliation, and harmony? In the following section, we discuss explicit and implicit intervention strategies that suggest successful interventions is possible.

Explicit Deradicalization

We often assume that violent extremists are fiery ideologues. Assuredly, some of them are and they are respected for it within the group. But could we say the same for the typical foot-soldier of the organization? Are all terrorists well-versed in the ideology they are fighting for? Interviews with terrorists across different ideologies suggest that this is not the case (e.g., Della Porta, 2013; Reinares, 2011). One striking comment on that subject comes from anthropologist Scott Atran. After interviewing ISIS fighters in Kirkuk, Iraq, he concluded that:

They knew nothing of the Quran or the Hadith, or of the early caliphs Omar and Othman, but had learned of Islam from Al-Qaida and ISIS propaganda, teaching that Muslims like them were targeted for elimination unless they first eliminated the impure.

(Atran, 2015)

If it is true that violent extremists have a cursory ideological comprehension of what they are fighting for, this lends credence to the idea that persuasion and re-education can be successful in helping them disengage from violence. And this is the purpose of explicit deradicalization.

Explicit deradicalization aims to delegitimize the use of violence through dialogue. In social cognitive terms, these efforts attempt to sever the relation between the means (e.g., being part of a violent group) and the goal (e.g., gaining significance). For instance, in the deradicalization programs developed in Saudi Arabia and Singapore, respected religious scholars (i.e., imams) engaged in theological discussion with jihadists to persuade them that violence is either immoral and/or ineffective to further their cause. This approach can be considered with jihadists, but imams are not always the best people to conduct these efforts when terrorists are not motivated by religious ideals (e.g., the Columbian FARC, the IRA, etc.). In this case, deradicalization programs have to turn to different epistemic authorities (see Kruglanski, 1989, Kruglanski et al., 2005) to persuade them. For instance, in the context of deradicalizing the Tamil Tigers in Sri Lanka (a group motivated by state independence), role models including respected business people, athletes, and movie stars attempted to convince them that "a shared future … is achievable through unity rather than division" (Hettiarachchi, 2014, p. 26). Sometimes dialogue is not enough to convince someone that violence is not the best route to long-lasting social changes. In fact, explicit deradicalization efforts can potentially create psychological reactance and frustration, especially if there are no alternatives means for the person to reach its goals. Hence, deradicalization programs utilize more subtle interventions to succeed their deradicalization efforts.

Implicit Deradicalization

Whereas explicit deradicalization attempts to sever the means–goal relationship (i.e., the use of violence to further one's cause) through dialogue, implicit deradicalization efforts attempt to reintroduce alternative means to significance and alternative goals compatible with those means. These efforts include a large repertoire of interventions, such as family counseling, vocational education, art therapy, and meditation. The intention of this approach is to shift the person's life from an ideological obsession to a more balanced lifestyle. One excellent example of implicit deradicalization is vocational education. Learning and developing new skills bestow significance (e.g., feeling competent and useful) and provide violent extremists with alternative means to personal significance (e.g., providing for their family). Similarly, family counseling allows for the creation of strong affective bonds that fulfill the need to belong (Baumeister & Leary, 1995; Koehler, 2013), while providing an alternative reference group to the radical one (which often played the role of a substitute family).

There are precedents in the social psychological literature supporting the notion that providing alternative means to a goal can be an effective way to promote disengagement from a given activity. Specifically, research on the dilution effect (Bélanger, Schori-Eyal, Pica, Kruglanski, & Lafrenière, 2015b; Zhang, Fishbach, & Kruglanski, 2007) has shown that introducing alternative means to a goal has two consequences. First, consistent with the concept of spreading of activation (Anderson, 1983), adding more means to a goal results in a weakening of the means–goal association. As a result, each means connected to the goal is perceived as less effective (i.e., instrumental) for goal-pursuit. In more concrete terms, if being part of a radical organization is a means to one's significance quest (goal), providing a substitutive means to that goal (e.g., maintaining good rapport with one's family) will result in both means being perceived as less instrumental than they would if only one means were available.

A second consequence of adding more means is that the weakening of the means–goal association results in people experiencing less intrinsic motivation and pleasure when engaging in the means. This hypothesis was borne out of a theoretical piece by Shah and Kruglanski (2000) in which they postulated that the stronger the means–goal association, the more one should have the impression that the activity and the goal are meshed together; hence, performing the activity amounts to accomplishing the goal for its own sake. Bélanger et al. (2015b) found support for that proposition: Adding more means to reaching a goal reduced the perceived instrumentality of the means (i.e., the dilution effect), which in turn reduced individuals' intrinsic motivation.

In sum then, the presence of alternative means promotes disengagement because the means (e.g., being part of a radical group) is perceived as: (1) less effective to reach the goal (e.g., significance); and (2) less psychologically satisfying.

A Groundbreaking Field Study

Although laboratory experiments provide proof of concept for Kruglanski and colleagues' (2014) theorizing on deradicalization, one critical question is whether similar effects pan out in real life. Since the emergence of deradicalization programs in the early 2000s, researchers have been unable to determine their effectiveness, either because these programs had no built-in assessment protocols or because governments have kept the data out of researchers' sight. As a consequence, researchers have had to rely on recidivism rates provided by government officials, which could not be independently verified. And even if they could have been checked, recidivism rates can only be a proxy measure of the effectiveness of these programs. In fact, even the best deradicalization program could yield outrageously high recidivism rates if the social environment is contaminated with charismatic ideologues working for an organization with decent operational capabilities and a large base of supporters. Alternatively, recidivism rates could be extremely low if no surveillance programs are put in place to detect people returning to radical groups.

What researchers have been waiting for—the gold standard—is a program whereby terrorists are assessed repeatedly over time and compared against a control group. Kruglanski and colleagues (2014) recently conducted such a study with thousands of Tamil Tigers detained in various deradicalization centers across Sri Lanka. The program aimed to (1) fulfill detainees' significance quest and (2) provide alternative means to a meaningful existence to prepare them for their eventual return to society. To achieve its objectives, staff and guards avoided stigmatizing the detainees by referring to them as "beneficiaries" (as opposed to "terrorists") as a way of providing them with dignity and respect. This approach thus assumed that these individuals had been *victims* misled by radical propaganda and charismatic leaders (Hettiarachchi, 2014). Further, leaders and followers were separated to break the group dynamic and to prevent vocal ideologues from radicalizing the more moderate members. Lastly, participants of the rehabilitation program had access to vocational training in order to learn a trade to become a significant and contributing member to society. The control group in this study did not have access to such opportunity.

Psychological surveys were administered twice over a nine-month period. At Time 1, the two groups did not differ on several psychological variables (e.g., need for closure, support for armed struggle, etc.). However, at Time 2, results indicated that Tamil Tigers' support for armed struggle significantly declined in the rehabilitation group, but not in the control condition. When Kruglanski and colleagues (2014) examined the ingredients related to that change, they noticed that the deradicalization effect observed in the rehabilitation group was stronger for those beneficiaries who had developed a positive attitude toward the center's program and personnel. Of note, Kruglanski and colleagues observed that the deradicalization effect was possible among the most hardcore members of the Tamil Tigers, thus demonstrating that those most psychologically entrenched in violent extremism can also benefit from the rehabilitation program (for a discussion see Kruglanski, Gelfand, Bélanger, Gunaratna, & Hettiararchchi, 2014).

One fascinating aspect of the Sri Lankan experience is the scale of its rehabilitation efforts. In her comprehensive report, Hettiarachchi (2014) states that the Sri Lankan program has reintroduced 11,902 Tamil Tigers into civil society— a staggering figure. But the unprecedented productivity of this program wouldn't be as impressive if its "beneficiaries" turned back to violence once in the community (i.e., the classic "revolving door" syndrome). However, everything seems to indicate that the quality of rehabilitation was not sacrificed to quantity. After several years of reintegration into civil society (i.e., 3 to 5 years depending on the individual), the recidivism rate of Tamil Tigers is currently 0% (see Dharmawardhane, 2013). However, one might object that the Sri Lankan context is a factor limiting the generalizability of the finding; so how do other programs catering to different extremists groups compare? In Germany, the Exit-Deutschland program, which provided similar aid to right-wing extremists, reported a recidivism rate of 3% (Exit-Deutschland, 2014). In Singapore, recidivism among jihadists is estimated at 0% (Sim, 2012). It thus seems that recidivism rates are remarkably low across different programs. The exception appears to be the Saudi program, which has reported recidivism rates between 10% and 20% (US Department of State, 2010). Even though the latter appears worrisome, it is relatively low compared to other forms of prison rehabilitation. To give a bit of perspective, a recent study by the US Bureau of Justice Statistics revealed that "67.8% of the 404,638 state prisoners released in 2005 in 30 states were arrested within 3 years of release, and 76.6% were arrested within 5 years of release" (Durose, Cooper, & Snyder, 2014, p. 1). A systematic review of rehabilitation programs in prisons—somewhat analog to those involving terrorists (vocational education, therapy, etc.)—revealed that they could reduce prisoners' recidivism rates by 10% to 20% (Aos, Miller, & Drake, 2006, see also Warren, 2007). In the same vein, a meta-analysis conducted by Lipsey and Cullen (2007) evinced that punitive approaches do not reduce recidivism rates, if anything, they increase them. Taken together, these results clearly indicate that "being tough on crime" doesn't work and that when it comes down to changing the hearts and mind of terrorists or criminals, the proverbial carrot appears more effective than the proverbial stick.

Preventing Violent Extremism: From Thought to Action

As the present chapter attests, we are starting to have a pretty decent theoretical and empirical understanding of radicalization and deradicalization. The findings discussed here are robust and, for the most part, have been replicated using different cultural samples and ideological groups. Thus far, however, our approach toward terrorism has mainly been *reactive*, and much could be done to *prevent* the tide of violent extremism from growing into a tsunami. In 2015, as a wave of teenagers was leaving Canada to fight for ISIS, the city of Montreal decided to take decisive actions by creating the Center for the Prevention of Radicalization Leading toward Violence (CPRLV). I was appointed to develop its prevention and intervention program. This was an opportunity to translate our thoughts into action with the intention of tackling homegrown terrorism and creating a safer society. Below, I describe some of the community-based interventions that were put in place.

Raising Awareness in the Community

Although law-enforcement agencies are imperative to preserve law and order, the community, I would argue, plays an even greater role. What is required from authorities to monitor a single person around the clock (more or less 20 officers) is fastidious and puts enormous strain on limited resources, whereas the community's ability to detect radicalization is far superior and less resource-dependent. At the heart of the community, there are parents and teachers who are uniquely positioned to detect behavioral changes and take concrete actions to help the youth disengage from violent ideologies. However, one hurdle preventing us from harnessing the power of the community is the lack of a common understanding of what radicalization is (e.g., a normal process experienced in varying degrees by everyone) and what it is not (e.g., a mental illness). This obstacle, however, can be easily overcome with: (1) a common vocabulary to facilitate communication and to avoid terminological confusion (the distinction between radicalization, fanaticism, and fundamentalism is a good example); and (2) an understanding of the empirically-based evidence to distinguish facts from fiction. Unfortunately, until recently, there was no off-the-shelf resource available to the community to develop a good understanding of violent extremism or to detect observable indicators of radicalization.

To fill this important gap, in collaboration with Arie, my team and I (Bélanger et al., 2015a) decided to summarize 50 years of research into a 24-page information toolkit. The toolkit, freely available online in French and English (trev.uqam.ca), gained momentum in the media and was disseminated to all college teachers in Quebec (Canada) through their newsletter. The toolkit (1) establishes common definitions to discuss violent extremism, (2) identifies factors that foster and stymie radicalization and deradicalization, (3) explains the early signs of radicalization, and (4) provides concrete ways to help people disengage from violent extremism. The toolkit also discusses real case studies, illustrates the process of radicalization with an infographic (see Figure 8.1), and offers useful contact information for those seeking help, including the Center's hotline, which is discussed next.

Hotline

Many communities throughout Canada have 24-hour, seven-day-a-week hotlines to refer residents to a vast array of social services. Yet, virtually none of these services have protocols in place to counter violent extremism by referring callers or their friends and loved ones to frontline workers (e.g., clerics, social workers, psychologists). This is a major problem. Consider the following. In a recent analysis of 119 cases of lone-actor terrorists, Gill and colleagues (Gill, Horgan, & Deckert, 2014) found that

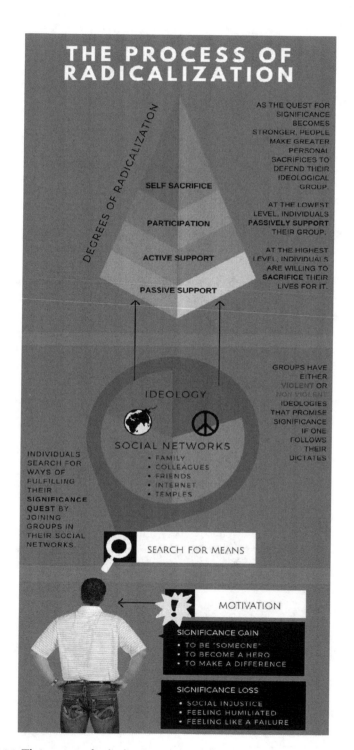

FIGURE 8.1 The process of radicalization

in 82.4% of the cases, other people were aware of the individual's grievance that spurred the terrorist plot, and in 79%, other individuals were aware of the individual's commitment to a specific extremist ideology. In 63.9% of the cases, family and friends were aware of the individual's intent to engage in terrorism-related activities *because the offender verbally told them.*

(emphasis added, p. 429)

What this research suggests is that terrorist attacks could potentially be prevented by establishing proper lines of communication within the community. Unfortunately, "families are not likely to report signs of radicalization to police or law enforcement due to the potential consequences, such as arrest or imprisonment" (Hedayah, 2014, p. 8). This is especially true for many immigrants whose relationship with the police has mainly been repressive (Ayache, 2009).

To address this challenge, the CPRLV created a hotline, entirely independent from law enforcement agencies, open 24/7 and manned by trained civilians. The community can call in to discuss their concerns and, except for extreme cases, the CPRLV does not share information with the police. Although the center has been in operation for a short period of time, the hotline has been immediately adopted by the community. Every day, worried citizens call the hotline to obtain information or request assistance. From March 2015 to February 2016:

the centre has received 612 calls on its hotline, 144 of which were worrisome enough for the centre's social workers and psychologists to 'directly intervene.' Nine cases were handed to the Montreal police because of either a perceived danger for the person's own security or a danger to others.

(Feith, 2016)

As discussed next, it is when the CPRLV intervenes that its true potential is unleashed. Below I describe some of the interventions put into practice to disrupt the radicalization process among youngsters and provide support to their families.

Creating Space for Dialogue

When cases are worrisome enough to warrant intervention, but not severe enough to call in the authorities, the CPRLV becomes an important intermediate step to prevent further radicalization within the community. Through friends and family, social workers and psychologists communicate with the referred person, to establish a bond of trust and create space for dialogue. Social workers and psychologists are uniquely positioned to carry out this work because of their training, but especially because they are less intimidating than police officers or, worse, secret services knocking at your door. Most cases received by the Center do not pose a threat to national security, such as when parents worry about their son's recent conversion to Islam. Other instances may raise a flag, such as when someone regularly consumes violent media online. In such a case, frontline workers can assess the extent to which the person is at ease (or defensive) about discussing this topic and get a better sense of what is happening. Akin to a suicide hotline, if sufficient evidence suggests that the person is at risk of self-harm or harming others, authorities may be called in. If this is not the case, follow-ups with the person and his or her entourage are encouraged to monitor the situation.

Creating a space for dialogue is essential for the Center to learn about the specific grievances individuals may have in the community (e.g., lack of employment) and find solutions with local community partners it is involved with (e.g., employment centers, schools, youth centers). Once these grievances are identified, frontline workers can propose alternatives tailored specifically to the individual's needs. For instance, if the person feels isolated, group activities (e.g., sports) might be suggested. In the case of political grievances (e.g., Syrian civil war), alternatives to traveling abroad can be discussed with the person (e.g., fundraising for Syrians, Médecins sans frontière, etc.). Spiritual leaders can also be brought into the conversation to delegitimize violence (e.g., reminding the person that jihad kills more innocent Muslims than anyone else). Without these interventions that propose prosocial alternatives, violence is likely to remain alluring, thus putting the community at risk.

Of course, it would be foolish to believe that one type of intervention fits all. And beyond looking into the ways radicalization occurs or how far it extends within certain communities, another important goal of the CPRLV is to collect information, develop more effective practices, and share these lessons with other programs worldwide. In the near future, this could even take the form of field-experiments with randomized groups to determine which intervention works best for whom. In that regard, the future looks extremely promising. Considering that scholars and practitioners have been historically fed high-quality information in dribs and drabs, the importance of having the CPRLV as a learning platform to improve our ability to counter violent extremism cannot be overstated.

Conclusion

For many years, researchers have struggled with understanding why and how people become terrorists. In a short period of time, social psychology has made great strides toward providing evidence-based methods to help practitioners and policy-makers curb the rise of violent extremism. This would not have been possible without the framework provided by the Quest for Personal Significance (Kruglanski et al., 2009; 2013a; 2014), which reconciled seemingly disparate findings into a coherent theoretical model.

Redirecting the youth's search for meaning toward something prosocial is promising and feasible, but we have yet to harness its true potential. In fact, while young people are searching for adventure, power, and meaning, we have been led by the idea that preaching abstention, safety, and moderation would work. Fortunately, this is changing, and because of the work discussed here, we are on our way to helping young people find meaningful ways of addressing their grievances and attaining a meaningful existence within our society. The old cliché about investing in our youth has never been truer: If we don't, violent groups will, because they need them to carry out their gruesome agenda.

Acknowledgement

I would like to thank Anastasia Lambrou for creating the infographics.

References

Anderson, J. R. (1983). *The architecture of cognition.* Cambridge, MA: Harvard University Press.

Aos, S., Miller, M. G., & Drake, E. (2006). *Evidence-based adult corrections programs: What works and what does not.* Olympia, WA: Washington State Institute for Public Policy.

Atran, S. (2004). Mishandling suicide terrorism. *Washington Quarterly, 27,* 67–90.

Atran, S. (2006). The moral logic and growth of suicide terrorism. *The Washington Quarterly, 29,* 127–147.

Atran, S. (2015). Here's what the social science says about countering violent extremism. *The Huffington Post.* Retrieved from http://www.huffingtonpost.com/scott-atran/violent-extremism-social-science_b_7142604.html.

Atran, S. (2016). The devoted actor: unconditional commitment and intractable conflict across cultures. *Current Anthropology, 57,* S000-S000.

Australian Government Attorney-General's Department (2015). *Preventing Violent Extremism and Radicalisation in Australia.* Retrieved from https://www.livingsafetogether.gov.au/ informationadvice/Documents/preventing-violent-extremism-and-radicalisation-in-australia.pdf.

Ayache, A. M. (2009). The role of 'cultural communities' in preventing terrorism in the West. *Building Terrorism Resistant Communities: Together Against Terrorism, 55,* 326.

Bandura, A. (1977). Self-efficacy: Toward a unifying theory of behavioral change. *Psychological Review, 84,* 191–215.

Bargh, J. A., Green, M., & Fitzsimons, G. (2008). The selfish goal: Unintended consequences of intended goal pursuits. *Social Cognition, 26,* 534.

Bargh, J. A. & Huang, J. Y. (2009). The selfish goal. In G. B. Moskowitz, & H. Grant (Ed.). *The psychology of goals* (pp. 127–50). New York: Guilford Press.

Baumeister, R. F., & Leary, M. R. (1995). The need to belong: desire for interpersonal attachments as a fundamental human motivation. *Psychological Bulletin, 117,* 497.

Bélanger, J. (2013). *The psychology of martyrdom* (Doctoral dissertation).

Bélanger, J. J., Caouette, J., Sharvit, K., & Dugas, M. (2014). The psychology of martyrdom: Making the ultimate sacrifice in the name of a cause. *Journal of Personality and Social Psychology, 107,* 494.

Bélanger, J. J., Lafrenière, M.-A. K., Vallerand, R. J., & Kruglanski, A. W. (2013a). When passion makes the heart grow colder: The role of passion in alternative goal suppression. *Journal of Personality and Social Psychology*, *104*, 126.

Bélanger, J. J., Lafrenière, M.-A. K., Vallerand, R. J., & Kruglanski, A. W. (2013b). Driven by fear: The effect of success and failure information on passionate individuals' performance. *Journal of Personality and Social Psychology*, *104*, 180.

Bélanger, J. J., Nociti, N., Chamberland, P.E., Paquette, V., Gagnon, D., Mahmoud, A., Carla, L., Lopes, M., Eising, C., & Kruglanski, A. W. (2015a). *Building a resilient community within a multicultural Canada: Information toolkit on violent extremism*. Retrieved from http://trev.uqam.ca/.

Bélanger, J. J., Chamberland, P.-E., Nociti, N., & Schumpe, B. M. (2017). Different pathways to political activism: The role of passion. Unpublished manuscript. Department of Psychology, New York University, Abu Dhabi.

Bélanger, J. J., Schori-Eyal, N., Pica, G., Kruglanski, A. W., & Lafrenière, M. A. (2015b). The "more is less" effect in equifinal structures: Alternative means reduce the intensity and quality of motivation. *Journal of Experimental Social Psychology*, *60*, 93–102.

Bélanger, J. J., Schumpe, B. Lafrenière, M.-A. K., Giacomantonio, M., Brizi, A., & Kruglanski, A. W. (2016). Beyond goal commitment: How expectancy shapes means evaluation. *Motivation Science*, *2*(2), 67.

Black Lives Matter. (n.d.). In *Wikipedia*. Retrieved from https://en.wikipedia.org/wiki/Black_Lives_Matter.

Bloom, M. (2005). *Dying to kill: The allure of suicide terrorism*. New York: Columbia University Press.

Bureau of Counterterrorism (BoC). (2014). Country reports on terrorism 2014. *National Consortium for the Study of Terrorism and Responses to Terrorism: Annex of statistical information*. Retrieved from http://go.usa.gov/3scv9.

Campbell, J. P., & Pritchard, R. D. (1976). Motivation theory in industrial and organizational psychology. In M. Dunnette (Ed.), *Handbook of industrial and organizational psychology* (pp. 63–130). Chicago: Rand McNally.

Canadian Security Intelligence Service (CSIS). (2015). *Personality Traits and Terrorism*. Retrieved from http://library.tsas.ca/media/TSASWP15-05_CSIS.pdf.

Corner, E., & Gill, P. (2015). A false dichotomy? Mental illness and lone-actor terrorism. *Law and Human Behavior*, *39*, 23.

Corrado, R. (1981). A critique of the mental disorder perspective of political terrorism. *International Journal of Law and Psychiatry*, *4*, 293–309.

Crocker, J., and Wolfe, C. (2001). Contingencies of worth. *Psychological Review*, *108*, 593–623.

Deci, E. L., and Ryan, R. M. (2000). The "what" and "why" of goal pursuits: Human needs and the self-determination of behavior. *Psychological Inquiry*, *11*, 227–268.

Della Porta, D. (1988). Recruitment processes in clandestine political organizations: Italian left-wing terrorism. *International Social Movement Research*, *1*, 155–169.

Della Porta, D. (2013). *Clandestine political violence*. Cambridge: Cambridge University Press.

Dharmawardane, I. (2013). Sri Lanka's post-conflict strategy: Restorative justice for rebels and rebuilding of conflict-affected communities. *Perspectives on Terrorism*, *7*, 1–10.

Dugas, M., Bélanger, J. J., Moyano, M., Schumpe, B. M., Kruglanski, A. W., Gelfand, M. J., Touchton-Leonard, K., & Nociti, N. (2016). The quest for significance motivates self-sacrifice. *Motivation Science*, *2*(1), 15.

Durose, M. R., Cooper, A. D., & Snyder, H. N. (2014). *Recidivism of Prisoners Released in 30 States in 2005: Patterns from 2005 to 2010*. Washington, DC: US Department of Justice, Office of Justice Programs, Bureau of Justice Statistics.

Echterhoff, G., Higgins, E. T., & Levine, J. M. (2009). Shared reality experiencing commonality with others' inner states about the world. *Perspectives on Psychological Science, 4*, 496–521.

The Economist. (2013, July 20). Where have all the burglars gone? Retrieved from http://www.economist.com/news/briefing/21582041-rich-world-seeing-less-and-less-crime-even-face-high-unemployment-and-economic.

Eisenberger, N. I., Lieberman, M. D., & Williams, K. D. (2003). Does rejection hurt? An fMRI study of social exclusion. *Science, 302*, 290–292.

Elster, J. (2005). Motivations and beliefs in suicide missions. In D. Gambetta (Ed.), *Making sense of suicide missions* (pp. 233–258). New York: Oxford University Press.

Exit-Deutschland (2014). *EXIT-Germany: We provide the way out: De-Radicalization and Disengagement*. Retrieved from http://www.exit-deutschland.de/file_download/29/Broschuere-EXIT-Engl_PDFDS_11.4.pdf.

Feith, J. (2016, February 14). UN secretary general praises Montreal's anti-radicalization efforts. *The Montreal Gazette*. Retrieved from http://montrealgazette.com/news/local-news/un-secretary-general-ban-ki-moon-mayor-denis-coderre-to-visit-radicalization-prevention-centre.

Frankl, V. E. (1985). *Man's search for meaning*. New York: Simon & Schuster.

Frankl, V. E. (2000). *Man's search for ultimate meaning*. New York: Basic Books.

Gambetta, D. (2005). *Making sense of suicide missions*. Oxford: Oxford University Press.

Gill, P., Horgan, J., & Deckert, P. (2014). Bombing alone: tracing the motivations and antecedent behaviors of lone-actor terrorists. *Journal of Forensic Sciences, 59*, 425–435.

Ginges, J., Atran, S., Medin, D., & Shikaki, K. (2007). Sacred bounds on rational resolution of violent political conflict. *Proceedings of the National Academy of Sciences, 104*, 7357–7360.

Gottschalk, M., & Gottschalk, S. (2004). Authoritarianism and pathological hatred: A social psychological profile of the middle eastern terrorist. *The American Sociologist, 35*, 38–59.

Greenberg, J., Pyszczynski, T., Solomon, S., Rosenblatt, A., Veeder, M., Kirkland, S., & Lyon, D. (1990). Evidence for terror management theory II: The effects of mortality salience on reactions to those who threaten or bolster the cultural worldview. *Journal of Personality and Social Psychology, 58*, 308.

Gurr, T. R. (1970). *Why men rebel*. Princeton, NJ: Princeton University Press.

Gurski, P. (2015). *The Threat from Within: Recognizing Al Qaeda-inspired Radicalization and Terrorism in the West*. Lanham, MD: Rowman & Littlefield.

Hardin, C. D., & Conley, T. D. (2001). A relational approach to cognition: Shared experience and relationship affirmation in social cognition. In G. B. Moskowitz (Ed.), *Cognitive Social Psychology: The Princeton Symposium on the Legacy and Future of Social Cognition* (pp. 3–17). Mahwah, NJ: Lawrence Erlbaum Associates.

Hardin, C. D., & Higgins, E. T. (1996). Shared reality: How social verification makes the subjective objective. In E. T. Higgins, & R. M. Sorrentino (Eds.), *Handbook of Motivation and Cognition: The Interpersonal Context* (Vol. 3, pp. 28–84). New York: Guilford Press.

Harris, G. T., Rice, M. E., & Quinsey, V. L. (1993). Violent recidivism of mentally disordered offenders the development of a statistical prediction instrument. *Criminal Justice and Behavior, 20*, 315–335.

Hecker, J., & Thorpe, G. (2015). *Introduction to clinical psychology*. London: Psychology Press.

Hedayah. (2014). *The roles of families and communities in strengthening community resilience against violent extremism*. Retrieved from http://www.hedayah.ae/pdf/the-roles-of-families-and-communities-in-building-resilience-meeting-report.pdf.

Hettiarachchi, M. (2014, February). *Sri Lanka's rehabilitation program: The humanitarian mission two*. Retrieved from http://www.sinhalanet.net/wp-content/uploads/2014/08/Sri-Lankas-Rehabilitation-Program.pdf.

Horgan, J. (2008). From profiles to pathways and roots to routes: Perspectives from psychology on radicalization into terrorism. *The Annals of the American Academy of Political and Social Science*, *618*, 80–94.

Horgan, J. (2009). *Walking away from terrorism: accounts of disengagement from radical and extremist movements*. London: Routledge.

Jost, J. T., Ledgerwood, A., & Hardin, C. D. (2008). Shared reality, system justification, and the relational basis of ideological beliefs. *Social and Personality Psychology Compass*, *2*, 171–186.

Kanfer, R., & Ackerman, P. L. (1989). Motivation and cognitive abilities: An integrative/aptitude-treatment interaction approach to skill acquisition. *Journal of Applied Psychology Monograph*, *74*, 657–690.

Koehler, D. (2013). Family counselling as prevention and intervention tool against 'foreign fighters'. The German 'Hayat'Program. *Journal Exit-Deutschland. Zeitschrift für Deradikalisierung und demokratische Kultur*, *3*, 182–204.

Köpetz, C., Faber, T., Fishbach, A., & Kruglanski, A. W. (2011). The multifinality constraints effect: How goal multiplicity narrows the means set to a focal end. *Journal of Personality and Social Psychology*, *100*, 810.

Köpetz, C., Hofmann, W., & Wiers, R. W. (2014). On the selection and balancing of multiple selfish goals. *Behavioral and Brain Sciences*, *37*, 147–148.

Krebs, V. E. (2002). Mapping networks of terrorist cells. *Connections*, *24*, 43–52.

Kruglanski, A. W. (1989). *Lay epistemics and human knowledge: Cognitive and motivational bases*. Plenum: New York.

Kruglanski, A. W., Bélanger, J. J., Chen, X., Köpetz, C., Pierro, A., & Mannetti, L. (2012). The energetics of motivated cognition: a force-field analysis. *Psychological Review*, *119*, 1.

Kruglanski, A. W., Bélanger, J. J., Gelfand, M., Gunaratna, R., Hettiarachchi, M., Reinares, F., Orehek, F., Sasota J., & Sharvit, K. (2013a). Terrorism—A (self) love story: Redirecting the significance quest can end violence. *American Psychologist*, *68*, 559.

Kruglanski, A. W., Chen, X., Dechesne, M., Fishman, S., & Orehek, E. (2009). Fully committed: Suicide bombers' motivation and the quest for personal significance. *Political Psychology*, *30*, 331–357.

Kruglanski, A. W., Gelfand, M. J., Bélanger, J. J., Hetiarachchi, M., & Gunaratna, R. (2015). Significance Quest Theory as the driver of radicalization towards terrorism. In Jerard, J. & Nasir S. M. (Ed.), *Resilience and Resolve: Community Engagement to Community Resilience*. London: Imperial College Press.

Kruglanski, A. W., Gelfand, M. J., Bélanger, J. J., Sheveland, A., Hettiarachchi, M., & Gunaratna, R. (2014). The psychology of radicalization and deradicalization: How significance quest impacts violent extremism. *Political Psychology*, *35*, 69–93.

Kruglanski, A. W., Köpetz, C., Bélanger, J. J., Chun, W. Y., Orehek, E., & Fishbach, A. (2013b). Features of multifinality. *Personality and Social Psychology Review*, *17*, 22–39.

Kruglanski, A. W., & Orehek, E. (2011). The role of quest for significance in motivating terrorism. In J. Forgas, A. Kruglanski, & K. Williams (Eds.), *Social Conflict and Aggression* (pp. 153–164). New York: Psychology Press.

Kruglanski, A. W., Raviv, A., Bar-Tal, D., Raviv, A., Sharvit, K., Bar, R., et al. (2005). Says who? Epistemic authority effects in social judgment. In M. P. Zanna (Ed.), *Advances in experimental social psychology* (pp. 346 –392). San Diego, CA: Academic Press.

Kruglanski, A. W., Shah, J. Y., Fishbach, A., Friedman, R., Chun, W. Y., & Sleeth-Keppler, D. (2002). A theory of goal systems. *Advances in experimental social psychology*, *34*, 331–378.

Lin, N. (2001). Building a network theory of social capital. In N. Lin, K. Cook, & R. S. Burt (Eds.), *Social capital: Theory and research* (pp. 3–29). New York: Aldine De Gruyter.

Lipsey, M. W., & Cullen, F. T. (2007). The effectiveness of correctional rehabilitation: A review of systematic reviews. *Annual Review of Law and Social Science*, *3*, 297–320.

Markus, H. R., & Kitayama, S. (1991). Culture and the self: Implications for cognition, emotion, and motivation. *Psychological Review*, *98*, 224.

Maslow, A. H. (1943). A theory of human motivation. *Psychological Review*, *50*, 370–396.

Maslow, A. H. (1965). *Eupsychian management*. Homewood, IL: Irwin.

McClelland, D., Atkinson, J., Clark, R., and Lowell, E. (1953). *The achievement motive*. New York: Appleton-Century-Crofts.

McVeigh, T. (2015, June 13). 'Recruiter' of UK jihadis: I regret opening the way to ISIS. *The Guardian*. Retrieved from https://www.theguardian.com/world/2015/jun/13/godfather-of-british-jihadists-admits-we-opened-to-way-to-join-isis.

Meehl, P. E., & Rosen, A. (1955). Antecedent probability and the efficiency of psychometric signs, patterns, or cutting scores. *Psychological Bulletin*, *52*, 194.

Ohnuki-Tierney, E. (2006). *Kamikaze diaries: Reflections of Japanese student soldiers*. Chicago: University of Chicago Press.

Orehek, E., Sasota, J. A., Kruglanski, A. W., Dechesne, M., & Ridgeway, L. (2014). Interdependent self-construals mitigate the fear of death and augment the willingness to become a martyr. *Journal of Personality and Social Psychology*, *107*, 265.

Pape, R. (2005). *Dying to win: The strategic logic of suicide terrorism*. New York: Random House.

Pedahzur, A. (2005). *Suicide terrorism*. London: Polity Press.

Pinder, C. C. (1984). *Work motivation*. Glenview, IL: Scott, Foresman.

Qin, J., Xu, J. J., Hu, D., Sageman, M., & Chen, H. (2005). Analyzing terrorist networks: A case study of the global salafi jihad network. In P. Kantor, F. Roberts, F. Y. Wang, & R. C. Merkle (Eds.), *Intelligence and security informatics* (pp. 287–304). Berlin, Germany: Springer.

Reinares, F. (2011). Exit from terrorism: A qualitative empirical study on disengagement and deradicalization among members of ETA. *Terrorism and Political Violence, 23,* 780–803.

Ricolfi, L. (2005). Palestinians, 1981–2003. In D. Gambetta (Ed.), *Making sense of suicide missions* (pp. 77–129). New York: Oxford University Press.

Royal Canadian Mounted Police (2009). *Radicalization: A guide for the perplexed*. Retrieved from http://publications.gc.ca/collections/collection_2012/grc-rcmp/PS64-102-2009-eng.pdf.

Sageman, M. (2004). *Understanding terror networks*. Philadelphia: University of Pennsylvania Press.

Sageman, M. (2008). *Leaderless Jihad: Terror networks in the twenty-first century*. Philadelphia: University of Pennsylvania Press.

Security Council. (2015). *Letter dated 13 May 2015 from the Chair of the Security Council Committee established pursuant to resolution 1373(2001) concerning counter-terrorism addressed to the President of the Security Council. United Nations.* Retrieved from http://www.un.org/ga/search/view_doc.asp?symbol=S/2015/338.

Shah, J. Y., Friedman, R., & Kruglanski, A. W. (2002). Forgetting all else: on the antecedents and consequences of goal shielding. *Journal of Personality and Social Psychology, 83*, 1261.

Shah, J., & Kruglanski, A. (2000). Aspects of goal networks: Implications for self-regulation. In M. Boekaerts, P. R. Pintrich, & M. Zeidner (Eds.), *Handbook of self-regulation* (pp. 85–110). San Diego, CA: Academic Press.

Silke, A. (1998). Cheshire-cat logic: The recurring theme of terrorist abnormality in psychological research. *Psychology, Crime and Law, 4*, 51–69.

Sim, S. (2012). Strategies for successful risk reduction programmes for violent extremists: Lessons from Singapore, Indonesia and Afghanistan. *Trends and Developments in Contemporary Terrorism, 103*, 55.

Steger, M. F., Frazier, P., Oishi, S., & Kaler, M. (2006). The meaning in life questionnaire: Assessing the presence of and search for meaning in life. *Journal of Counseling Psychology, 53*, 80.

Stern, J. (2003). *Terror in the name of God: Why religious militants kill.* New York: Ecco/Harper Collins.

Taarnby, M. (2005). *Recruitment of Islamist terrorists in Europe: Trends and perspectives. Research report sunded by the Danish Ministry of Justice.* Retrieved from http://www.investigative-project.org/documents/testimony/58.pdf .

Tajfel, H., & Turner, J. C. (1979). An integrative theory of intergroup conflict. *The Social Psychology of Intergroup Relations, 33*, 74.

US Department of State. (2010). *Country reports on Terrorism 2010.* Retrieved from http://www.state.gov/j/ct/rls/crt/2010/170257.htm.

Vallerand, R. J., Blanchard, C., Mageau, G. A., Koestner, R., Ratelle, C., Léonard, M., Gagne, M., & Marsolais, J. (2003). Les passions de l'âme: on obsessive and harmonious passion. *Journal of Personality and Social Psychology, 85*, 756.

Warren, R. K. (2007). *Evidence-based practice to reduce recidivism: Implications for state judiciaries.* Washington, DC: The Crime and Justice Institute and National Institute of Corrections, Community Corrections Division.

Zhang, Y., Fishbach, A., & Kruglanski, A. W. (2007). The dilution model: how additional goals undermine the perceived instrumentality of a shared path. *Journal of personality and social psychology, 92*, 389.

9

EXTREMIST REHABILITATION – OPPORTUNITIES AND CHALLENGES

Rohan Gunaratna

Synopsis

The world is facing an acute and a growing threat from the rise of the Islamic State (IS). The foreign fighter threat is unprecedented in terms of numbers. Despite efforts by the international community, military, diplomatic, political, economic and informational strategies have failed to curb the threat of IS. While an effective military response is crucial to dismantling IS in the theatre of Iraq and Syria, governments working with their partners should also craft a strategy to fight IS globally. The goal should be to create a multinational, multipronged, multiagency, and a multijurisdictional framework to fight upstream counter radicalization and downstream deradicalization of returning foreign fighters for their home countries.

This research is inspired by the work done together with Muslim clerics at the International Centre for Political Violence and Terrorism Research (ICPVTR) in Singapore and the START research team spearheaded by Professor Kruglanski. Professor Kruglanski developed an index to administer radicalization and deradicalization, which eventually became a standard tool in the field and was steadily modified to measure the detainee and inmate transformation. In the Philippines, both Professor Kruglanski and Professor Gelfand worked in prison and community settings to conduct interviews. In Indonesia they worked with Muhammad Taufiq to collect data on the attitudes and opinions of Indonesians. Moreover, Professor Kruglanski and Professor Michele Gelfand have worked together with Malkanthi Hettiarachchi to build the terrorist rehabilitation program in Sri Lanka in 2009. This comprehensive program allowed access to 12,000 detainees. During this program, they collected the data on the changing attitudes and opinions of the detainees together with a Sri Lankan team led by

Ms Hettiarachchi. The Sri Lankan case is the most complete dataset available and its analysis helped to refine future interventions and the program.

Moreover, in building terrorist rehabilitation programs worldwide, the quest for significance, a theory developed by Professor Kruglanski was of exceptional value. As such, the interventions attempted to restore the significance of detainees and inmates. Similarly, in the design and development of community engagement programs in regions and countries affected by conflict, our aim was to restore their significance together. Professor Kruglanski and Ms Hettiarachchi had joined me for training the intelligence services in Oman (2014) and UAE (2015) so they could effectively rehabilitate their terrorists and extremists. Professor Kruglanski's quest for significance theory became a central theme of discussion among practitioners in Asia and the Middle East. There was a lack of a holistic theory that could either supplant or rebut the quest for significance theory. Moreover, the pioneer work and the sustained commitment of Professor Kruglanski strengthened the capabilities of our institute and researchers. However, the more pertinent value of this theory lies within saving the lives of countless terrorists and extremists in custodial and community settings. Professor Kruglanski, who is a pathfinder of knowledge, also assisted us in developing a rare template to bring back those who stepped out of the mainstream. Future generations of researchers and practitioners will utilize Professor Kruglanski's theory to help individuals through such rehabilitation and community engagement programs that have proved successful. The success and effort within these programs have allowed the strategies of rehabilitation and deradicalization to develop further.

As such, rehabilitation and community engagement are vital in the fight against terrorism and extremism. As the IS threat is global, the threat can be managed only by embracing and implementing rehabilitation and community engagement strategies and practices at national and international levels. To engage and protect vulnerable communities, while rehabilitating returning terrorists and extremists, the governments need to work with the civil society and private firms. As Joseph Nye has argued, it is not possible to achieve smart power, without integrating hard and soft power (Nye 2009). To contain and counter the threat of IS at its core, periphery and in the virtual domain, the challenge today is to build global rehabilitation and community engagement infrastructures and capabilities. Overall, this chapter presents the argument that using military might to target terrorist groups such as IS, will only have limited gains. However, in order to see lasting gains and counter the ideology of IS, deradicalization and rehabilitation are a necessity.

The Influence of Professor Kruglanski

At a time when western centric scholars wrote about deradicalization, Professor Kruglanski travelled to Singapore and studied rehabilitation. As such, rehabilitation entailed deradicalization, which calls for engaging the detainee and inmates using clerics, psychologists, social workers, teachers and other specialists to change the outlooks, attitudes and opinions. As the mind is critical in this scenario, the focus was to transform the person's thoughts as that would transform his or her words and actions. However, Professor Kruglanski knew that in order for that to succeed the heart of the detainees needed to be engaged. He understood the need for building a rapport first by inviting the beneficiary to sit with us, asking about his health. Professor Kruglanski understood why we spent an extraordinary amount of time listening to the beneficiary to listen to his side of the story and talking to his family members and helping both the family and extended family to win his trust. The terrorist or the terrorist suspect we engaged understood why we cared for his children and others who mattered to him.

Professor Kruglanski spent time with us both in detention and inmate facilities observing and talking to those incarcerated and the ones engaging them. Until Professor Kruglanski came to the scene, matrix and measurement was not our focus. We understood its importance, but we had no tools to measure motivation. By putting together research teams to measure the changing attitudes and opinions over time of the incarcerated population, Professor Kruglanski defined the field of rehabilitation and created a new subfield in the discipline of terrorism studies. Professor Kruglanski demonstrated research leadership, securing grants for research, authored, edited and published, and organized conferences. Unlike other academics and practitioners, he approached the subject with an open mind.

Introduction

Understanding the nature of threat is important while studying any terrorist group and the same logic applies to IS. A new global threat landscape has emerged with the rise of IS. Now, the Al Qaeda-centric threat landscape is eclipsed by an Al Qaeda–IS hybrid global threat. Within the context of this threat, the four components of IS are (1) IS theatre of Iraq and Syria; (2) IS provinces overseas; (3) IS associated groups in Asia, Africa, the Middle East and the Caucasus; and (4) IS home grown cells. Western security and intelligence services estimate the number of Sunni foreign fighters in the theatre of operations at 20,000 from nearly 100 countries. In comparison, Afghanistan attracted about 10,000 IS fighters in its ten years of war. In other words, Syria has managed to attract double that number in its first five years. IS has become a global threat because the caliphate has a symbolic and global resonance, propagated through its social media content that extols its large pool of foreign fighters (Islamic State (ISIS) Dabiq Magazine). In addition to the group's vast resource base, its graphic violence appeals to a segment of radicalized and militarized youth. Moreover, based on the frequency of traffic to IS digital platforms, IS has politicized, radicalized, and mobilized thousands of supporters and sympathizers worldwide. The scale and magnitude of threat posed by IS has surpassed Al Qaeda, in terms of its associated groups and home grown cells. Unsurprisingly, IS now eclipses Al

Qaeda as the leader of the global terrorist movement. Moreover, each of the factors points towards the significant threat posed from the thousands of returning foreign fighters and extremists to their home countries.

Like the threat posed by Al Qaeda, a much smaller group with lesser resources, IS threat is likely to grow and affect regions beyond the Iraqi-Syrian theatre. In Egypt's Sinai, Libya, northern Nigeria, Russia's Dagestan, Afghanistan–Pakistan border and in Eastern Indonesia, IS has established a robust infrastructure. To mitigate the growing threat, a global strategy is needed specifically as concerns IS's proven ability to activate home grown cells and to mobilize returning foreign fighters to carry out attacks in their native lands.

Taking into account the complexity and severity of the global threat that IS poses, it is necessary to complement the efforts of the military, law enforcement and national security agencies, with a parallel strategy of counter-radicalization and de-radicalization. It is impractical for thousands of returning foreign fighters and their supporters to be put to death or prosecuted. By countering the IS ideology, IS indoctrination can be disrupted. Successful re-integration of IS's foreign fighters into the society will prevent reradicalization. In addition to non-IS fighters, governments in partnership with civil society and business firms should build an enterprise to rehabilitate those who support the IS cause.

Kinetic means of deterring terrorism through arresting supporters, disrupting their operational capabilities and killing the terrorists, though necessary aren't the complete solution. In order to curb the long-term threat of terrorism, governments should focus on dismantling the infrastructure that is creating the terrorists. The propaganda, recruitment, fundraising, procurement, safe houses, transportation, travel, communication, training and other support networks should be relentlessly targeted. Furthermore, governments should work with the civil society and business community to rehabilitate and reintegrate captured or surrendered terrorists within the broader society.

Success in the fight depends on the ability and willingness of military, law enforcement and national security agencies to work in partnership with a range of actors to build a capacity to deliver a full spectrum response. At the hard end of the spectrum, lethal and kinetic forces should weaken the operational capabilities of fighters on the ground in Iraq and Syria. At the soft end of the spectrum, communities vulnerable to extremist ideas should be engaged. This represents a preventive approach, where those who are susceptible to the messages of IS are targeted. Most importantly, surrendered or captured foreign fighters should be made to repent, regret and express remorse and re-join mainstream society as productive citizens. If these steps are not taken then IS will continue the cycle of recruitment despite the numbers of terrorists killed, and thus will still possess regeneration capabilities. In addition, the foreign fighters will not only continue to grow in number, but they will also pose a threat when they return endowed with battlefield experience and crowned with the glory of returning heroes.

Lessons from History

The world's most pivotal conflict theatres, Afghanistan and Iraq, offer important lessons in governments' failure to rehabilitate and reintegrate their returning fighters. Al Qaeda (previously Maktabal-Khidamat) was the child of the anti-Soviet multinational Afghan mujahidin campaign (1979–1989). Pending Soviet withdrawal, a proposal by US Congressman Charlie Wilson to fund the rehabilitation of the mujahidin succumbed to Congressional reluctance to invest more. Furthermore, many Arab countries were reluctant to bring back their nationals fearing that they will seek to replicate the Afghan experience in their home countries. As a result, many fighters' best option appeared to be to continue doing what they knew best, namely fight, which they did in Kashmir, Chechnya, Bosnia and other conflict zones. The Palestinian ideologue Abdullah Azzam, touted as the "Father of Global Jihad," envisioned creating "a pioneering vanguard of the Islamic movements," and his Saudi protégé, Osama bin Laden brought together foreign fighters to create Al Qaeda in Peshawar on August 11, 1988 (Bergen 2001; Jacquard 2002).

After Al Qaeda attacked America's most iconic landmarks, the threat proliferated. Some governments did build rehabilitation capabilities, but the US itself failed to do so. Its failure in Bagram and Guantanamo Bay resulted in those released forming new groups, and/or joining or supporting existing groups. While the US had built a credible rehabilitation program in Iraq, it did not have an integration program. Following the US withdrawal from Iraq in 2010, the failure of the new Iraqi administration to continue to rehabilitate and reintegrate the fighters led to them joining the ranks of the Islamic State of Iraq (ISI) and other terrorist groups. With the depletion of experienced fighters, ISI and its successor, the Islamic State of Iraq and Sham (ISIS), turned their attention to those who had spent time in custody. Most notably, Abu Umar al Baghdadi (leader of ISI) and Abu Bakr al Baghdadi (leader of ISIS), were previous detainees of Camp Bucca in Iraq. Today, the leadership of IS includes a significant proportion of detainees who served either in terrorist groups or in the Saddam Hussein's Baathist Administration.

Detention of violent extremists can produce further radicalization but under the appropriate conditions it can also allow de-radicalization and rehabilitation. Prisons can be "petrie dishes" for radicalization if the detainees are treated disrespectfully, thus fuelling their quest for significance restoration (Kruglanski et al., 2013, 2014), if the group of violent extremists is kept together in the detention facility, intact with their influential leaders who espouse the extremist ideology. Such were the conditions in a Philippine prison where I collaborated with Arie Kruglanski, Michele Gelfand and their Maryland based team (Kruglanski, Gelfand, Babush, Hettiarachchi, Bonto & Gunaratna, in press). In this situation, we observed a significant increase in radicalization over a two-year term. Specifically, the detainees increased their support for Islamic extremism measured by their tendency to legitimize suicide bombing, endorse the establishment of the Caliphate and express enmity toward the West and a condemnation of the Western lifestyle.

But we also observed that detention can provide a window of opportunity to deradicalize the detainees, particularly if they are extricated from their group's sphere of influence, exposed to a compelling counter-radical ideology, and are given means for an alternative attainment of respect and self-significance. Such conditions prevailed in Sri Lanka following the defeat of the Liberation Tigers of Tamil Eelam (LTTE) among the most ruthless and best organized terror organizations in history. Following their defeat by the Sri Lankan military in 2009, about 12,000 LTTE members surrendered and were placed in special detention centers where an intense program of deradicalization was implemented. The "beneficiaries" were not explicitly exposed to an ideology that favored a unified Sri Lanka rather than an independent Tamil state on the island, but rather were involved in vocational courses as well as allowed a free expression of their individuality in art, yoga and religion. The collaboration between myself and the Kruglanski team (Webber, Chernikova, Kruglanski, Gelfand, Hettiarachchi, Gunaratna, Lafreniere, & Belanger, 2017) yielded that as compared to a control group that received only a minimal rehabilitation program, the full treatment group manifested significant deradicalization evident by their improved attitudes toward the Sinhalese majority, and their diminished readiness to use violence as means to their end. Of even greater interest, in a follow up study that examined the beneficiaries' success in reintegration into society following their release – we found that former beneficiaries were more conciliatory and moderate in their attitudes toward the Sinhalese and more reluctant to return to violence than members of the Tamil community that never participated in the LTTE struggle.

Even before 9/11, a few governments invested in the rehabilitation of terrorists and returning foreign fighters. Working with clerics from al Azhar, Egypt was the first country to rehabilitate Muslim terrorists and extremists. While other governments built their own rehabilitation initiatives, only a few programs were comprehensive enough. For instance, in Egypt and Yemen, the lack of state patronage led to the collapse of such programs. In Indonesia, the ad hoc nature of the program suffered as a result. Attempts made in Afghanistan also failed due to a lack of support and understanding from the US military leadership. Efforts in the UK, Maldives, Morocco, and Australia to send clerics to engage terrorists and extremists also failed to build successful national programs. Most countries like the Philippines, Thailand and Bangladesh have visions for rehabilitation initiatives but few have leaders with the will power to build and sustain them. There are a few countries that had built capabilities in custodial rehabilitation but failed to build capabilities in reintegration. The aftercare component was therefore either absent or lacking (Horgan and Altier 2012, pp. 83–90).

The Challenges of Rehabilitating Foreign Fighters

Terrorists use violence to achieve specific political goals, and are not born but instead created through grievances towards governments or international institutions. As such, foreign fighters are also terrorists, but choose to cross geographical boundaries to achieve their political goals through violence. Despite the presence of political goals, most governments dispense with the idea of strategic counterterrorism, even though the threat is directly facing them. The dominant strategy of the West, viz., through lethal and kinetic response, has met only with partial successes. The most evident instances of the West employing these approaches are the US operations in Afghanistan and Iraq as a part of the global War on Terror. Moreover, the utilization of drone strikes against terrorist groups also signifies kinetic responses. Traditionally, counterterrorism practitioners continue to prefer the shorter route. Most governments therefore lack the visionary leadership, knowledge and resources to invest in strategic counterterrorism programs that work towards sustained peace and prevention.

Governments should work in partnership with civil society and the business firms to counter terrorist ideology and rehabilitate these foreign fighters once they return to home soil. However, most civil servants are uncomfortable with developing a whole of society approach. Community engagement initiatives to build community resilience rehabilitate and reintegrate terrorists and extremists must occur simultaneously with the fight against terrorism. Countries with no rehabilitation programs should develop a vision to build rehabilitation capabilities. Those with ad hoc rehabilitation programs should transform them into permanent rehabilitation programs. Others with rehabilitation programs should build community engagement programs.

No custodial rehabilitation program will succeed without an effective reintegration program. Post-release monitoring and after care determine the success of custodial rehabilitation and prevent reradicalisation. In parallel with deradicalization efforts, there should be an investment in countering the radicalization of the masses. Counter-radicalization should seek to create an environment that is hostile to terrorists and unfriendly to terrorist supporters by immunizing the general public. Thus, even if these foreign fighters come back, the unity and harmony within the society will deter their efforts toward polarization. In this sense, they won't be able to recruit further, as effective counter-radicalization prevents ordinary citizens from being transformed into extremists and terrorists. Unless terrorist's ideological capabilities that empower and motivate terrorists to legitimize and justify violence are countered, the threat will continue to linger and manifest itself violently (S. Rajaratnam School of International Studies and The Religious Rehabilitation Group, 2009).

When a foreign fighter comes back and surrenders or is captured, the government has a narrow window of opportunity to deradicalize him. Even if incarcerated for life or held incommunicado, he can influence and radicalize others through contact with prison staff or visitors. Consequently, terrorists who are eventually released may perpetuate the vicious cycle of violence. The ideas of extremism and ideology of violence will continue to create a landscape of instability and insecurity. In this regard, both terrorist rehabilitation and community engagement are powerful tools in deradicalization and counter-radicalization respectively.

Why Rehabilitate Foreign Fighters?

Failure to rehabilitate released terrorists can pose a security threat as they could infect others or re-join terrorist groups. If terrorists reflect, repent and express remorse, they could possibly re-enter society as productive citizens. To support the transformation of a returning IS terrorist from the extreme to the mainstream, governments in partnership with civil society and business firms can play a pivotal role (Stern 2010, pp. 95–108).

When to Rehabilitate Foreign Fighters?

When foreign fighters return, after their surrender or arrests, their eventual reintegration into society must be a top agenda item. The initial shock of arrest should be exploited to gain a cognitive opportunity to both investigate their activities and background, and transform them. There is a need for counter-terrorism investigators to be trained in motivational interviewing. While terrorists in custody are a valuable source of insight into terrorist leadership, ideology and operation, the focus to determine the threat and how to prevent the next attack should not be neglected. But, beyond this focus, their reintegration must not be neglected. In this sense, a foreign fighter who accepts rehabilitation should be referred to as a beneficiary and not as a terrorist or an ex-terrorist. There should be provisions in the legal and administrative framework of rehabilitation for early release of those who cooperate and genuinely repent, to be clearly differentiated from those who are uncooperative and unwilling to reject violence and extremism.

Where to Rehabilitate Foreign Fighters?

As most prisons and detention centers worldwide are overcrowded, rehabilitation of returning foreign fighters should be ideally conducted in a rehabilitation center with a conducive environment needed to facilitate such programs. However, as most governments lack the monetary resources to build a specialist center, the public and private sector can be invited to invest in building such platforms in prisons and detention centers. Prisons guards should be trained to professionally work with inmates and detainees to ensure that the beneficiaries are treated with care. When a beneficiary is visited by a religious cleric, psychological counselor, social worker or his family members, there should be a room dedicated for such visits. Such a room should be comfortable enough to create a relaxed friendly atmosphere and thus promote rehabilitation. The beneficiary should be treated with respect and never undermined or humiliated, especially in front of his visitors. These are some of the steps that can be taken to actively ensure proper rehabilitation of incarcerated extremists as well as returning foreign fighters.

Who Will Rehabilitate Foreign Fighters?

The government should enlist the support of both the public and private sector to build a rehabilitation program by tapping into their pool of talents. Rehabilitation is an enterprise where experts and specialists from diverse fields come together to form a common platform. As mentors, they seek to bring members of their society back to mainstream society. Rehabilitation is conducted by psychologists, counselors, social workers, teachers, vocational instructors, sports instructors, artistes, religious clerics and others passionate about transforming lives. They will come from government agencies, NGOs, academia, community organizations, religious bodies, business community and others. To anticipate and achieve success, rehabilitation staff should assess each beneficiary. Together with case officers, specialists and experts should meticulously plan and prepare a series of interventions vis-à-vis each detainee and inmate. Assessments on progress in rehabilitation by the case officers, counselors, clerics, prison/rehabilitation center and other staff will be forwarded to the review board that will determine release. The staff that work on rehabilitation need to be trained on handling terrorists and extremists. This needs to be done to ensure that the staff are not cleverly manipulated by the terrorists.

How to Rehabilitate Foreign Fighters?

To transform returning foreign fighters to productive citizens, governments should partner with a range of actors to create a rehabilitation enterprise. There needs to be an attempt to win their hearts and minds through three distinct but interrelated components. The components of a comprehensive rehabilitation enterprise is providing services in (1) custodial rehabilitation to the beneficiary, (2) aftercare services to their families, and (3) successful reintegration back to the community. To administer the different modes of rehabilitation, there should be a resource panel with dedicated staff that will implement the rehabilitation interventions. The seven modes of rehabilitation are (1) religious and spiritual rehabilitation, (2) educational rehabilitation, (3) vocational rehabilitation, (4) social and family rehabilitation, (5) psychological rehabilitation, (6) recreational rehabilitation and (7) creative arts in rehabilitation. Each mode of rehabilitation should have a manual of instruction and an accompanying guide of administrative instructions on how to implement the interventions.

All modes of rehabilitation are important but to engage Muslim terrorists, religious rehabilitation will offer the required benefits. This is an effective process of deradicalization that involves theological refutation and ideological debates between religious scholars and the detained beneficiaries. For extremist and violent Muslim groups such as Al Qaeda and IS, religious concepts such as jihad (struggle), hijrah (migration) and Al-Wala' wal Bara' (Loyalty and Disavowal) are used as key doctrines in the movement ideology. These ideas are also ingrained within the mind-set of returning foreign fighters. According to the Religious Rehabilitation Group of Singapore, these concepts are manipulated and their inter-pretations are being twisted to justify the actions of the politico-religious move-ments. As such, there is a critical need to address these misunderstandings for a more effective rehabilitation. Ultimately, the religious rehabilitation will effect change in their mental paradigm, which will open the doors for prevention of future violent acts. By correcting the misinterpretations of these religious concepts, the rehabilitated foreign fighters can be guided not only to refrain from committing violent acts, but to also recognize and accept the deeds as wrong.

Primacy of Reintegration

To ensure maximum success during custodial rehabilitation phase and to prevent relapse, rehabilitation interventions for foreign fighters should be comprehensive. Otherwise, returning foreign fighters could revert back to their old ways. Similarly, terrorists who surrender should also be enlisted and engaged both in the custodial and community phases. Without going through a comprehensive rehabilitation program, complete transformation is unlikely for the returning foreign fighters that have surrendered after leaving IS for personal and not ideological reasons. When in custody, the government and the society should take the lead. Custodial and com-munity rehabilitation are golden opportunities that the government and society should focus on in order to influence a person's actions and behavior positively.

Terrorist rehabilitation starts from the point of capture, but does not end with the point of release. The rehabilitation process should continue from the custodial phase into the community phase, where the beneficiary is constantly engaged by deradicalization agents at work, in his private life as well as in the community. A case officer should facilitate, support and guide the beneficiary to overcome any obstacles he may face due to his incarceration. There should be periodic visits by the case officer to ensure that the beneficiary is not harassed and does not come into contact with terrorists or extremists. Similarly, the case worker should remain in contact with the family, notably the wife and children, to ensure that the beneficiary readapts to the society. Both the case officer and case worker should ensure a smooth transition from the status of a detained terrorist or returning foreign fighter to an active and peaceful member of the society (Stern 2010).

Digital Rehabilitation of Foreign Fighters

In parallel with rehabilitating and reintegrating returning foreign fighters or incarcerated terrorists, governments should build capacities and capabilities to engage the communities. By educating communities, they become immunized against extremist ideas and ideologies. By empowering communities to better understand the threat, they become the eyes and the ears of the state. By building trusted networks, community leaders emerge as stakeholders and protect community constituents. In parallel to working in the physical space, the virtual space should also be the primary focus as well.

With the rise of Al Qaeda and IS, the online terrorist threat has proliferated numerically. To counter terrorist influence on communities through the Internet, governments should work with the community and other partners. In order to counter the attempts to replenish the fighters' rank and file, the online counter-ideology platforms should engage in digital rehabilitation. Governments working with their community partners should invest in vulnerable communities by creating attractive counter-ideology platforms. With the rise of social media in 2005, threat groups worldwide use Facebook, Twitter, Instagram, YouTube and other platforms. With IS mastery of social media, the worldwide threat is shifting to IS-inspired and – instigated attacks worldwide. From Ottawa to Paris, Copenhagen to Sydney, those vulnerable to IS ideology disseminated via social media platforms killed, maimed and injured civilians. Although the threat of IS and Al Qaeda-directed attacks persists, the dominant threat outside the IS core area and provinces is posed by self-radicalized home-grown cells and individuals. A new frontier in the fight against online extremism and terrorism should be digital rehabilitation to bring back those from the extreme to the mainstream.

Future Threat

Today, two conglomerates – IS and Al Qaeda – fight the US, their allies and friends. Operating both in cyber and real space, the ideology of global jihad inspired Muslims and instigated their movements worldwide. In the battlefield and off-the-battlefield, Al Qaeda and IS use terrorism, guerrilla warfare and semi-conventional warfare. The response of governments has been largely kinetic and lethal. Governments and their partners have realized albeit late, the grave need to counter the ideology – the center of gravity – of the threat groups. Having realized the limitations of a military and law enforcement centric approach, governments are working with their partners to build programs in community engagement to counter extremism and rehabilitation to deradicalize those radicalized by the extremist message. With no structured and comprehensive community engagement and rehabilitation programs, ideologies of incitement and hate grew among Afghan veterans. Moreover, most leaders of IS were radicalized or reradicalized in detention or in prison. Today, both inside and outside prison, in cyber and real space, radicalization and potential for radicalization remains an enduring challenge.

With the rise of IS, Islamization is taking place openly and behind closed doors. Often in its early non-violent manifestations, radicalization does not attract government attention. Most countries have no harmony laws for security forces to crack down on radicalization activities. As government and partners lack tools to detect and counter, extremism often progresses to terrorism. The fundamentalists and radicals are taking over publishing industries, mosques and religious schools. A segment of the Muslim community is becoming less tolerant and increasingly radicalized. Its members want to suppress the minorities and attack fellow Muslims who disagree with their views. The drift towards excommunication (takfirism) and the labeling of government as transgressors (thogud) is becoming common place. In addition, the youth may excitedly identify with the global ummah rather than with the nation-state.

IS threatens unity between diverse communities and precipitate the disintegration of the nation. Rather than rely solely on hard methods of catch and kill – it is necessary to build new and expand existing strategic communications capabilities. Failure to do so will give strength to Salafism and its strains – Wahabism and Takfirism in comparison to traditional and local Islam. Al Qaeda, IS and Ikhwan (Muslim Brotherhood) and their associates present a continuing and a severe challenge. At present, exploiting the confusion caused by the rise of IS, other groups are imposing their version of Islam on Muslim groups through the threat of excommunicating them on charges of blasphemy (takfirism).

Since 9/11, most governments built or expanded existing counter terrorism capabilities to detect and counter the threat using existing tools. Here, there is also a need to recognize the gap between Al Qaeda and IS capabilities. IS is a bigger group that presents a much larger threat and the government should build stronger capabilities to counter it. The governments worldwide have not yet built sufficient legal, intelligence and operational capabilities to fight IS.

For instance, in Indonesia, there is no law to prosecute those who join IS. The Indonesian authorities are unable to arrest returnees from conflict zones including from Syria and Iraq. States need to create adequate legal mechanisms to ensure that the returning foreign fighters are properly convicted.

Moreover, a new generation is growing up lacking nationalism but following IS brand of global Islam. A reason for this is the high numbers of recruits who are attracted to travel to Syria and Iraq and join IS due to the high monthly salary IS offered, alongside the opportunity to defend Islam. In this sense, there is a switch of allegiances and the efforts to defend Indonesian nationalism (Pancasila) are declining, while the desire to defend Islam is on the rise. The recruitment narrative of migration to the caliphate and its territories (wilayat), negates the state ideologies of the Pancasila, through the rhetoric of man versus God. To counter this narrative both in the real and virtual spaces, civic education by training and retraining teachers is imperative. Such measures, even for countries other than Indonesia will prevent the recruitment of foreign fighters, and allow long-term integration of retaining foreign fighters as well.

Conclusion

The Global War on Terror (GWOT) led to a million deaths and produced generations of jihadists, now the threat has escalated. With the proliferation of the threat, many thousands are willing to kill and die for God. The overwhelming military response did not help to restore stability and security in conflict zones of the global south. The developments in Asia, Africa, and the Middle East are now also affecting the Muslim migrant and diaspora communities by further escalating the crisis of foreign fighter recruitment and return. Today, the ideology of jihad has spread worldwide generating millions of supporters and sympathizers not only for Al Qaeda, that was the original target of the Global War on Terror, but also for IS and other groups.

The success in the fight against terrorism depends on the integration of hard and soft power. As mentioned earlier, kinetic means of counter-terrorism are not a sufficient strategy to defeat terrorist ideology. To defeat terrorism, governments should continue working in partnership with the civil society and businesses to counter terrorist ideology and rehabilitate the terrorists and extremists. Upstream counter-radicalization and downstream deradicalization are game changers in counter-terrorism. Most governments are yet to build the capabilities to counter the threat strategically. The twin approaches to fight terrorism strategically are to develop community engagement initiatives, to build community resilience and rehabilitate and reintegrate both terrorists and extremists. Governments need to get the strategy right by thinking and acting beyond the catch, kill and disrupt paradigm. The international community should develop the will to address the challenges confronting the world. The legitimate grievances of those fighting should be addressed and their perceived grievances should be challenged through the means of counter-narratives.

A lesson from history is pertinent in this case. While kinetic operations weakened Al Qaeda, they did not eliminate the group completely. However, the group's associates and affiliates including IS emerged stronger. While hard power is essential to dismantle the terrorist infrastructure and decapitate leaders and operatives, soft power is essential to engage communities vulnerable to radicalization and to deradicalize captured and surrendered foreign fighters.

Community leaders, especially religious clerics, should work with government to influence and shape the community that the foreign fighters belong to. There should also be a greater emphasis on upstream intervention, where the role of family, friends and community is engaged by government to identify early indicators of radicalization, in order to prevent individuals from traveling as foreign fighters.

Acknowledgement

I would like to thank Sarah Mahmood at the International Centre for Political Violence and Terrorism Research in Singapore for her help in reviewing this paper.

References

Bergen, Peter L. (2001). *Holy war, Inc: Inside the secret of Osama Bin Laden.* London: Weidenfeld & Nicolson.

Horgan, John and Altier, M. B. (2012). The future of terrorist de-radicalization programs. *Conflict & Security,* 83–90.

Jacquard, Roland. (2002). *In the name of Osama Bin Laden: Global terrorism & the Bin Laden brotherhood.* Durham and London: Duke University Press.

Kruglanski, A. W., Bélanger, J. J., Gelfand, M., Gunaratna, R., Hettiarachchi, M., Reinares, F., & Sharvit, K. (2013). Terrorism—A (self) love story: Redirecting the significance quest can end violence. *American Psychologist,* 68, 559.

Kruglanski, A. W., Gelfand, M. J., Sheveland, A., Babush, M., Hetiarachchi, M., Bonto, M., & Gunaratna, R. (in press). What a difference two years make: Patterns of radicalization in a Philippine jail. *Dynamics of Asymmetric Conflict.*

Kruglanski, A. W., Gelfand, M. J., Bélanger, J. J., Sheveland, A., Hetiarachchi, M., & Gunaratna, R. (2014). The psychology of radicalization and deradicalization: How significance quest impacts violent extremism. *Political Psychology,* 35, 69–93.

Nye, Joseph S. (2009). Get smart: Combining hard and soft power. *Foreign Affairs.* https://www.foreignaffairs.com/articles/2009-07-01/get-smart.

S. Rajaratnam School of International Studies and The Religious Rehabilitation Group. (2009). *International Conference on Terrorist Rehabilitation (ICTR).* Singapore: Nanyang Technological University.

Stern, Jessica. (2010). Mind over matter: How to deradicalize Islamist extremists. *Foreign Affairs,* 89(1), 95–108.

Webber, D., Chernikova, M., Kruglanski, A., Gelfand, M., Hetiarachchi, M., Gunaratna, R., Lafreniere, M.-A. & Belanger, J. (2017). Deradicalizing detained terrorists. *Political Psychology.* doi:10.1111/pops.12428

INDEX